DINOSAUR
ULTIMATE HANDBOOK

DK LONDON
Editor Katie Lawrence
Project Art Editors Charlotte Jennings, Lucy Sims
Managing Editor Laura Gilbert
Managing Art Editor Diane Peyton Jones
Production Editor Dragana Puvacic
Production Controller Basia Ossowska
Publishing Coordinator Issy Walsh
Jacket Designers Charlotte Jennings, Sonny Flynn
Publishing Manager Francesca Young
Deputy Art Director Mabel Chan
Publishing Director Sarah Larter

DK DELHI
Senior Editor Roohi Sehgal
Senior Art Editor Chhaya Sajwan
Project Art Editor Roohi Rais
Art Editor Bhagyashree Nayak
Managing Editor Monica Saigal
Managing Art Editor Ivy Sengupta
Picture Researcher Rituraj Singh
Senior DTP Designer Neeraj Bhatia
DTP Designer Dheeraj Singh
Delhi Creative Heads Glenda Fernandes,
Malavika Talukder

DYNAMO
Project management, editing, and design by Dynamo Limited

First published in Great Britain in 2021 by
Dorling Kindersley Limited
DK, One Embassy Gardens, 8 Viaduct Gardens,
London, SW11 7BW

The authorised representative in the EEA is
Dorling Kindersley Verlag GmbH. Arnulfstr. 124,
80636 Munich, Germany

A CIP catalogue record for this book
is available from the British Library.
ISBN: 978-0-2415-1962-2

Printed and bound in China

For the curious
www.dk.com

DINOSAUR
ULTIMATE HANDBOOK

Written by Andrea Mills, Catherine Saunders,
Lizzie Munsey, Shari Last
Expert consultant Dr. Dean Lomax

Contents

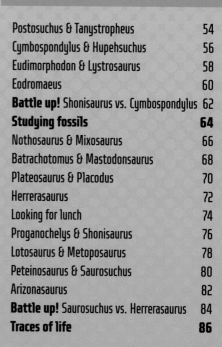

JURASSIC

CRETACEOUS

CENOZOIC

How this book works

Ready to read about the incredible prehistoric world of the dinosaurs? Here is some information to help you find your way around this book.

Profiles

Dinosaurs and other prehistoric animals are introduced on these fact-packed profile pages. The profiles sit within different chapters, which are in chronological order.

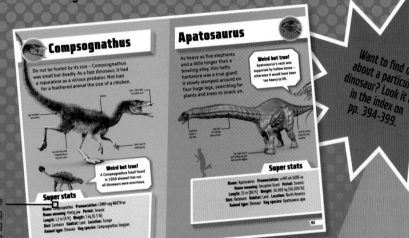

Want to find out about a particular dinosaur? Look it up in the index on pp. 394–399.

Super stats panels are filled with amazing information, including what the names mean and how to say them.

Not sure what a word means? Look it up in the glossary on pp. 390–393.

Scale silhouettes show how big some creatures were, compared to an average 10-year-old child.

Battle up!

These pages set two creatures against each other in an imaginary battle to the death.

Key attack and defence features are highlighted.

Two animals face each other across the page.

The winner is announced at the bottom of the page.

Special features

Feature pages give you extra information about the prehistoric world.
What is a dinosaur? How were fossils made? Read on and find out.

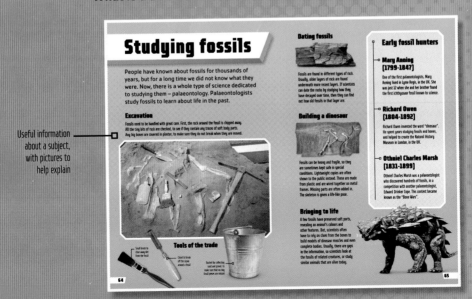

Useful information about a subject, with pictures to help explain

What is a dinosaur?

About 235 million years ago, some reptiles developed in ways that set them apart from the rest. This group of animals became incredibly varied. Some were huge, while others were tiny. Some were ferocious meat eaters, others giant plant eaters. Some had spikes, feathers, or scales. These "terrible lizards" ruled the Earth for 170 million years.

Dinosaurs were vertebrates, which means they had a backbone like humans.

Giganotosaurus

What makes a dinosaur a dinosaur?

Although dinosaurs could look very different from each other, they did share some things in common. They were all vertebrates, had their legs directly under their body, had a tail of some kind, and laid eggs.

Many fossilized dinosaur eggs have been discovered.

Their legs were directly underneath their bodies, not pointing out to the sides, like a lizard or crocodile.

Feathers or scales?

Dinosaurs were covered in scales, feathers, or both. Fossils have been found that show the texture of both of these. This is amazing, considering how long they have been buried!

All types of dinosaur

Just because they shared some features, that does not mean all dinosaurs looked the same. There were a lot of differences between them. Take a closer look at these two creatures.

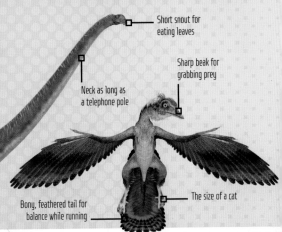

Short snout for eating leaves

Sharp beak for grabbing prey

Neck as long as a telephone pole

Long, whip-like tail for defence against predators

Bony, feathered tail for balance while running

The size of a cat

	Mamenchisaurus	Archaeopteryx
Length	26 m (85 ft)	50 cm (20 in)
Stance	Quadruped (walked on four legs)	Biped (walked on two legs)
Skin	Scaled	Feathered
Diet	Herbivore	Carnivore
Teeth	Wide and blunt	Sharp
Special features	Long neck for reaching treetop leaves	Wings and ability to fly

Not so ancient

Dinosaurs developed over 170 million years. Whether a hunter using clever tactics, like Tyrannosaurus, or a well-defended plant eater, like Ankylosaurus, each type of dinosaur was perfectly suited to its lifestyle.

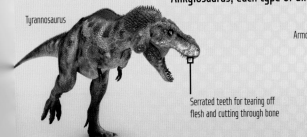

Tyrannosaurus

Armoured body

Ankylosaurus

Serrated teeth for tearing off flesh and cutting through bone

Timeline

PRECAMBRIAN ERA (4.6 billion–541 MYA)

4.6 billion years ago

The Earth formed from a cloud of gas and dust, which was joined together by a pulling force, called gravity.

3.5 billion years ago

The first life on Earth appeared. These were simple organisms with just a single cell, called bacteria.

MYA is short for million years ago.

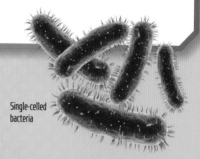

Single-celled bacteria

Permian
299–252 MYA

Reptiles eventually ruled the land. This period ended with most of the existing animals dying out. As much as 90 per cent of all known animal species became extinct.

Dimetrodon

Carboniferous
359–299 MYA

Swamps developed on land. With them came bugs that ate plants. These bugs were hunted by large amphibians and the first reptiles.

Meganeura

Prehistoric animals did not all live at the same time – they developed and then died out over millions and billions of years. To help us keep track of these huge time spans, Earth's history is divided into eras. Each era is split up further, into sections called periods.

PALEOZOIC ERA (541-252 MYA)

Cambrian
541-485 MYA

In the oceans, life forms with more than one cell appeared. These included invertebrates (animals without a backbone), who had tough outer layers called exoskeletons.

Marrella

Ordovician
485-444 MYA

Over time, more life forms appeared in the ocean. There were many types of fish, and lots of species of invertebrates, including many species of trilobites.

Astraspis

Devonian
419-359 MYA

As more fish appeared, some of them left the water. They gradually became the first amphibians on land.

Drepanaspis

Silurian
444-419 MYA

Plants, such as cooksonia, began spreading far and wide on land. They were green and had no roots, leaves, or flowers. Coral reefs began to form in the warm oceans.

Cooksonia

MESOZOIC ERA (252-66 MYA)

Triassic
252-201 MYA

It took millions of years for Earth to recover from events at the end of the Permian period. Eventually, new animals appeared, including pterosaurs, ichthyosaurs, and the first dinosaurs.

Jurassic
201-145 MYA

Dinosaurs continued to develop. There were many new types, and they spread out across the Earth. Giant plant-eating dinosaurs were hunted by powerful, meat-eating predators.

Cryolophosaurus

Eoraptor

Quaternary
2 MYA-today

Some mammals died out, while others developed. Modern humans appeared in Africa around 200,000 years ago, then slowly spread around the world.

There are more humans on Earth than any other mammal.

Elephant

Cretaceous
145-66 MYA

Dinosaurs were the most powerful animals on Earth. The first flowering plants appeared. Then a space rock, called an asteroid, hit the Earth, wiping out almost all of the dinosaurs and ending the Cretaceous period.

An incredible 99 per cent of all the life forms that have ever existed on Earth are now extinct.

Baryonyx

CENOZOIC ERA (66 MYA-today)

Neogene
23-2 MYA

Animals that still exist today began to appear. Around 4 million years ago, early humans developed in east Africa.

Palaeogene
66-23 MYA

With no dinosaurs left, apart from birds, mammals ruled the Earth. They got bigger, and more types appeared. Huge whales swam in the sea, and land mammals, such as Uintatherium, walked on the land.

Deinotherium

Uintatherium

15

Pre-Mesozoic

Billions of years ago, tiny living things like bacteria existed on Earth. These developed into the first animals – hundreds of millions of years before dinosaurs roamed the planet. This was when animals started to become different from one another. The oceans teemed with fish, molluscs, and arthropods – creatures with a hard outer shell and no back bone. On land, plants grew, insects swarmed, and amphibians scuttled. Eventually, the rise of the reptiles also began.

Anomalocaris

The curious-looking Anomalocaris was one of the first ever super predators. This sea creature used the hook-shaped parts of its mouth to grab prey, then shoved its meal into its mouth.

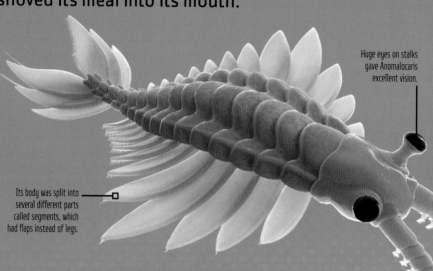

Huge eyes on stalks gave Anomalocaris excellent vision.

Its body was split into several different parts called segments, which had flaps instead of legs.

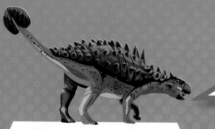

Weird but true!
It might look like an insect, but Anomalocaris grew to around the same size as a raccoon.

Super stats

Name: Anomalocaris   **Pronunciation:** a-NOM-a-low-CAR-iss
Name meaning: Abnormal shrimp   **Period:** Cambrian
Length: 1 m (3 ft)   **Weight:** 5 kg (11 lb)   **Diet:** Carnivore
Habitat: Ocean   **Location:** Asia, North America, and Oceania
Animal type: Prehistoric creature
Key species: Anomalocaris canadensis

Cotylorhynchus

The lizard-like Cotylorhynchus had stumpy legs and a tiny head compared to its large, barrel-shaped body. It could grow up to an astonishing 6 m (20 ft) long, which is about as big as a speedboat.

Weird but true!
Cotylorhynchus was one of the largest animals from the Permian period.

Snout hangs over a row of large, blunt teeth

Cotylorhynchus may have had paddle-like feet.

Super stats

Name: Cotylorhynchus   **Pronunciation:** coe-TY-low-RIN-kus
Name meaning: Cup snout   **Period:** Permian
Length: 6 m (20 ft)   **Weight:** 1,500 kg (3,300 lb)
Diet: Herbivore   **Habitat:** Land / Water
Location: North America   **Animal type:** Prehistoric creature
Key species: Cotylorhynchus romeri

Amphibamus

The newt–sized Amphibamus, as its name suggests, was a prehistoric amphibian. It is thought to be a close relative of modern frogs and salamanders. Amphibamus fossils often show the soft parts of the body, such as the body outline, tail, and foot pads.

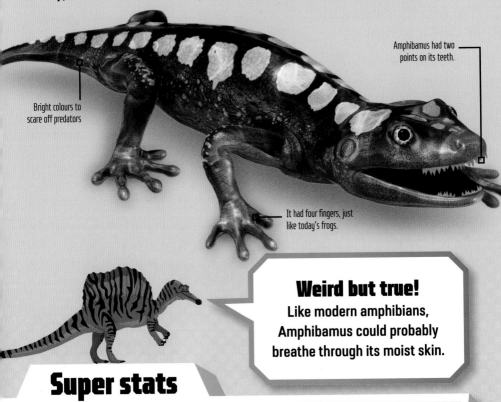

Amphibamus had two points on its teeth.

Bright colours to scare off predators

It had four fingers, just like today's frogs.

Weird but true!
Like modern amphibians, Amphibamus could probably breathe through its moist skin.

Super stats

Name: Amphibamus   **Pronunciation:** AM-fee-bah-muss
Name meaning: Equal legs   **Period:** Carboniferous
Length: 20 cm (8 in)   **Weight:** 1 kg (2 lb)   **Diet:** Carnivore
Habitat: Swamps   **Location:** North America and Europe
Animal type: Prehistoric creature
Key species: Amphibamus grandiceps

Dendrerpeton

This early amphibian was a toothy, lizard–like creature. It had about 40–50 small, spiky teeth, which it used to catch insects and larger animals, such as fish.

Back feet slightly paddle-shaped for swimming

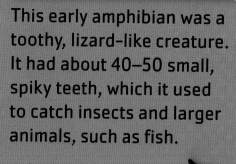

Eyes on either side of its head gave Dendrerpeton a wide range of vision.

Spiky teeth lined the top and bottom jaws

Weird but true!
Dendrerpeton means "tree-creeper" because many of its fossils were found inside tree trunks.

Super stats

Name: Dendrerpeton **Pronunciation:** DEND-rerp-et-on
Name meaning: Tree-creeper **Period:** Carboniferous
Length: 35 cm (14 in) **Weight:** 0.9 kg (2 lb) **Diet:** Carnivore
Habitat: Land **Location:** North America and Europe
Animal type: Prehistoric creature
Key species: Dendrerpeton acadianum

Edaphosaurus

Edaphosaurus was a large, lizard–like creature. It had a small head and a unique, large sail on its back. The sail had small spikes jutting out of it, which looked similar to little twigs.

Its mouth was full of blunt teeth – including on the roof of its mouth.

Back-sail might have been brightly coloured to help attract a mate

Weird but true!
Edaphosaurus was a herbivore, but, at the size of a rhinoceros, it must have looked pretty scary.

Super stats

Name: Edaphosaurus **Pronunciation:** ed-A-fo-SORE-uss
Name meaning: Pavement lizard **Period:** Carboniferous to Permian
Length: 3.5 m (11.5 ft) **Weight:** 300 kg (660 lb) **Diet:** Herbivore
Habitat: Land **Location:** North America and Europe
Animal type: Prehistoric creature **Key species:** Edaphosaurus pogonias

Diplocaulus

Have you ever seen a creature with a boomerang–shaped head? Well, here's one! Meet Diplocaulus, an aquatic prehistoric creature. It used its horns to control water currents so it could easily float up and down.

Long, thin tail used to move through water

Small, flat body, often described as looking like a "fat salamander"

Horns are long and flattened, and point backwards

Weird but true!

Diplocaulus has no living relatives, so you will not see any animals with these horns today.

Super stats

Name: Diplocaulus **Pronunciation:** DIP-low-CAWL-us
Name meaning: Double caul **Period:** Permian
Length: 1 m (3 ft) **Weight:** 9 kg (20 lb)
Diet: Carnivore **Habitat:** Swamps **Location:** North America and Africa
Animal type: Prehistoric creature **Key species:** Diplocaulus magnicornis

Dimetrodon

You are looking at one of the earliest land predators that ever walked the Earth – Dimetrodon. With its bony back-sail, Dimetrodon looks similar to a dinosaur, but it is a synapsid, and is more closely related to mammals than to reptiles. This car-sized carnivore had sharp teeth and powerful jaws, giving it a deadly bite.

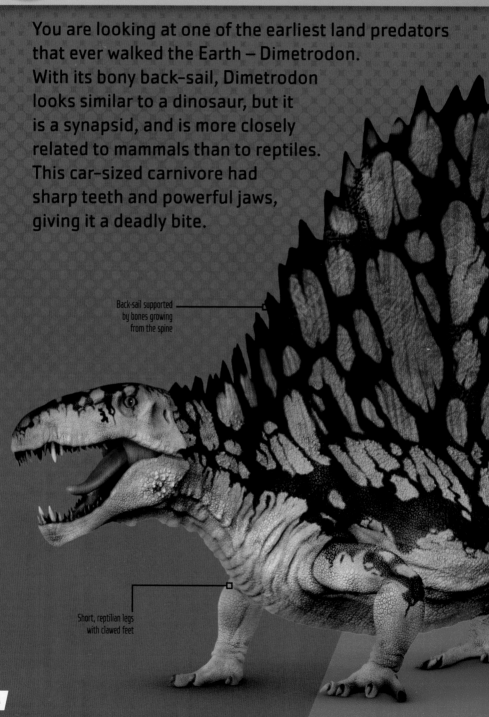

Back-sail supported by bones growing from the spine

Short, reptilian legs with clawed feet

Super stats

Name: Dimetrodon
Pronunciation: die-MET-roe-don
Name meaning: Two measures of teeth   **Period:** Permian
Length: 4 m (13 ft)   **Weight:** 250 kg (550 lb)
Diet: Carnivore   **Habitat:** Land
Location: Europe and North America
Animal type: Prehistoric creature
Key species: Dimetrodon incisivus

Back-sail patterned
with striking colours
to scare away
predators

Weird but true!
Dimetrodon had 80 sharp teeth
in its mouth, including fangs that
were larger than the rest of its
teeth. This is why its name
means "two measures of teeth".

Dimetrodon's large tail
was about as long as
the rest of its body.

Sharp fangs for
tearing meat

Anomalocaris

Big and bold, Anomalocaris was a scary predator. With its long mouthparts, it could grab and pull prey straight into its mouth, where its sharp, tooth-like plates were ready to chomp! It may not have been able to crack through tough Calymene shells, but Anomalocaris could seek out the uncovered, soft parts of its prey.

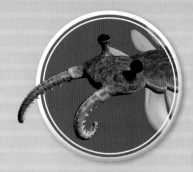

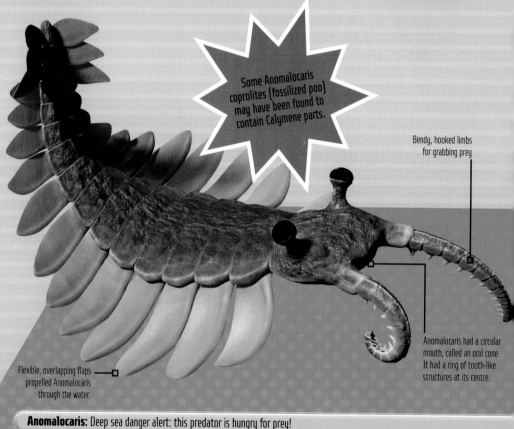

Some Anomalocaris coprolites (fossilized poo) may have been found to contain Calymene parts.

Bendy, hooked limbs for grabbing prey

Anomalocaris had a circular mouth, called an oral cone. It had a ring of tooth-like structures at its centre.

Flexible, overlapping flaps propelled Anomalocaris through the water.

Anomalocaris: Deep sea danger alert: this predator is hungry for prey!

Battle up!

Super predator Anomalocaris searched the depths of the Cambrian oceans for a tasty Calymene. Once cornered, would Calymene's defensive features be enough to protect it from its large, hungry enemy?

Calymene

Calymene was smaller than Anomalocaris, and it came in many shapes and sizes. Some hunted for food scraps, some were predators, and others fed on tiny sea creatures called plankton. Most were slow-moving and would have been an easy target. However, they had a tough exoskeleton, and when attacked, some Calymene could roll up into a ball to protect their soft underbellies.

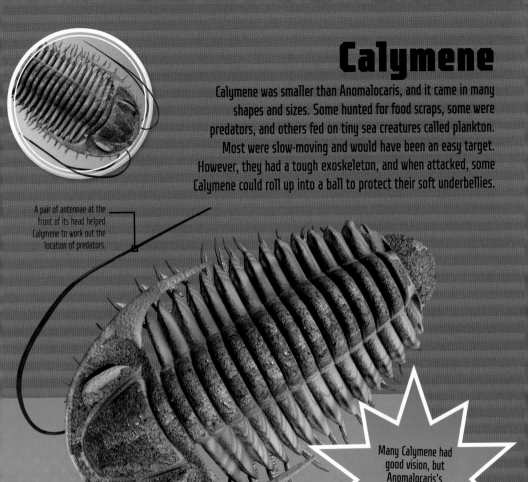

A pair of antennae at the front of its head helped Calymene to work out the location of predators.

Some types of Calymene could see well, but others were blind.

Many Calymene had good vision, but Anomalocaris's eyesight was 30 times better!

Calymene: This armoured arthropod is ready to roll into a ball!

Who would win?

Anomalocaris was larger, faster, and much more vicious than Calymene. It would not have had a hard time finding and trapping its prey. But, Calymene's hard exoskeleton could withstand the bite of its attacker. Rolling into a ball, Calymene hoped to stay safe, but Anomalocaris would use its mouthparts to roll its victim over until the soft areas were exposed. Game over!

Winner!

Fossil finds

Our understanding of prehistoric life comes from incredible discoveries of fossils from all over the world. Fossils are the preserved remains of living things, including dinosaurs, mammals, plants, insects, and anything else that ever lived. They are buried under layers of rock and sand over millions of years.

Bones

Scientists use bones to work out the size, diet, movement, and lifestyle of a creature. They occasionally find complete skeletons, but most discoveries are single bones or bone fragments.

Amber

From time to time an insect or other organism gets stuck in sticky resin from a tree trunk. This hardens to form amber, and perfectly preserves the creature inside.

Ice

Fossils frozen in blocks of ice date back to the Ice Age, which began about 2.6 million years ago. Woolly mammoths may have fallen in pits or got stuck in the mud where they were frozen by the cold.

Feathers

Fossilized feathers are tough, so they survive for a long time. Feathers have helped scientists find the link between dinosaurs and birds.

Skin and hair

It is very rare to find soft body parts, like skin and hair. However, the Messel quarry in Germany has revealed some amazing fossils with both skin and hair.

Weird but true!

The largest fossil ever found is a tree in Thailand. It was more than 72 m (236 ft) long.

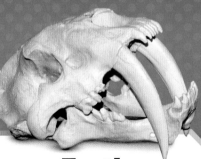

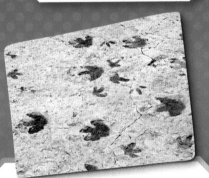

Teeth

The hard outside of a tooth can last long after soft body parts disappear. One tooth can be used to identify an animal, and shows whether it ate meat or plants.

Footprints

Fossilized footprints reveal a lot about the creature that made them. They tell us its size, whether it walked on two or four legs, and if it travelled alone or in a group.

Orthacanthus

A dangerous marine predator, Orthacanthus looked a bit like an eel, but was in fact an early type of shark. It would attack its prey with sharp, double-fanged teeth.

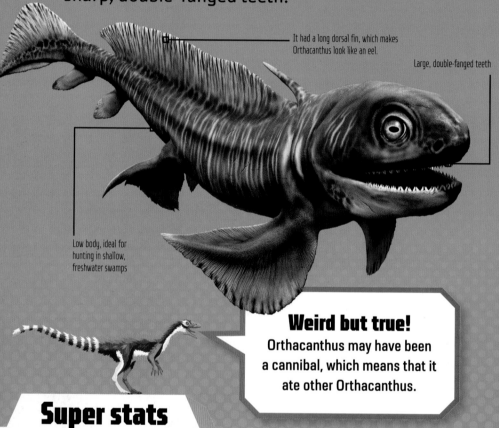

It had a long dorsal fin, which makes Orthacanthus look like an eel.

Large, double-fanged teeth

Low body, ideal for hunting in shallow, freshwater swamps

Weird but true!
Orthacanthus may have been a cannibal, which means that it ate other Orthacanthus.

Super stats

Name: Orthacanthus **Pronunciation:** ORF-ah-CAN-fus
Name meaning: Vertical spike **Period:** Carboniferous to Permian
Length: 3 m (10 ft) **Weight:** 100 kg (220 lb)
Diet: Carnivore **Habitat:** Ocean
Location: Europe and North America **Animal type:** Prehistoric creature
Key species: Orthacanthus cylindricus

Eryops

Eryops was an early predator that looked like a small, fat alligator. It had a long face, bumpy skin, and very short legs.

Weird but true!
Eryops is special – it is one of the only early amphibians whose entire skeleton survived in fossilized form.

Skin covered in oval bumps

Short, narrow tail – probably not used for swimming

Curved teeth, like a frog

A human would have outrun heavy, plodding Eryops, which struggled to lift itself off the ground.

Super stats

Name: Eryops   **Pronunciation:** EH-ree-ops
Name meaning: Drawn-out face   **Period:** Carboniferous to Permian
Length: 2 m (6.5 ft)   **Weight:** 90 kg (200 lb)
Diet: Carnivore   **Habitat:** Land / Water
Location: North America   **Animal type:** Prehistoric creature
Key species: Eryops megacephalus

Calymene

This tiny creature was a type of trilobite. It had a segmented body and lots of little legs. There were more than 20,000 different types of trilobite. Some had eyes on stalks, some were blind, and some even had spiny, tail-like limbs that stuck out from their body.

The body was split into different pieces, or segments, to allow for flexible movement.

Trilobites were among the first animals known to have eyes.

Antennae to sense the surrounding environment

A hard exoskeleton provided protection from predators.

Weird but true!

Trilobites might be extinct now, but they survived on Earth for almost 300 million years.

Super stats

Name: Calymene **Pronunciation:** CA-lih-ME-nee
Name meaning: Beautiful crescent **Period:** Silurian
Length: 10 cm (4 in) **Weight:** 0.04 kg (0.08 lb)
Diet: Carnivore **Habitat:** Ocean **Location:** Europe
Animal type: Prehistoric creature
Key species: Calymene blumenbachii

Dunkleosteus

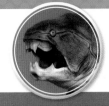

This beastly armoured fish was one of the largest predators of its time. It could open its mouth really quickly and bite with a fierce amount of force – its prey stood no chance of escaping.

Weird but true!
Dunkleosteus fossils show bite and puncture marks. This suggests that these predators were also hunted.

It had bony plates for protection that were up to 5 cm (2 in) thick.

Bony fangs that sharpened themselves developed at the corners of the lower and upper jaws.

Large tail fin for speedy swimming

Super stats

Name: Dunkleosteus **Pronunciation:** DUN-kell-OSS-tee-us
Name meaning: Dunkle's Bone **Period:** Devonian
Length: 10 m (33 ft) **Weight:** 3,500 kg (7,700 lb)
Diet: Carnivore **Habitat:** Ocean
Location: North America, Europe, and Africa
Animal type: Prehistoric creature **Key species:** Dunkleosteus terrelli

Inostrancevia

Inostrancevia was a fierce carnivore with a slender body, bulky legs, a short tail, and huge fangs. It was similar in size and weight to a large motorbike. It was a top predator.

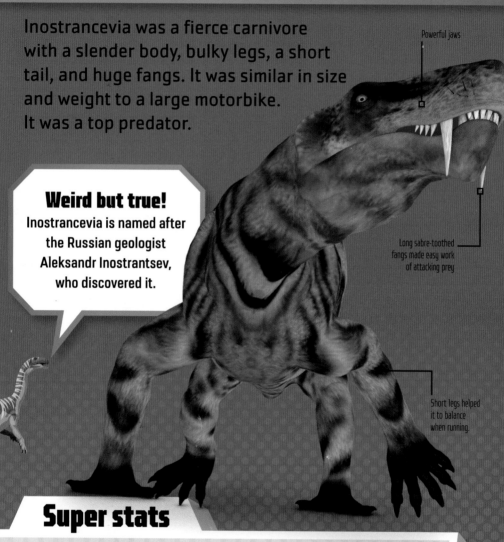

Powerful jaws

Long sabre-toothed fangs made easy work of attacking prey

Short legs helped it to balance when running.

Weird but true!

Inostrancevia is named after the Russian geologist Aleksandr Inostrantsev, who discovered it.

Super stats

Name: Inostrancevia **Pronunciation:** ee-NOS-tran-see-VEE-a
Name meaning: After Aleksandr Inostrantsev **Period:** Permian
Length: 3 m (10 ft) **Weight:** 500 kg (1,100 lb) **Diet:** Carnivore
Habitat: Land **Location:** Europe and Asia
Animal type: Prehistoric creature **Key species:** Inostrancevia alexandri

Helicoprion

The shark-like Helicoprion fish had a very unusual feature in its mouth – a tooth whorl. Its teeth were set in a spiral, with smaller teeth on the inside of its jaw and larger ones at the edges.

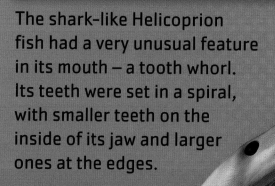

Tooth whorl

Its powerful, streamlined body made Helicoprion a fast swimmer.

Similar gills to modern-day sharks

Weird but true!

Experts have mostly identified Helicoprion from fossilized tooth whorls – the only body part to survive.

Super stats

Name: Helicoprion   **Pronunciation:** HELL-ee-coe-PRY-on
Name meaning: Spiral saw   **Period:** Permian
Length: 10 m (33 ft)   **Weight:** 500 kg (1,100 lb)   **Diet:** Carnivore
Habitat: Ocean   **Location:** Worldwide
Animal type: Prehistoric creature   **Key species:** Helicoprion bessonovi

Estemmenosuchus

Estemmenosuchus was an early relative of mammals. It had a rather large head, with an elaborate head crest. The crest was similar to antlers, but much shorter, and it could grow out from the sides of the head. Scientists think that Estemmenosuchus may have used its head crest to communicate with others of its kind, through visual displays.

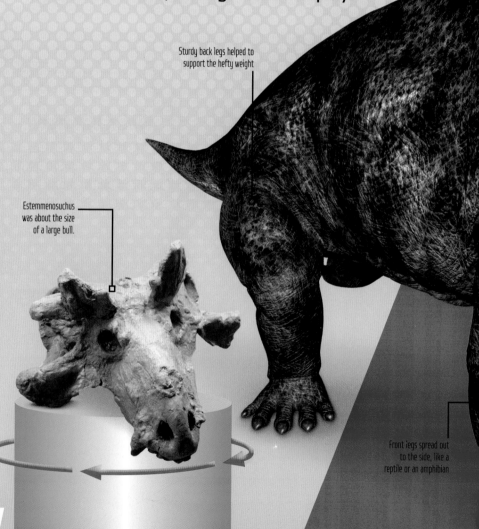

Sturdy back legs helped to support the hefty weight

Estemmenosuchus was about the size of a large bull.

Front legs spread out to the side, like a reptile or an amphibian

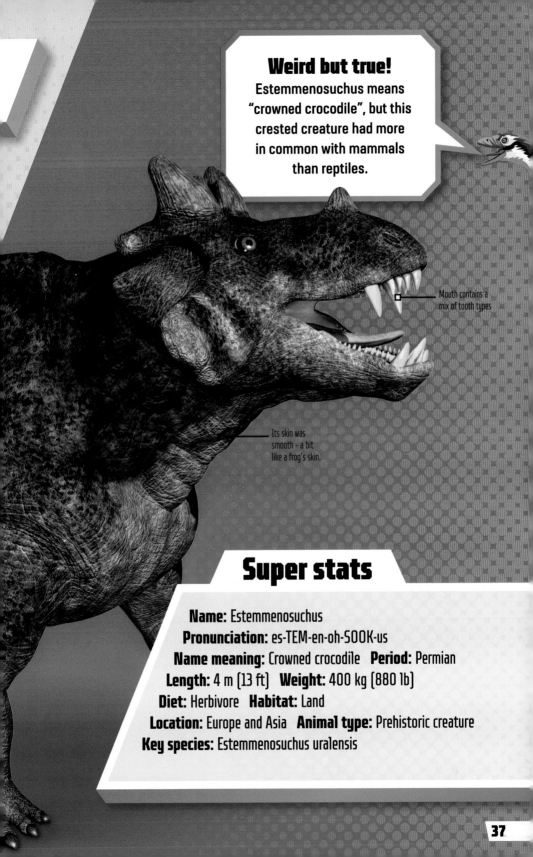

Weird but true!
Estemmenosuchus means "crowned crocodile", but this crested creature had more in common with mammals than reptiles.

Mouth contains a mix of tooth types

Its skin was smooth – a bit like a frog's skin.

Super stats

Name: Estemmenosuchus
Pronunciation: es-TEM-en-oh-SOOK-us
Name meaning: Crowned crocodile   **Period:** Permian
Length: 4 m (13 ft)   **Weight:** 400 kg (880 lb)
Diet: Herbivore   **Habitat:** Land
Location: Europe and Asia   **Animal type:** Prehistoric creature
Key species: Estemmenosuchus uralensis

Watch out!

Lurking in the lush wetlands, this animal looked like a dinosaur, but it was not. Edaphosaurus was around before the dinosaurs, and was actually more closely related to mammals. It was a herbivore and had strong jaw muscles for biting and chewing tough plants.

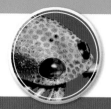

Pterygotus

Pterygotus was a giant, aquatic creature, also known as a sea scorpion. Its body was split into different pieces, or segments, and it could grow as long as the average adult human. Its huge pincers were covered in sharp teeth.

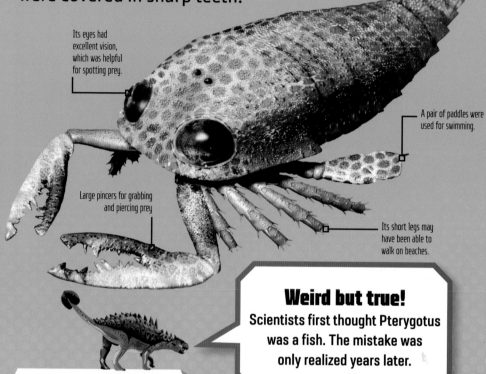

Its eyes had excellent vision, which was helpful for spotting prey.

A pair of paddles were used for swimming.

Large pincers for grabbing and piercing prey

Its short legs may have been able to walk on beaches.

Weird but true!
Scientists first thought Pterygotus was a fish. The mistake was only realized years later.

Super stats

Name: Pterygotus   **Pronunciation:** terry-GOAT-us
Name meaning: Winged fish   **Period:** Silurian to Devonian
Length: 1.75 m (5.75 ft)   **Weight:** 10 kg (22 lb)
Diet: Carnivore   **Habitat:** Ocean
Location: Europe and North America   **Animal type:** Prehistoric creature
Key species: Pterygotus anglicus

Eogyrinus

With a long, eel-like shape and short legs, Eogyrinus's body was perfect for hunting in shallow waters and swamps. It could easily snatch prey without getting caught in reeds and tree roots. Eogyrinus sometimes goes by another name, Pholiderpeton.

Long tail aided swimming

Narrow snout for grabbing prey out of small spaces

Scaly body

Webbed feet for paddling

Weird but true!
One of the largest four-legged animals of its time, Eogyrinus was bigger than a car.

Super stats

Name: Eogyrinus **Pronunciation:** e-O-gy-RIN-us
Name meaning: Dawn tadpole **Period:** Carboniferous
Length: 4 m (13 ft) **Weight:** 450 kg (990 lb)
Diet: Carnivore **Habitat:** Water **Location:** Europe
Animal type: Prehistoric creature
Key species: Eogyrinus attheyi

Arthropleura

This huge millipede scuttled through the forests of Scotland and North America on 120 little legs. Despite its large size, it was a herbivore, not a carnivore.

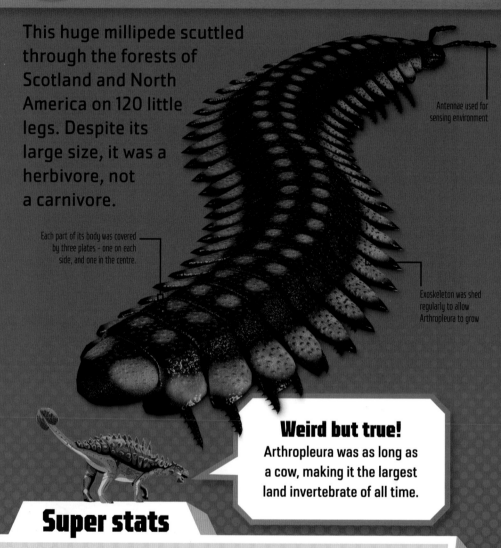

Antennae used for sensing environment

Each part of its body was covered by three plates – one on each side, and one in the centre.

Exoskeleton was shed regularly to allow Arthropleura to grow

Weird but true!

Arthropleura was as long as a cow, making it the largest land invertebrate of all time.

Super stats

Name: Arthropleura   **Pronunciation:** arth-row-PLOO-ra
Name meaning: Jointed ribs   **Period:** Carboniferous
Length: 2.5 m (8 ft)   **Weight:** 20 kg (44 lb)   **Diet:** Herbivore
Habitat: Land   **Location:** Europe and North America
Animal type: Prehistoric creature   **Key species:** Arthropleura armata

Meganeura

Meganeura looked like a dragonfly, but it was the size of a large bird. A deadly predator, it caught other insects – and maybe even small fish – by trapping them in the spines that lined its legs.

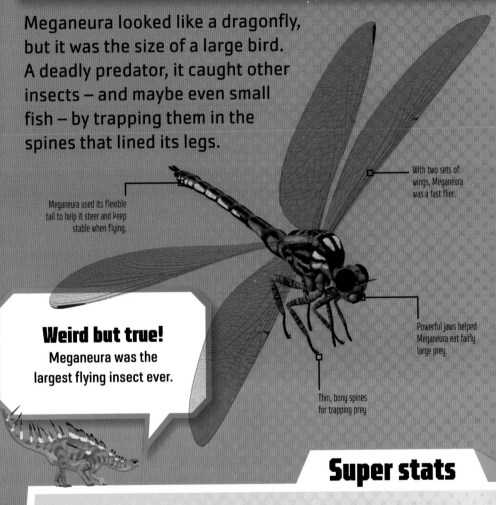

With two sets of wings, Meganeura was a fast flier.

Meganeura used its flexible tail to help it steer and keep stable when flying.

Powerful jaws helped Meganeura eat fairly large prey.

Thin, bony spines for trapping prey

Weird but true!
Meganeura was the largest flying insect ever.

Super stats

Name: Meganeura   **Pronunciation:** MEGA-new-ra
Name meaning: Large-veined   **Period:** Carboniferous
Wingspan: 75 cm (30 in)   **Weight:** 0.5 kg (1 lb)
Diet: Carnivore   **Habitat:** Land   **Location:** Europe
Animal type: Prehistoric creature   **Key species:** Meganeura brongniarti

Dipterus

With a scaly body, two dorsal fins far down its back, and a shark–like tail, Dipterus was a prehistoric lungfish. It had strong jaws and several rows of tooth–like plates.

Head covered in a thick pattern of bones

Gills protected by a bony plate

Long, muscly limb-like fins

Its scales were coated in a hard layer of cosmine, similar to the substance our teeth are made of.

Weird but true!

Dipterus was one of the first fish to develop the ability to breathe air.

Super stats

Name: Dipterus **Pronunciation:** DIP-ter-us
Name meaning: Two wings **Period:** Devonian
Length: 40 cm (16 in) **Weight:** 3.4 kg (7.5 lb)
Diet: Carnivore **Habitat:** Water **Location:** Europe and North America
Animal type: Prehistoric creature **Key species:** Dipterus valenciennesi

Tiktaalik

Tiktaalik was a large fish, but it had strong, limb–like fins that enabled it to walk. It was one of the first ever fish to come out from the water and walk on land.

Hind fins could support body weight

Wide, flat head, similar to a crocodile

Strong fins with wrist bones

Weird but true!

Tiktaalik is the earliest known link between fish and tetrapods – it has the nickname "fishapod".

Super stats

Name: Tiktaalik   **Pronunciation:** tik-TAA-lick
Name meaning: Large freshwater fish
Period: Devonian   **Length:** 3 m (10 ft)   **Weight:** 23 kg (50 lb)
Diet: Carnivore   **Habitat:** Land / Water   **Location:** North America
Animal type: Prehistoric creature   **Key species:** Tiktaalik roseae

Mesosaurus

Mesosaurus was among the first reptiles that could live in the oceans. Its long, thick tail and webbed feet made it a powerful swimmer. Mesosaurus had needle-like teeth that were too delicate for tearing large prey, so it would sweep its head from side to side in the water to catch small fish and crustaceans.

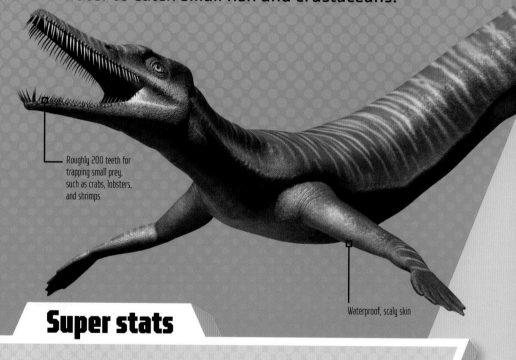

Roughly 200 teeth for trapping small prey, such as crabs, lobsters, and shrimps

Waterproof, scaly skin

Super stats

Name: Mesosaurus **Pronunciation:** MEE-so-SORE-us
Name meaning: Middle lizard **Period:** Permian **Length:** 1 m (3 ft)
Weight: 9 kg (20 lb) **Diet:** Carnivore **Habitat:** Ocean
Location: Africa and South America
Animal type: Prehistoric creature
Key species: Mesosaurus tenuidens

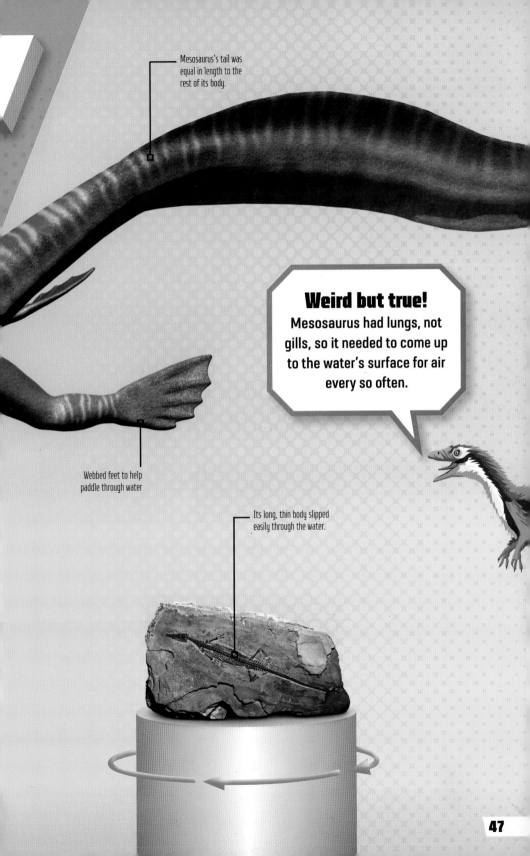

Mesosaurus's tail was equal in length to the rest of its body.

Weird but true!
Mesosaurus had lungs, not gills, so it needed to come up to the water's surface for air every so often.

Webbed feet to help paddle through water

Its long, thin body slipped easily through the water.

Dimetrodon

A predator needs sharp teeth, and Dimetrodon had plenty. Its front fangs were long and sharp, perfect for stabbing prey. A set of serrated, or jagged, teeth helped to saw through flesh, too. It even had teeth hidden on the roof of its mouth to stop smaller prey from escaping. With these toothy weapons and strong jaw muscles, this creature's bite was fearsome.

Its impressive back sail was used to show off to other Dimetrodons – not as a weapon.

Dimetrodon tooth fossils are among the earliest known examples of serrated teeth.

Dimetrodon: This toothy terror lines up its next meal and prepares to strike!

Battle up!

Dimetrodon and Edaphosaurus roamed the Earth almost 300 million years ago. Both were lizard–like, with small heads, bulky legs, and large back sails. But, Edaphosaurus was a herbivore, while Dimetrodon was a vicious predator.

Edaphosaurus

Edaphosaurus was almost as big as Dimetrodon, but nowhere near as aggressive. It spent most of its time eating low-growing plants. For this reason, its peg-like teeth were short and blunt, which is great for munching on plants, but not for defending itself against predators. Edaphosaurus had a unique back sail, with small spines poking out from it. These spines broke easily, so offered little protection.

A long, heavy tail was not made for whipping at predators, and would have meant Edaphosaurus was a rather slow mover.

Edaphosaurus means "pavement lizard". The name refers to its blunt, tightly packed teeth.

Edaphosaurus: The herbivore with a prickly sail may be in trouble...

Who would win?

If Edaphosaurus spotted Dimetrodon first, it probably would have tried to escape. If trapped, it might have attempted to use its sail as camouflage to hide. But, if that failed to fool Dimetrodon, the battle would not have lasted long. Edaphosaurus might manage a few blows, but that would not be enough to seriously injure its opponent. As soon as Dimetrodon's deadly teeth came out, the battle was won.

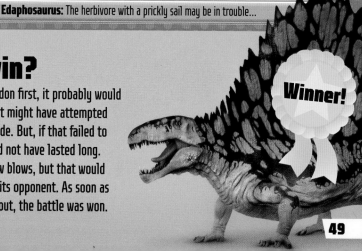

Winner!

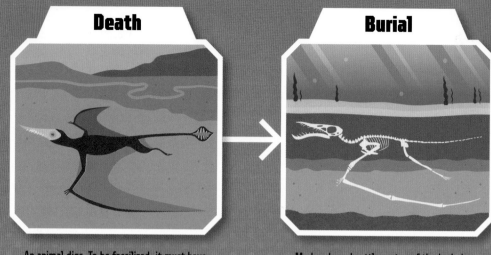

Death

An animal dies. To be fossilized, it must have died near to, or in water. The softer parts of its body usually rot away or are eaten by other creatures.

Burial

Mud and sand settle on top of the body in the water. More and more layers are added over time. This means that the weight and pressure on top of the body increases.

How are fossils made?

Long ago, Earth was home to very different animals and plants from those that live now. We know this because we have found their remains, preserved as fossils. Only a tiny number of them become fossils. To become fossils, they had to be preserved in very specific ways. Then, their remains would have gone through a process that takes millions of years to complete.

Weird but true!
Some fossils even show us prehistoric animals' fur, feathers, or skin.

Becoming rock

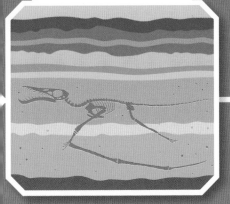

Slowly, the body is buried deeper and deeper. The layers of mud or sand turn into rock. Minerals from water in the rock seep into the bones, turning them into stone.

Finding fossils

Millions of years later, water and wind wear away the land, revealing the fossil. It might be spotted by a fossil hunter and carefully removed from the rock.

Fossil forms

Most fossils are made from hard body parts, such as shells or bones, that have turned to stone. It is very rare for softer parts of an animal, such as feathers, hair, or skin, to be preserved.

Body fossils

Most dinosaur fossils are body fossils. These are hard, bony parts that have taken in minerals and turned to stone.

Sometimes a creature turns to rock, making a mould of its shape. Over time, mud fills the mould, creating a copy of the animal's shape.

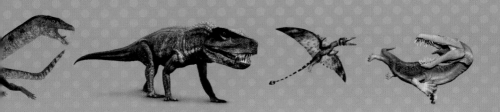

Triassic

At the beginning of the Triassic, the world was recovering from a huge extinction event that had destroyed much of the life on Earth. Without any competition, the animals that had survived grew in large numbers for a short while. Over time, new animals appeared, including marine reptiles, flying pterosaurs, and the first dinosaurs. These early dinosaurs were small, walked on two legs, and many ate meat.

Postosuchus

Among the biggest and most powerful predators in the late Triassic period was Postosuchus. This ancient, armoured reptile looked a little like a long-legged crocodile and weighed the same as six adult humans.

Large eyes for sharp, long-distance vision

Bony plates provided body armour along its back and tail.

Its teeth were a mix of longer old teeth and shorter new teeth.

Weird but true!
Postosuchus dined on other dinosaurs, maybe even its own species.

Super stats

Name: Postosuchus   **Pronunciation:** POST-oh-SOOK-us
Name meaning: Crocodile from Post   **Period:** Triassic
Length: 4.5 m (14.5 ft)   **Weight:** 680 kg (1,500 lb)
Diet: Carnivore   **Habitat:** Land   **Location:** North America
Animal type: Prehistoric creature
Key species: Postosuchus kirkpatricki

Tanystropheus

Meet Tanystropheus, a marine reptile with an incredibly long neck. Tanystropheus could extend its neck without warning to launch a surprise attack on fish and reptiles in the shallow Triassic waters.

The neck made up about half of its total body length.

Weird but true!
Although Tanystropheus spent most of its time in shallow waters, it may have come to shore to lay eggs.

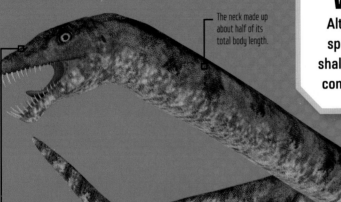

Nostrils on top of the snout allowed it to breathe on the surface of the water.

Super stats

Name: Tanystropheus   **Pronunciation:** tan-EE-stro-FEE-us
Name meaning: Long hinged   **Period:** Triassic
Length: 6 m (20 ft)   **Weight:** 136 kg (300 lb)   **Diet:** Carnivore
Habitat: Ocean   **Location:** Europe and Asia
Animal type: Prehistoric creature
Key species: Tanystropheus longobardicus

Cymbospondylus

Colossal Cymbospondylus measured more than twice the length of a great white shark. The enormous size of its lizard-like body made sure that this species had very few predators while hunting in deep water.

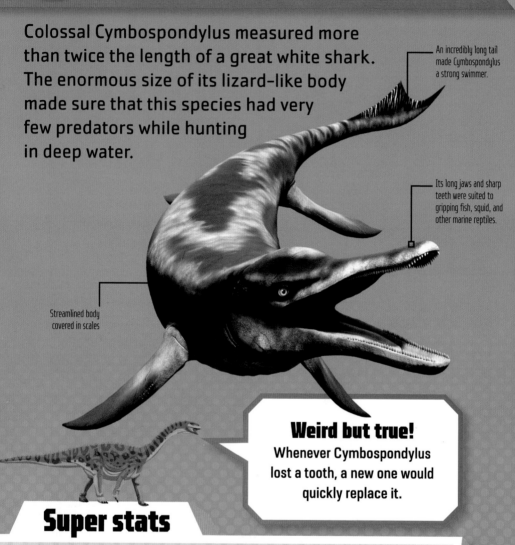

An incredibly long tail made Cymbospondylus a strong swimmer.

Its long jaws and sharp teeth were suited to gripping fish, squid, and other marine reptiles.

Streamlined body covered in scales

Weird but true!
Whenever Cymbospondylus lost a tooth, a new one would quickly replace it.

Super stats

Name: Cymbospondylus **Pronunciation:** SIM-boe-SPON-dil-lus
Name meaning: Boat spine **Period:** Triassic
Length: 10 m (33 ft) **Weight:** 3,200 kg (7,000 lb)
Diet: Carnivore **Habitat:** Ocean **Location:** North America and Europe
Animal type: Prehistoric creature
Key species: Cymbospondylus piscosus

Hupehsuchus

This small marine reptile was about half the size of a dolphin. It relied on its sharp teeth to catch prey and to protect it against predators in the Triassic seas.

Strips of armour running along its back provided extra protection.

A long snout crammed with short teeth was used to grab hold of fish.

Fan-like front flippers for paddling through water

Weird but true!

It is unlikely that Hupehsuchus was able to move around on land because of its body shape.

Super stats

Name: Hupehsuchus
Pronunciation: HU-peh-SOO-kus
Name meaning: Hubei crocodile **Period:** Triassic **Length:** 1 m (3 ft)
Weight: 45 kg (99 lb) **Diet:** Carnivore **Habitat:** Ocean
Location: Asia **Animal type:** Prehistoric creature
Key species: Hupehsuchus nanchangensis

Eudimorphodon

Eudimorphodon was among the first of the pterosaurs to take flight in the Triassic. Although it was as small as a crow, its big wings and stiff tail made it a strong flier, allowing it to swoop down to hunt fish.

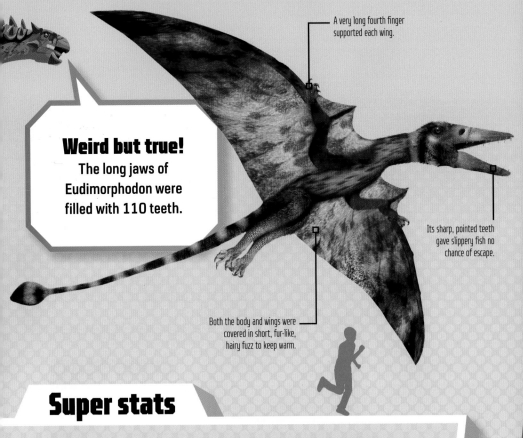

A very long fourth finger supported each wing.

Weird but true!
The long jaws of Eudimorphodon were filled with 110 teeth.

Its sharp, pointed teeth gave slippery fish no chance of escape.

Both the body and wings were covered in short, fur-like, hairy fuzz to keep warm.

Super stats

Name: Eudimorphodon **Pronunciation:** YOU-die-MOR-fo-don
Name meaning: Two truly different forms of teeth **Period:** Triassic
Wingspan: 1 m (3 ft) **Weight:** 10 kg (22 lb)
Diet: Carnivore **Habitat:** Land / Sky **Location:** Europe
Animal type: Prehistoric creature
Key species: Eudimorphodon ranzii

Lystrosaurus

This curious, chunky creature was not a dinosaur, but an ancient type of mammal relative. Sturdy Lystrosaurus spent its days wandering around, and it built burrows to sleep in at night.

Weird but true!
Lystrosaurus was toothless, except for two upper canines, which were shaped like walrus tusks.

Tough beak could tear through the strongest plants and leaves

Sharp claws on the powerful front legs were used to dig underground burrows.

Super stats

Name: Lystrosaurus   **Pronunciation:** LIS-trow-SORE-us
Name meaning: Shovel lizard   **Period:** Permian to Triassic
Length: 2.5 m (8 ft)   **Weight:** 120 kg (265 lb)   **Diet:** Herbivore
Habitat: Land   **Location:** Africa, Asia, and Antarctica
Animal type: Prehistoric creature   **Key species:** Lystrosaurus murrayi

Eodromaeus

Small, but fast and fierce, Eodromaeus appeared at the dawn of the dinosaur era, sprinting across the land in pursuit of small reptiles. This dinosaur was named in 2011, when a nearly complete skeleton was discovered in Argentina.

Its long tail was used for balance when running at top speed.

Weird but true!

Despite being a speedy hunter, Eodromaeus only weighed about the same as a large domestic cat.

Super stats

Name: Eodromaeus   **Pronunciation:** ee-oh-dro-MAY-uss
Name meaning: Dawn runner   **Period:** Triassic
Length: 1 m (3 ft)   **Weight:** 5 kg (11 lb)   **Diet:** Carnivore
Habitat: Land   **Location:** South America
Animal type: Dinosaur   **Key species:** Eodromaeus murphi

It is thought to have been one of the earliest members of the theropod group of dinosaurs, which includes the likes of Tyrannosaurus.

A lightweight body kept Eodromaeus quick on its feet.

Three sharp claws on each hand gripped hold of prey before clawing it apart.

Long legs helped Eodromaeus to chase prey or outrun predators.

Shonisaurus

This huge predator is the biggest known reptile to have ever existed. Its sheer size meant it was unlikely to be hunted – it was the length of a swimming pool. Shonisaurus was the first truly gigantic predator to develop in the ocean, and it was the biggest predator in the world at the time.

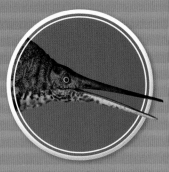

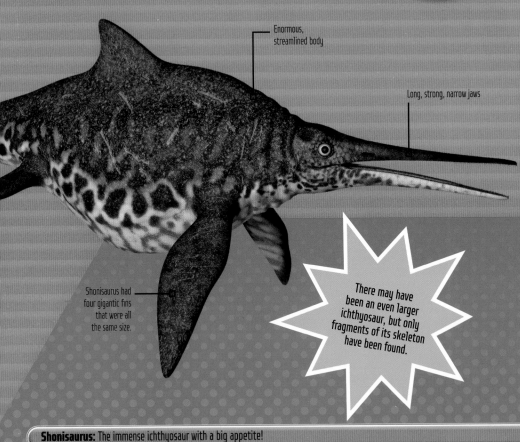

Enormous, streamlined body

Long, strong, narrow jaws

Shonisaurus had four gigantic fins that were all the same size.

There may have been an even larger ichthyosaur, but only fragments of its skeleton have been found.

Shonisaurus: The immense ichthyosaur with a big appetite!

Battle up!

The Triassic oceans were bursting with life, including lots of types of fish and ancient squid-like creatures. Chasing after this plentiful prey were shark-shaped ichthyosaurs, including Shonisaurus and Cymbospondylus.

Cymbospondylus

This large reptile looked a little like a modern dolphin. It was a strong, fast swimmer, with an eel-like tail that made up half of its body length. Cymbospondylus had rows of teeth in its long, narrow jaws, and hunted small, soft prey.

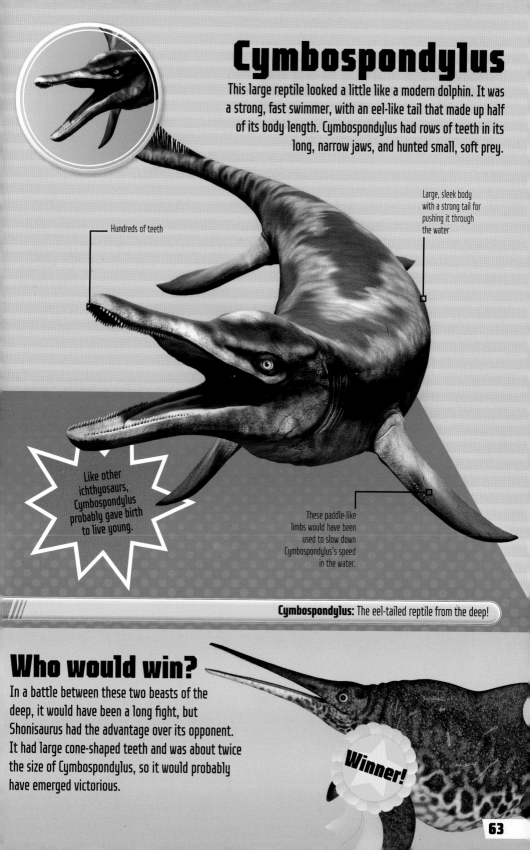

Large, sleek body with a strong tail for pushing it through the water

Hundreds of teeth

Like other ichthyosaurs, Cymbospondylus probably gave birth to live young.

These paddle-like limbs would have been used to slow down Cymbospondylus's speed in the water.

Cymbospondylus: The eel-tailed reptile from the deep!

Who would win?

In a battle between these two beasts of the deep, it would have been a long fight, but Shonisaurus had the advantage over its opponent. It had large cone-shaped teeth and was about twice the size of Cymbospondylus, so it would probably have emerged victorious.

Winner!

Studying fossils

People have known about fossils for thousands of years, but for a long time we did not know what they were. Now, there is a whole type of science dedicated to studying them – palaeontology. Palaeontologists study fossils to learn about life in the past.

Excavation

Fossils need to be handled with great care. First, the rock around the fossil is chipped away. All the tiny bits of rock are checked, to see if they contain any traces of soft body parts. Any big bones are covered in plaster, to make sure they do not break when they are moved.

Tools of the trade

Small brush to clear away dirt from the fossil

Chisel to break off the stone around a fossil

Bucket for collecting sand and gravel, to make sure that no tiny fossil pieces are missed

Dating fossils

Fossils are found in different types of rock. Usually, older layers of rock are found underneath more recent layers. If scientists can date the rocks by studying how they have decayed over time, then they can find out how old fossils in that layer are.

Building a dinosaur

Fossils can be heavy and fragile, so they are sometimes kept safe in special conditions. Lightweight copies are often shown to the public instead. These are made from plastic and are wired together on metal frames. Missing parts are often added in. The skeleton is given a life-like pose.

Bringing to life

A few fossils have preserved soft parts, revealing an animal's colours and other features. But, scientists often have to rely on clues from the bones to build models of dinosaur muscles and even complete bodies. Usually, there are gaps in the information, so scientists look at the fossils of related creatures, or study similar animals that are alive today.

Early fossil hunters

Mary Anning (1799-1847)

One of the first palaeontologists, Mary Anning lived in Lyme Regis, in the UK. She was just 12 when she and her brother found the first ichthyosaur fossil known to science.

Richard Owen (1804-1892)

Richard Owen invented the word "dinosaur". He spent years studying fossils and bones, and helped to create the Natural History Museum in London, in the UK.

Othniel Charles Marsh (1831-1899)

Othniel Charles Marsh was a palaeontologist who discovered hundreds of fossils, in a competition with another palaeontologist, Edward Drinker Cope. This contest became known as the "Bone Wars".

Nothosaurus

This dagger-toothed reptile spent most of its time in water, hunting fish. It could also use its short, sturdy legs to walk on land and may have made nests on beaches like modern turtles.

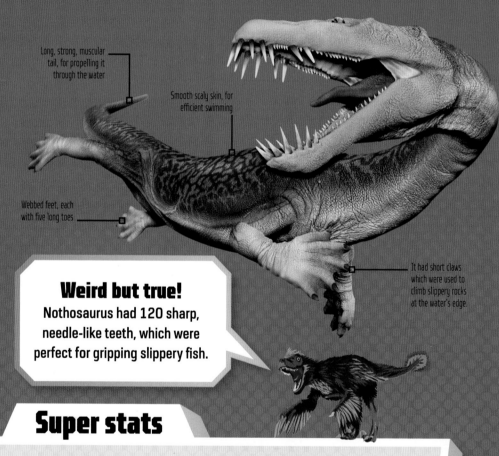

Long, strong, muscular tail, for propelling it through the water

Smooth scaly skin, for efficient swimming

Webbed feet, each with five long toes

It had short claws which were used to climb slippery rocks at the water's edge.

Weird but true!
Nothosaurus had 120 sharp, needle-like teeth, which were perfect for gripping slippery fish.

Super stats

Name: Nothosaurus **Pronunciation:** NO-tho-SORE-us
Name meaning: False reptile **Period:** Triassic
Length: 5 m (16.5 ft) **Weight:** 200 kg (440 lb) **Diet:** Carnivore
Habitat: Ocean **Location:** Europe and Asia
Animal type: Prehistoric creature **Key species:** Nothosaurus mirabilis

Mixosaurus

Mixosaurus looked similar to a modern dolphin. It used its flipper–like limbs to expertly steer through the water as it chased fish to eat. Its fossils have been found all over the world.

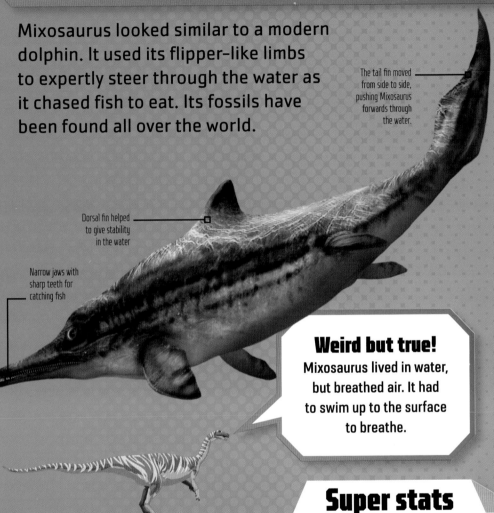

The tail fin moved from side to side, pushing Mixosaurus forwards through the water.

Dorsal fin helped to give stability in the water

Narrow jaws with sharp teeth for catching fish

Weird but true!
Mixosaurus lived in water, but breathed air. It had to swim up to the surface to breathe.

Super stats

Name: Mixosaurus   **Pronunciation:** MIX-oh-SORE-us
Name meaning: Mixed lizard   **Period:** Triassic   **Length:** 2 m (6.5 ft)
Weight: 30 kg (66 lb)   **Diet:** Carnivore   **Habitat:** Ocean
Location: Europe and Asia   **Animal type:** Prehistoric creature
Key species: Mixosaurus cornalianus

Batrachotomus

Most of the time, this creature walked around on four legs. However, it may have been able to rear up on its back legs for short periods to attack smaller animals that it wanted to eat.

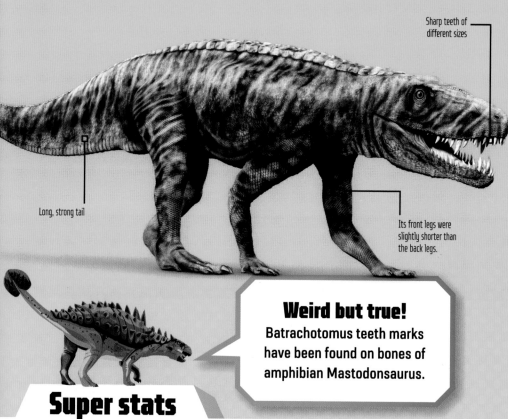

Sharp teeth of different sizes

Long, strong tail

Its front legs were slightly shorter than the back legs.

Weird but true!
Batrachotomus teeth marks have been found on bones of amphibian Mastodonsaurus.

Super stats

Name: Batrachotomus **Pronunciation:** ba-TRAK-o-TO-mus
Name meaning: Frog slicer **Period:** Triassic
Length: 6 m (20 ft) **Weight:** 1,100 kg (2,400 lb)
Diet: Carnivore **Habitat:** Land
Location: Europe **Animal type:** Prehistoric creature
Key species: Batrachotomus kupferzellensis

Mastodonsaurus

Colossal Mastodonsaurus spent most of its life in water. It used its limbs to pull itself through forests of underwater plants in search of fish. It is one of the largest amphibians known to have ever existed.

Large, triangle-shaped head

Its webbed back feet and fin-like tail would have helped this amphibian to push itself through the water.

Weird but true!

Mastodonsaurus's two front teeth were so big that it had special openings in its gums for them, to help it shut its mouth.

Two large teeth at the front of the lower jaw

Super stats

Name: Mastodonsaurus **Pronunciation:** mas-TOE-don-SORE-us
Name meaning: Breast-toothed lizard **Period:** Triassic
Length: 6 m (20 ft) **Weight:** 1,400 kg (3,100 lb)
Diet: Carnivore **Habitat:** Ocean
Location: Europe and Asia **Animal type:** Prehistoric creature
Key species: Mastodonsaurus giganteus

Plateosaurus

This plant eater walked on its two back legs, then used its powerful arms and hands to gather leaves. Plateosaurus was one of the first larger-bodied dinosaurs to exist, and is one of the best-known Triassic dinosaurs.

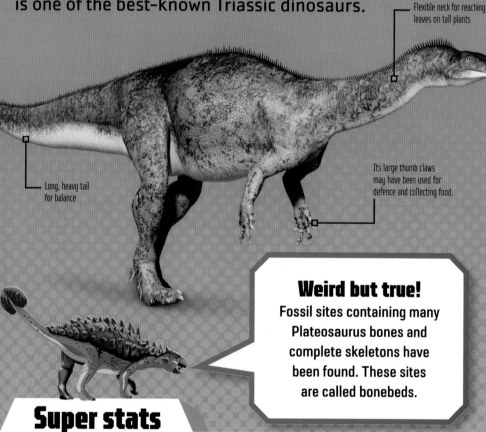

Flexible neck for reaching leaves on tall plants

Its large thumb claws may have been used for defence and collecting food.

Long, heavy tail for balance

Weird but true!

Fossil sites containing many Plateosaurus bones and complete skeletons have been found. These sites are called bonebeds.

Super stats

Name: Plateosaurus **Pronunciation:** PLATE-ee-oh-SORE-us
Name meaning: Broad lizard **Period:** Triassic
Length: 10 m (33 ft) **Weight:** 4,000 kg (8,800 lb) **Diet:** Herbivore
Habitat: Land **Location:** Europe **Animal type:** Dinosaur
Key species: Plateosaurus trossingensis

Placodus

Pladocus might look like an awkward mover, but it was perfect in water and was an effective swimmer. It probably spent time out of the water, too, but would have found it harder to move about on land.

Weird but true!
Placodus had small, sharp front teeth for snatching prey, and a mouth full of large, round, flat teeth for crushing shellfish.

Large eyes and nostrils on top of its head

Large, barrel-chested body

Strong tail to push through water

Paddle-like, webbed hands and feet

Super stats

Name: Placodus   **Pronunciation:** PLAK-oh-dus
Name meaning: Flat tooth   **Period:** Triassic
Length: 3 m (10 ft)   **Weight:** 227 kg (500 lb)   **Diet:** Carnivore
Habitat: Ocean   **Location:** Europe and Asia
Animal type: Prehistoric creature   **Key species:** Placodus gigas

Herrerasaurus

This fearsome carnivore was one of the first dinosaurs to exist. It had all the features needed to be a dangerous predator: sharp teeth, hands with large claws, and a long, strong tail. This tail helped Herrerasaurus to balance its weight across its back legs, so it could speed after prey.

Backward-facing, serrated teeth for slicing flesh

Hands with three long, clawed fingers

Weird but true!
Herrerasaurus had a flexible bottom jaw. This allowed its jaw bones to slide back and forth, so it could keep a firm grip on struggling prey.

Super stats

Name: Herrerasaurus
Pronunciation: heh-RARE-ra-SAW-russ
Name meaning: Herrera's lizard   **Period:** Triassic
Length: 6 m (20 ft)   **Weight:** 260 kg (575 lb)
Diet: Carnivore   **Habitat:** Land   **Location:** South America
Animal type: Dinosaur   **Key species:** Herrerasaurus ischigualastensis

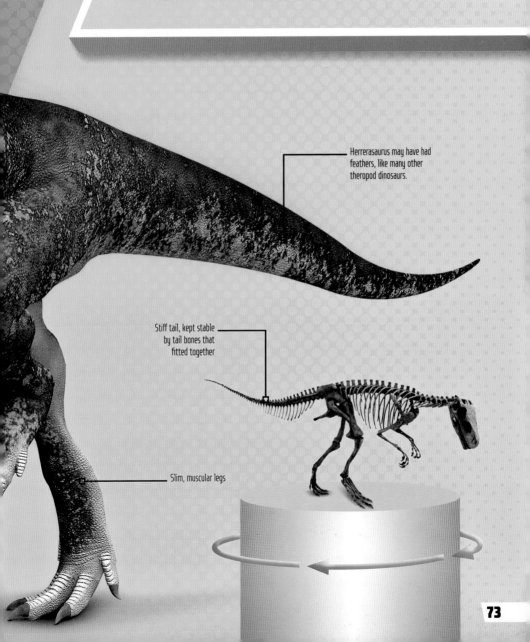

Herrerasaurus may have had feathers, like many other theropod dinosaurs.

Stiff tail, kept stable by tail bones that fitted together

Slim, muscular legs

Looking for lunch

The swampy landscape of the Triassic was home to a wide range of early animals. Here, a hungry Arizonasaurus is about to launch an attack on a herd of plant-eating Placerias.

Proganochelys

This ancient turtle could not pull its head into its shell to hide, but it was not completely defenceless. A row of spikes around Proganochelys's neck warned predators not to take a bite.

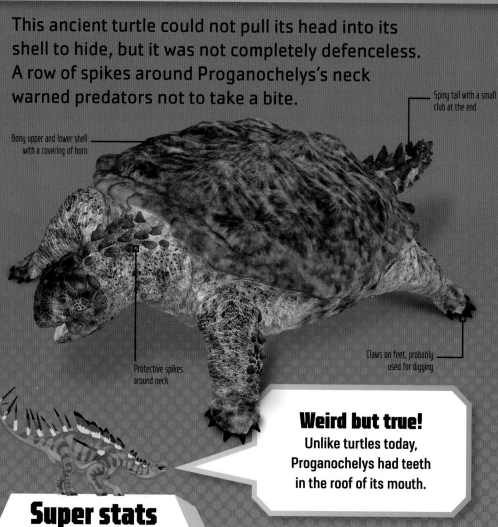

Spiny tail with a small club at the end

Bony upper and lower shell with a covering of horn

Protective spikes around neck

Claws on feet, probably used for digging

Weird but true!
Unlike turtles today, Proganochelys had teeth in the roof of its mouth.

Super stats

Name: Proganochelys   **Pronunciation:** pro-GAN-o-CHELL-iss
Name meaning: Before brightness turtle   **Period:** Triassic
Length: 1 m (3 ft)   **Weight:** 100 kg (220 lb)   **Diet:** Herbivore
Habitat: Land   **Location:** Europe, North America, and Asia
Animal type: Prehistoric creature
Key species: Proganochelys quenstedti

Shonisaurus

This immense ichthyosaur is the largest sea reptile to be discovered so far. It may have grown to the same size as a blue whale – the biggest animal on Earth today.

Weird but true!
Some giant jaw bones found in the UK may belong to an ichthyosaur that was bigger than a blue whale.

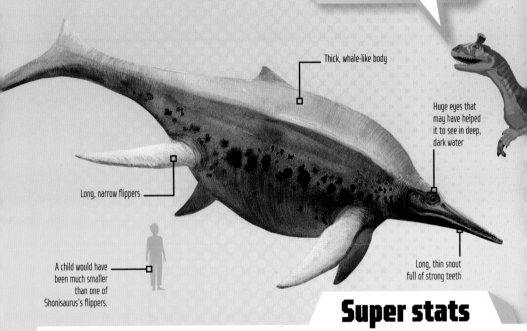

Thick, whale-like body

Huge eyes that may have helped it to see in deep, dark water

Long, narrow flippers

A child would have been much smaller than one of Shonisaurus's flippers.

Long, thin snout full of strong teeth

Super stats

Name: Shonisaurus **Pronunciation:** SHON-ee-SORE-us
Name meaning: Lizard from the Shoshone Mountains
Period: Triassic **Length:** 21 m (70 ft)
Weight: 70,000 kg (154,000 lb) **Diet:** Carnivore **Habitat:** Ocean
Location: North America **Animal type:** Prehistoric creature
Key species: Shonisaurus sikanniensis

Lotosaurus

This bulky, round–bodied creature had no teeth, so it used its beak to break off plants. As it could not chew, it had to swallow its food whole. Members of the Lotosaurus group of animals spread all over the world when the Earth's continents were still joined together.

Sail on back may have been used for temperature control

Toothless, beaky jaws

Big, round body

Super stats

Name: Lotosaurus   **Pronunciation:** low-toe-SORE-us
Name meaning: Lotus lizard   **Period:** Triassic
Length: 2.5 m (8 ft)   **Weight:** 150 kg (330 lb)
Diet: Herbivore   **Habitat:** Land
Location: Asia   **Animal type:** Prehistoric creature
Key species: Lotosaurus adentus

Metoposaurus

On land, this amphibian was clumsy, but in water it was a super predator. Metoposaurus was one of the largest animals in its watery world, snapping at prey with hundreds of sharp, pointed teeth.

Weird but true!

Metoposaurus lived at the same time as the earliest dinosaurs, and is likely to have eaten them.

Large, flat head

Small, weak limbs

Large, broad feet

Super stats

Name: Metoposaurus **Pronunciation:** meh-top-oh-SORE-uss
Name meaning: Front lizard **Period:** Triassic
Length: 2 m (6.5 ft) **Weight:** 300 kg (660 lb)
Diet: Carnivore **Habitat:** Water
Location: Europe **Animal type:** Prehistoric creature
Key species: Metoposaurus diagnosticus

Peteinosaurus

This small pterosaur was one of
the first flying backboned animals
to exist, so Peteinosaurus ruled
the skies before others appeared.
Light yet strong bones helped
it to soar through the air
on its leathery wings.

Needle-sharp,
tiny teeth

Wingspan similar width
to a modern magpie

Saurosuchus

This large reptile was among the biggest
and most dangerous predators
of its period. It spent most
of its time on all fours,
but could pull itself up
onto its back legs to
run short distances.

Bony lumps, called
osteoderms, covered its
back from head to tail for
protection against attackers.

Weird but true!
Saurosuchus looks like a dinosaur,
but it is actually more closely
related to modern crocodiles.

Thin wing membrane supported by extra-long fourth finger

Super stats

Name: Peteinosaurus
Pronunciation: peh-TAIN-oh-SORE-us
Name meaning: Winged lizard
Period: Triassic   **Wingspan:** 60 cm (24 in)
Weight: 200 g (7 oz)   **Diet:** Carnivore
Habitat: Land / Sky   **Location:** Europe
Animal type: Prehistoric creature
Key species: Peteinosaurus zambelli

Long, stiff but flexible tail

Weird but true!

Peteinosaurus had strong limbs and claws, suggesting that it may have climbed trees to search for food.

Super stats

Name: Saurosuchus
Pronunciation: SORE-oh-SOO-kus
Name meaning: Lizard crocodile
Period: Triassic   **Length:** 7 m (23 ft)
Weight: 1,800 kg (4,000 lb)   **Diet:** Carnivore
Habitat: Land   **Location:** South America
Animal type: Prehistoric creature
Key species: Saurosuchus galilei

Saurosuchus's enormous size meant that it would have moved at a slow pace most of the time.

Strong neck and jaw muscles, giving a powerful bite

Long, curved, jagged teeth

Arizonasaurus

Arizonasaurus was a sharp-toothed meat eater, named after Arizona, the place in the USA where it was found. For a long time, the only known fossils were a handful of teeth and a single jawbone. Then, in 2002, more bones were found that showed Arizonasaurus had a large, spiny backbone.

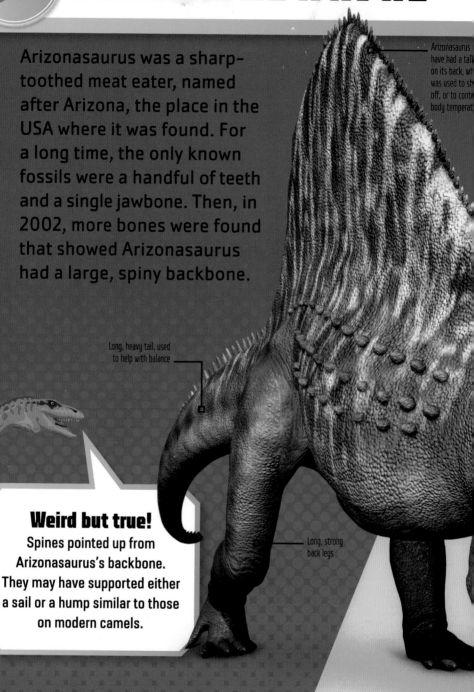

Arizonasaurus have had a tall on its back, wh was used to sh off, or to contr body temperat

Long, heavy tail, used to help with balance

Long, strong back legs

Weird but true!
Spines pointed up from Arizonasaurus's backbone. They may have supported either a sail or a hump similar to those on modern camels.

Super stats

Name: Arizonasaurus
Pronunciation: AH-ree-ZO-nah-SORE-us
Name meaning: Arizona lizard
Period: Triassic **Length:** 3 m (10 ft)
Weight: 700 kg (1,550 lb) **Diet:** Carnivore **Habitat:** Land
Location: North America **Animal type:** Prehistoric creature
Key species: Arizonasaurus babbitti

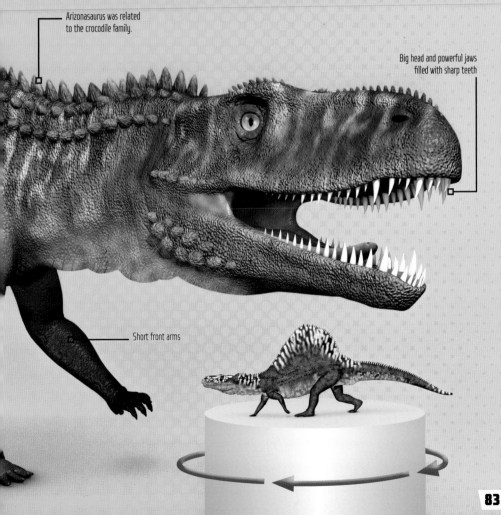

Arizonasaurus was related to the crocodile family.

Big head and powerful jaws filled with sharp teeth

Short front arms

Saurosuchus

This mega reptile was the top predator of its day – among the biggest, baddest carnivores on Earth. It ate anything that it could find, including dinosaurs and other carnivores. Saurosuchus's teeth constantly regrew, meaning its weapons never ran out, and it had super strong jaw muscles that let it keep a tight grip on struggling prey.

Armour along Saurosuchus's back protected it from attack.

Strong neck and jaw muscles

Long, curved, jagged teeth regrew as they wore out

Saurosuchus was not a dinosaur – this reptile is an ancestor of modern crocodiles.

Saurosuchus: The reptilian super predator is ready for the fight!

Battle up!

When Herrerasaurus first appeared, some deadly carnivores already roamed the Earth – Saurosuchus was among the biggest predators of its time. A skull of Herrerasaurus was found with bite marks that may belong to Saurosuchus.

Herrerasaurus

Three large curving claws on each hand let this carnivore grasp its prey. It was able to keep hold of any animals unfortunate enough to find themselves within reach. A double hinge in its jaw let Herrerasaurus grasp tightly onto prey. Those jaws were not opening once they were clamped shut around something tasty!

Large, curving teeth for gripping on to prey

Small bones have been found in what is thought to be Herrerasaurus fossilized poo, showing that they could digest bone.

Long, curved claws

Herrerasaurus: Has this clawed contender bitten off more that it can chew?

Who would win?

Fierce though it was, Herrerasaurus was no match for Saurosuchus. Saurosuchus may have actively hunted Herrerasaurus or have eaten its dead body, but either way Saurosuchus was too big for Herrerasaurus to take on in a fight. If a battle could not be avoided, Saurosuchus would almost certainly have been the victor.

Winner!

Traces of life

Not all fossils are parts of animals or plants. Trace fossils are fossils of things that animals did when they were alive. They can show us where animals have been and how they behaved. Sometimes, plants and animals left prints in the ground, called impressions, or were preserved in ice, tar, or hardened tree resin.

Footprints

These can be found in all types of rocks. Studying footprints can show us if animals walked or ran, and if they travelled in groups.

Coprolites

Coprolites are fossilized poo. They preserve bits of food and bone, so scientists can see what dinosaurs ate.

Nests

Dinosaur nests have been found with eggs in. These show that the eggs had hard shells and were different shapes. Some were just about to hatch.

Gastroliths

Some animals swallowed these stones to help them digest their food. The stones stayed in their stomachs, grinding up tough food to help digestion.

Burrows

Some animals dug holes in the ground or underwater for protection from weather or other creatures. These burrows give clues about animals' habits.

Impression

Sometimes a shell, leaf, or piece of skin makes an impression in the mud. Then the mud slowly turns to stone, preserving the imprint as a fossil.

Tar

Animals could get trapped in tar pits. The remains of short-faced bears, American lions, and other creatures have been found at La Brea Tar Pits in Los Angeles, USA.

Jurassic

This was the golden age of the dinosaurs. In the Triassic, dinosaurs had been just a small part of animal life, but now they grew in size and number. Dinosaurs dominated the land. They developed into a huge range of shapes and sizes, from massive herbivores to tiny, feathery carnivores. Insects, lizards, the first birds, and early mammals lived among them. The oceans were ruled by massive marine reptiles, such as ichthyosaurs.

Gigantspinosaurus

There's a reason its name means "giant–spined lizard" – just look at those shoulder spines! Gigantspinosaurus was an unusual looking stegosaur. It was similar to, but smaller than, Stegosaurus, and was not related to Spinosaurus.

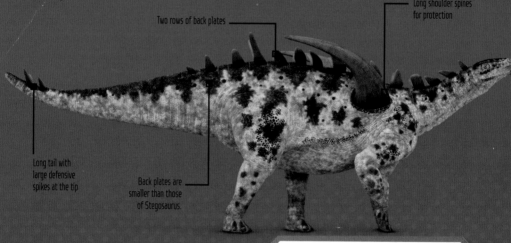

Long shoulder spines for protection

Two rows of back plates

Long tail with large defensive spikes at the tip

Back plates are smaller than those of Stegosaurus.

Weird but true!

Experts argue whether the shoulder spines on the reconstruction have been placed upside down.

Super stats

Name: Gigantspinosaurus **Pronunciation:** ji-GANT-SPY-noe-SORE-us
Name meaning: Giant-spined lizard **Period:** Jurassic
Length: 4 m (13 ft) **Weight:** 850 kg (1,900 lb)
Diet: Herbivore **Habitat:** Land **Location:** Asia
Animal type: Dinosaur **Key species:** Gigantspinosaurus sichuanensis

Huayangosaurus

They might be relatives, but Huayangosaurus lived 10 million years before Stegosaurus, making it one of the earliest stegosaurs discovered. It had a small head, large body, spiky back plates, and a long, spike-tipped tail.

Weird but true!
A stegosaur's tail spike is known as a "thagomizer" – a word invented by a cartoonist and adopted by experts.

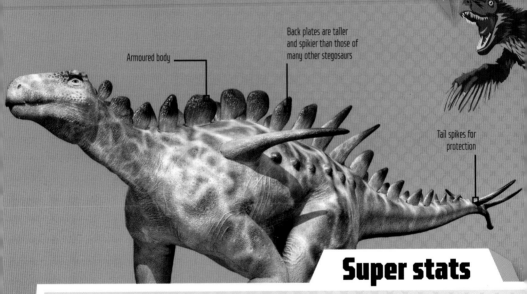

Back plates are taller and spikier than those of many other stegosaurs

Armoured body

Tail spikes for protection

Super stats

Name: Huayangosaurus   **Pronunciation:** HWAH-YANG-oh-SORE-us
Name meaning: Huayang lizard   **Period:** Jurassic
Length: 4.5 m (15 ft)   **Weight:** 1,000 kg (2,200 lb)
Diet: Herbivore   **Habitat:** Land   **Location:** Asia
Animal type: Dinosaur   **Key species:** Huayangosaurus taibaii

Compsognathus

Do not be fooled by its size – Compsognathus was small but deadly. As a fast dinosaur, it had a reputation as a vicious predator. Not bad for a feathered animal the size of a chicken.

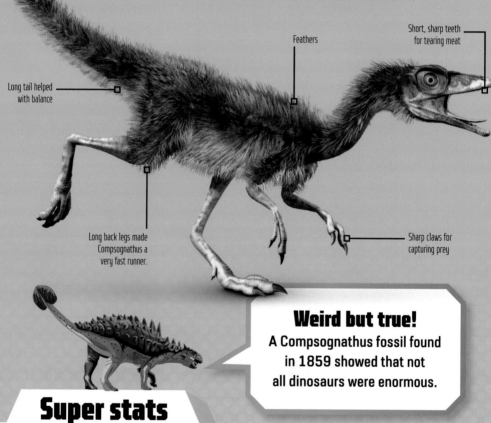

Feathers

Short, sharp teeth for tearing meat

Long tail helped with balance

Long back legs made Compsognathus a very fast runner.

Sharp claws for capturing prey

Weird but true!
A Compsognathus fossil found in 1859 showed that not all dinosaurs were enormous.

Super stats

Name: Compsognathus   **Pronunciation:** COMP-sog-NAITH-us
Name meaning: Pretty jaw   **Period:** Jurassic
Length: 1.2 m (4 ft)   **Weight:** 3 kg (6.5 lb)
Diet: Carnivore   **Habitat:** Land   **Location:** Europe
Animal type: Dinosaur   **Key species:** Compsognathus longipes

Apatosaurus

As heavy as five elephants and a little longer than a bowling alley, this hefty herbivore was a true giant! It slowly stomped around on four huge legs, searching for plants and trees to snack on.

Weird but true!
Apatosaurus's neck was supported by hollow bones – otherwise it would have been too heavy to lift.

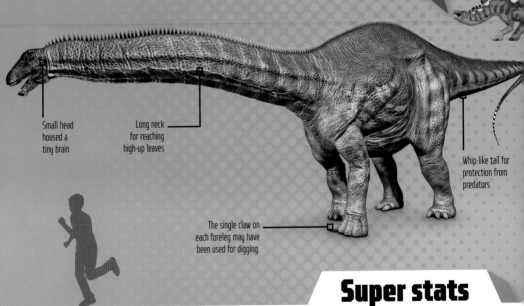

Small head housed a tiny brain

Long neck for reaching high-up leaves

Whip-like tail for protection from predators

The single claw on each foreleg may have been used for digging.

Super stats

Name: Apatosaurus   **Pronunciation:** a-PAT-oh-SORE-us
Name meaning: Deceptive lizard   **Period:** Jurassic
Length: 25 m (80 ft)   **Weight:** 30,000 kg (66,000 lb)
Diet: Herbivore   **Habitat:** Land   **Location:** North America
Animal type: Dinosaur   **Key species:** Apatosaurus ajax

Mamenchisaurus

Yes, it's a sauropod, just like Brachiosaurus, but you can tell Mamenchisaurus apart by its enormous neck! Its neck is supported by 19 huge vertebrae filled with air pockets.

Domed forehead

Tiny head

Its neck was as long as a bus.

Weird but true!
Mamenchisaurus had the longest neck of any animal ever – it was 9 m (30 ft) long.

Long, whip-like tail, used to fight off predators

Legs as big as tree trunks

Inward-pointing front claw

Toe claws

Super stats

Name: Mamenchisaurus **Pronunciation:** ma-MEN-chee-SORE-us
Name meaning: Mamenchi lizard **Period:** Jurassic to Cretaceous
Length: 26 m (85 ft) **Weight:** 35,000 kg (77,000 lb)
Diet: Herbivore **Habitat:** Land **Location:** Asia
Animal type: Dinosaur **Key species:** Mamenchisaurus constructus

Metriorhynchus

Metriorhynchus looked like a crocodile, but was not built for life on land. This fast, powerful swimmer hunted for prey in the open ocean. It pushed through the water by using its large, paddle–like limbs and tail.

Weird but true!

Fossil remains show Metriorhynchus had a dolphin-like tail fluke that would have helped it swim.

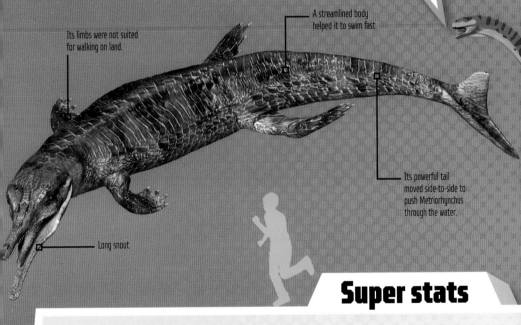

Its limbs were not suited for walking on land.

A streamlined body helped it to swim fast.

Its powerful tail moved side-to-side to push Metriorhynchus through the water.

Long snout

Super stats

Name: Metriorhynchus **Pronunciation:** met-ree-OH-RINK-us
Name meaning: Moderate snout **Period:** Jurassic
Length: 3 m (10 ft) **Weight:** 25 kg (55 lb) **Diet:** Carnivore
Habitat: Ocean **Location:** Europe **Animal type:** Prehistoric creature
Key species: Metriorhynchus brevirostris

Allosaurus

Allosaurus was one of the most fearsome dinosaurs of all time. It was smart, fast, and fearless, with serrated teeth and razor–sharp claws. Lots of large dinosaur bones have Allosaurus teeth marks. This tells us that Allosaurus was not afraid of attacking larger prey.

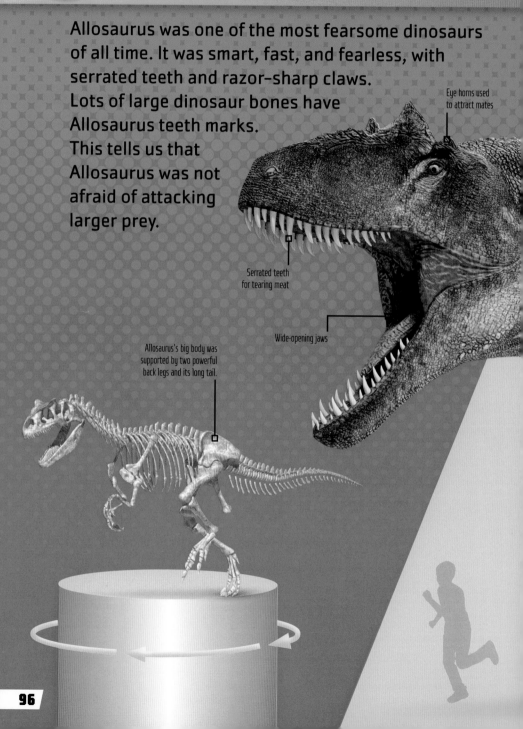

Eye horns used to attract mates

Serrated teeth for tearing meat

Wide-opening jaws

Allosaurus's big body was supported by two powerful back legs and its long tail.

Super stats

Name: Allosaurus Pronunciation: AL-oh-SORE-us
Name meaning: Different lizard   Period: Jurassic
Length: 10.5 m (34 ft) Weight: 2,300 kg (5,000 lb)
Diet: Carnivore Habitat: Land
Location: North America and Europe
Animal type: Dinosaur
Key species: Allosaurus fragilis

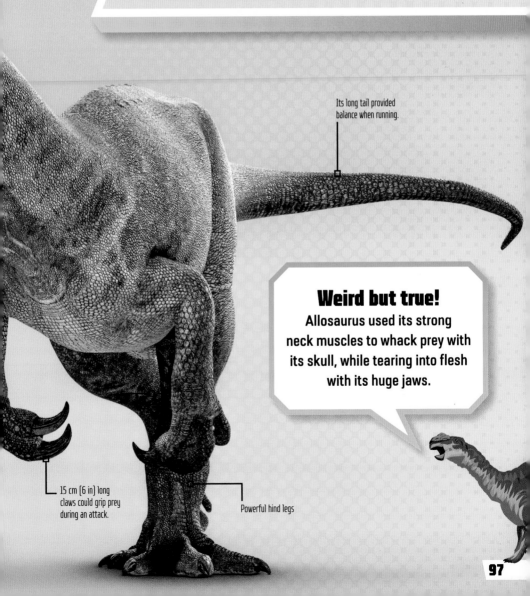

Its long tail provided balance when running.

Weird but true!
Allosaurus used its strong neck muscles to whack prey with its skull, while tearing into flesh with its huge jaws.

15 cm (6 in) long claws could grip prey during an attack.

Powerful hind legs

Allosaurus

An accomplished hunter, Allosaurus was fearless in a fight. It would attack its prey without mercy. This massive beast had sharp, serrated, or jagged, teeth that could rip through even the toughest of skin, and curved claws for holding its prey tight during a battle. It was fast and moved easily, able to chase down its prey and attack.

Allosaurus had powerful thighs. Some scientists think it could reach speeds of up to 55 kph (34 mph).

An Allosaurus fossil was found with a puncture wound matching the size and shape of a Stegosaurus tail spike.

Allosaurus: This fearless foe has the drive to keep on attacking, again, and again, and again...

Battle up!

Two Jurassic heavyweights – fierce Allosaurus and armoured Stegosaurus – were known enemies, and would often engage in battle. Stegosaurus fossils have been found with bite and puncture marks matching the teeth of Allosaurus.

Stegosaurus

What Stegosaurus lacked in speed, it more than made up for in power. As big as a tank and immensely strong, its most important defensive weapon was its mighty, spike-tipped tail. Stegosaurus relied on its armoured body and large, bony back plates for protection. When a predator lashed out, thick armour bought Stegosaurus enough time to fight back with its strong tail!

Back plates would stop a taller predator from biting down onto Stegosaurus from above.

Unlike Allosaurus, Stegosaurus's head was close to the ground, near the plants it ate.

Stegosaurus: This tank with a tail squares up to its attacker. Watch out for the spikes!

Who would win?

You might think that a battle between a cunning carnivore and a heavy herbivore would be pretty one-sided. However, despite Allosaurus's speed and razor-sharp claws, its bite let it down. Its jaws opened really wide, but the force of its bite was nothing special. This gave Stegosaurus time to fight back with its spike-tipped tail. Unless a group of Allosauruses overcame Stegosaurus by attacking it together, the herbivore would win the contest!

Winner!

Classifying dinosaurs

More than 1,000 different types of dinosaur have been found. Fast, ferocious, or feathery – you name it and it probably existed. Scientists have grouped dinosaurs with others that shared similar features. Here are the different dinosaur groups.

Start with the hips

Dinosaurs are split into two main groups, depending on what their pelvis, or hip bone, is like. A dinosaur can either be a saurischian, with hips like a lizard, or an ornithischian, with hips like a bird.

Saurischians

These fearsome predators with lizard-like hips are divided into two main groups: theropods (three-toed dinosaurs) and sauropods (lizard-footed). Theropods are the only group of saurischians to include carnivores, while sauropods include the biggest animals to ever walk the planet.

Theropods

Stomping around on their two strong legs, theropods were mostly meat eaters, such as Velociraptor and Tyrannosaurus.

Sauropods

These dinosaurs are recognizable by their long necks, long tails, and staggering size. These slow-moving herbivores include Diplodocus and Brachiosaurus.

Ornithischians

These bird-hipped beasts are divided into five major groups: stegosaurs, ankylosaurs, ceratopsians, pachycephalosaurs, and ornithopods.

Ankylosaurs

Known for their thick body armour, these club-tailed quadrupeds had bony plates and spikes across their backs for protection. Some, such as Ankylosaurus and Euoplocephalus, also had a bony club at the end of their tail.

Stegosaurs

Stegosaurs are known for their bony plates and spikes that ran down their backs. Famous members of this group include Stegosaurus and Kentrosaurus.

Ceratopsians

Ceratopsians are recognizable for their head frills, pointy beaks, and long, sharp horns. Triceratops, Pentaceratops, and Protoceratops belong to this group.

Ornithopods

Ornithopod means "bird feet". Dinosaurs in this group, such as Iguanodon and Parasaurolophus, also shared other bird-like features, including beaks.

Pachycephalosaurs

These dinosaurs had thick, bony skulls. They were used for head-ramming during battle by dinosaurs such as Pachycephalosaurus and Stegoceras.

Coelophysis

Coelophysis was an expert hunter. It was a fast runner with excellent eyesight, and three flexible fingers on each hand that could grip small prey.

Long, narrow snout, perfect for reaching prey in burrows

Slim build for speed

Long, flexible S-shaped neck

Its saw-like teeth pointed backwards. This made it almost impossible for prey to escape once caught.

Weird but true!

One Coelophysis fossil was found in such good condition that we can see what its last meal was – a Hesperosuchus.

Super stats

Name: Coelophysis **Pronunciation:** SEE-low-FYE-sis
Name meaning: Hollow form **Period:** Triassic
Length: 3 m (10 ft) **Weight:** 45 kg (100 lb) **Diet:** Carnivore
Habitat: Land **Location:** North America
Animal type: Dinosaur **Key species:** Coelophysis bauri

Dilophosaurus

Dilophosaurus was one of the largest predators of its time. It had two head crests on top of its skull and a strange notch in its upper jaw, possibly for catching small prey.

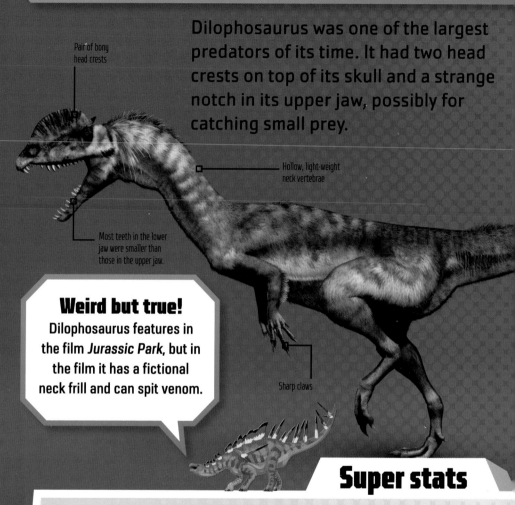

Pair of bony head crests

Hollow, light-weight neck vertebrae

Most teeth in the lower jaw were smaller than those in the upper jaw.

Sharp claws

Weird but true!

Dilophosaurus features in the film *Jurassic Park*, but in the film it has a fictional neck frill and can spit venom.

Super stats

Name: Dilophosaurus **Pronunciation:** die-LOAF-oh-SORE-us
Name meaning: Two-crested lizard **Period:** Jurassic
Length: 6 m (20 ft) **Weight:** 450 kg (1,000 lb) **Diet:** Carnivore
Habitat: Land **Location:** North America **Animal type:** Dinosaur
Key species: Dilophosaurus wetherilli

Scutellosaurus

Scutellosaurus is one of the earliest known relatives of the famous armoured dinosaurs, such as Ankylosaurus. This armoured dinosaur would have spent a lot of time running away from predators.

Rows of bony plates ran along the back and tail to protect it from predators.

Long tail

Long neck for reaching high leaves and plants

Strong, long hind legs made Scutellosaurus a speedy runner.

Weird but true!
Scutellosaurus mostly scurried around on two legs, but may have also walked on all fours.

Super stats

Name: Scutellosaurus **Pronunciation:** scu-tella-SAW-us
Name meaning: Little-shielded lizard **Period:** Jurassic
Length: 1.2 m (4 ft) **Weight:** 10 kg (22 lb) **Diet:** Herbivore
Habitat: Land **Location:** North America **Animal type:** Dinosaur
Key species: Scutellosaurus lawleri

Dorygnathus

Dorygnathus was a fish–eating pterosaur with a short neck and a long tail. Its front teeth acted like a sieve to trap small fish and sea creatures in its beak, before swallowing them.

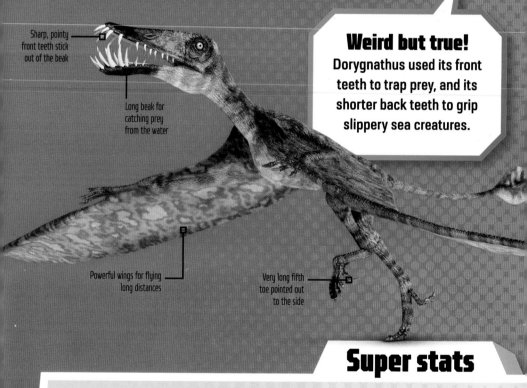

Sharp, pointy front teeth stick out of the beak

Long beak for catching prey from the water

Powerful wings for flying long distances

Very long fifth toe pointed out to the side

Weird but true!

Dorygnathus used its front teeth to trap prey, and its shorter back teeth to grip slippery sea creatures.

Super stats

Name: Dorygnathus   **Pronunciation:** dor-EE-ga-NAY-thuss
Name meaning: Spear jaw   **Period:** Jurassic
Wingspan: 1.5 m (5 ft)   **Weight:** 8 kg (18 lb)   **Diet:** Carnivore
Habitat: Sky   **Location:** Europe   **Animal type:** Prehistoric creature
Key species: Dorygnathus banthensis

Dimorphodon

Dimorphodon was a flying reptile, but was not particularly good at flying – it was quite clumsy on land, too. It spent most of its time scurrying up cliffs and trees, like a large squirrel with wings!

Large, curved claws helped when climbing.

Short wings were not well-adapted for flying.

The beak and head were similar in shape to a puffin's.

Smaller teeth on lower jaw

Larger teeth on upper jaw

Weird but true!
With short wings and a stocky body, Dimorphodon only flew as a last resort.

Super stats

Name: Dimorphodon   **Pronunciation:** die-MOR-foe-don
Name meaning: Two formed tooth   **Period:** Jurassic
Wingspan: 1.5 m (5 ft)   **Weight:** 4 kg (9 lb)
Diet: Carnivore   **Habitat:** Land
Location: Europe   **Animal type:** Prehistoric creature
Key species: Dimorphodon macronyx

Atlasaurus

Atlasaurus was similar to Brachiosaurus, with its long front legs and downwards–sloping back. It had a shorter neck, though, and was roughly half the size of its giant cousin.

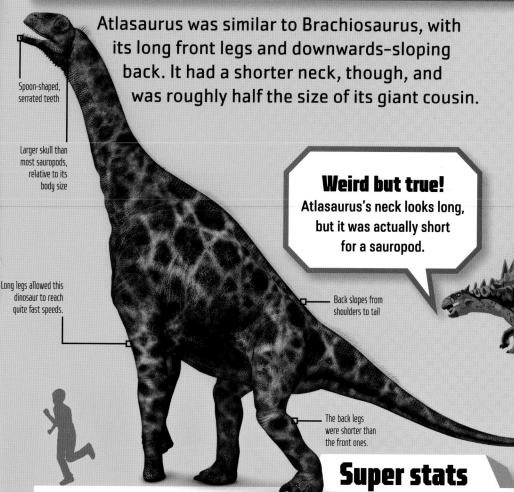

Spoon-shaped, serrated teeth

Larger skull than most sauropods, relative to its body size

Long legs allowed this dinosaur to reach quite fast speeds.

Weird but true!
Atlasaurus's neck looks long, but it was actually short for a sauropod.

Back slopes from shoulders to tail

The back legs were shorter than the front ones.

Super stats

Name: Atlasaurus   **Pronunciation:** AT-las-SORE-us
Name meaning: Atlas lizard   **Period:** Jurassic
Height: 15 m (50 ft)   **Weight:** 14,000 kg (30,800 lb)
Diet: Herbivore   **Habitat:** Land
Location: Africa   **Animal type:** Dinosaur
Key species: Atlasaurus imelakei

Brachiosaurus

You can imagine the ground shaking near you each time this colossal creature took a step. Brachiosaurus had front legs that were taller than usual for a sauropod. That meant its back sloped down towards its tail. Its incredibly long neck gave Brachiosaurus a reach most other dinosaurs could not get close to.

Super stats

Name: Brachiosaurus
Pronunciation: brack-ee-oh-SORE-us
Name meaning: Arm lizard   **Period:** Jurassic
Length: 23 m (75 ft)   **Weight:** 30,000 kg (66,000 lb)
Diet: Herbivore   **Habitat:** Land
Location: North America   **Animal type:** Dinosaur
Key species: Brachiosaurus altithorax

Tail shorter than most other sauropods

Protective eye crest

Weird but true!
Brachiosaurus could not stand on only its back legs – its body was too heavy. But with its long neck, it probably did not need to.

Back slopes down from shoulders to tail

Its neck was almost as long as a telegraph pole.

Wide snout and mouth filled with spoon-like teeth

Tall front legs

Finding food

Brachiosaurus might have lived in herds and travelled over the forests and floodplains of North America. Using their long necks to reach high-up leaves, these dinosaurs would strip the nearby trees, before moving on to munch in a new spot.

Jobaria

Big, heavy, and sturdy on its feet, Jobaria was an early sauropod from northern Africa. It had spoon-shaped teeth, and its flexible neck was shorter than most sauropods.

Its tail could not whip sharply at predators.

Weird but true!
Jobaria's fossils were originally thought to be the bones of a mythical African monster named Jobar.

Hind legs could bear its full body weight

Super stats

Name: Jobaria **Pronunciation:** jo-BA-RE-ah
Name meaning: Jobar
Period: Jurassic **Length:** 20 m (66 ft)
Weight: 18,200 kg (40,000 lb) **Diet:** Herbivore **Habitat:** Land
Location: Africa **Animal type:** Dinosaur
Key species: Jobaria tiguidensis

Cryptoclidus

This was a graceful marine reptile with a long neck and powerful flippers. Cryptoclidus had a delicate skull and teeth, so it was unable to grapple with large prey.

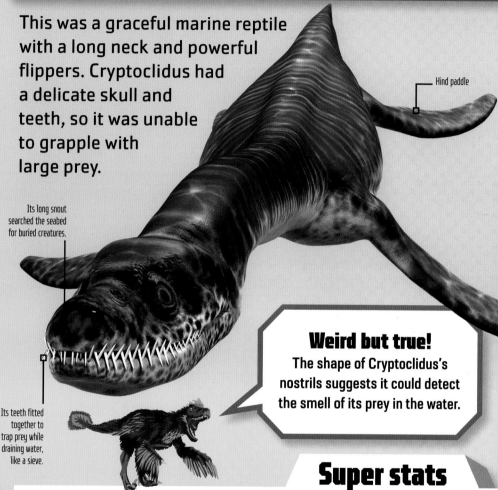

Hind paddle

Its long snout searched the seabed for buried creatures.

Its teeth fitted together to trap prey while draining water, like a sieve.

Weird but true!
The shape of Cryptoclidus's nostrils suggests it could detect the smell of its prey in the water.

Super stats

Name: Cryptoclidus   **Pronunciation:** CRIP-toe-CLEID-us
Name meaning: Hidden collarbones   **Period:** Jurassic
Length: 8 m (26 ft)   **Weight:** 6,000 kg (13,000 lb)
Diet: Carnivore   **Habitat:** Water   **Location:** Europe
Animal type: Prehistoric creature
Key species: Cryptoclidus eurymerus

Archaeopteryx

Meet Archaeopteryx, one of the oldest bird–like dinosaurs. It had some distinctly dinosaur–like features, including sharp teeth, wing claws, and a bony tail.

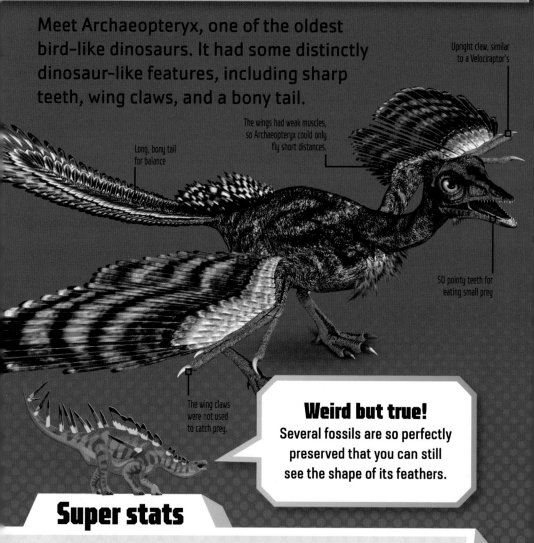

Upright claw, similar to a Velociraptor's

The wings had weak muscles, so Archaeopteryx could only fly short distances.

Long, bony tail for balance

50 pointy teeth for eating small prey

The wing claws were not used to catch prey.

Weird but true!

Several fossils are so perfectly preserved that you can still see the shape of its feathers.

Super stats

Name: Archaeopteryx   **Pronunciation:** ar-kee-OP-ter-ix
Name meaning: Ancient wing   **Period:** Jurassic
Length: 50 cm (20 in)   **Weight:** 1 kg (2 lb)
Diet: Carnivore   **Habitat:** Land / Sky
Location: Europe   **Animal type:** Dinosaur
Key species: Archaeopteryx lithographica

Dicraeosaurus

This spiky sauropod was about half the size of Brachiosaurus. Its name means "double-forked lizard", which describes the Y-shaped spikes running down its back and tail.

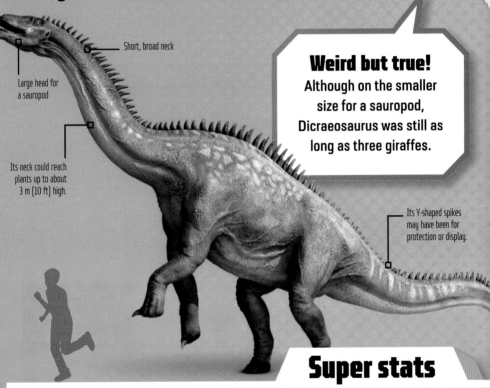

Short, broad neck

Large head for a sauropod

Its neck could reach plants up to about 3 m (10 ft) high.

Weird but true!
Although on the smaller size for a sauropod, Dicraeosaurus was still as long as three giraffes.

Its Y-shaped spikes may have been for protection or display.

Super stats

Name: Dicraeosaurus **Pronunciation:** DIH-cray-oh-SORE-us
Name meaning: Double-forked lizard **Period:** Jurassic
Length: 15 m (50 ft) **Weight:** 6,000 kg (13,000 lb)
Diet: Herbivore **Habitat:** Land
Location: Africa **Animal type:** Dinosaur
Key species: Dicraeosaurus hansemanni

Hesperornithoides

Hesperornithoides, a fluffy, bird–like theropod, had wings and feathers, but it did not fly – its wings were too short. It had sharp teeth and a large, curved claw on each of its feet.

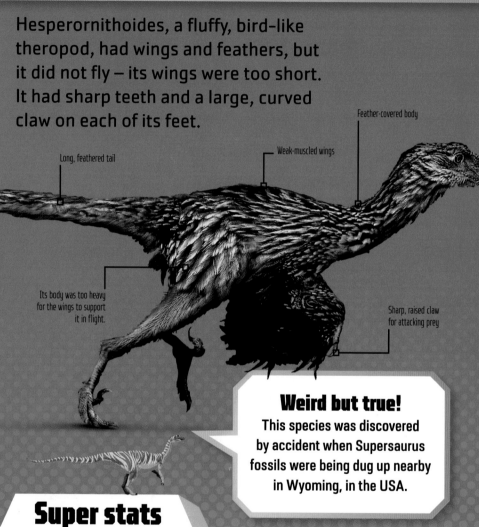

Feather-covered body

Long, feathered tail

Weak-muscled wings

Its body was too heavy for the wings to support it in flight.

Sharp, raised claw for attacking prey

Weird but true!

This species was discovered by accident when Supersaurus fossils were being dug up nearby in Wyoming, in the USA.

Super stats

Name: Hesperornithoides   **Pronunciation:** hes-PER-or-NIF-oy-dees
Name meaning: Western bird   **Period:** Jurassic
Length: 1 m [3 ft]   **Weight:** 6 kg [13 lb]
Diet: Carnivore   **Habitat:** Land
Location: North America   **Animal type:** Dinosaur
Key species: Hesperornithoides miessleri

Dryosaurus

This small plant eater may have stored its food in its cheeks. Dryosaurus had strong, slender legs, which made running away from predators, such as Allosaurus, easy work.

Super stats

Name: Dryosaurus
Pronunciation: DRY-oh-SORE-us
Name meaning: Oak lizard
Period: Jurassic
Length: 3 m (10 ft)
Weight: 100 kg (220 lb)
Diet: Herbivore   **Habitat:** Land
Location: North America
Animal Type: Dinosaur
Key species: Dryosaurus altus

Narrow beak for eating leaves

Thick, bumpy skin

Side-facing eyes to keep watch for predators

Long, stiff tail

Weird but true!

Dryosaurus lived alongside giant dinosaurs, such as Stegosaurus and Diplodocus.

Cryolophosaurus

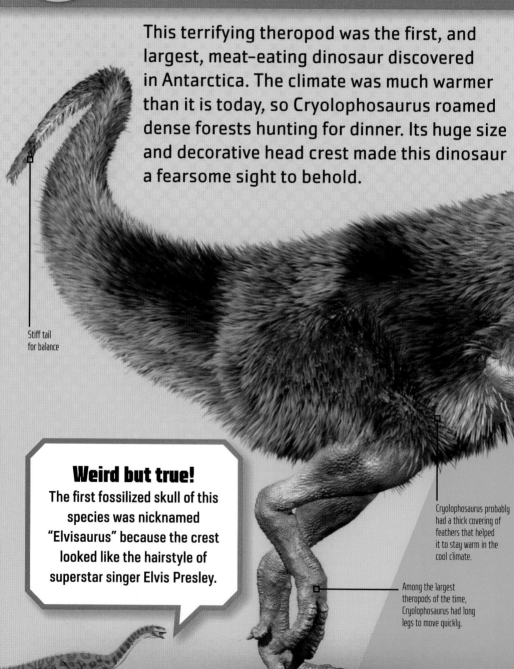

This terrifying theropod was the first, and largest, meat-eating dinosaur discovered in Antarctica. The climate was much warmer than it is today, so Cryolophosaurus roamed dense forests hunting for dinner. Its huge size and decorative head crest made this dinosaur a fearsome sight to behold.

Stiff tail for balance

Weird but true!
The first fossilized skull of this species was nicknamed "Elvisaurus" because the crest looked like the hairstyle of superstar singer Elvis Presley.

Cryolophosaurus probably had a thick covering of feathers that helped it to stay warm in the cool climate.

Among the largest theropods of the time, Cryolophosaurus had long legs to move quickly.

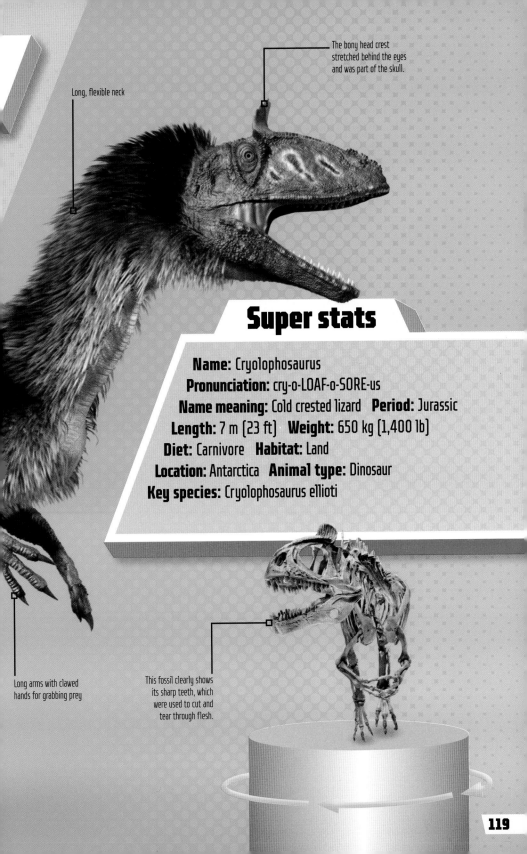

The bony head crest stretched behind the eyes and was part of the skull.

Long, flexible neck

Super stats

Name: Cryolophosaurus
Pronunciation: cry-o-LOAF-o-SORE-us
Name meaning: Cold crested lizard   **Period:** Jurassic
Length: 7 m (23 ft)   **Weight:** 650 kg (1,400 lb)
Diet: Carnivore   **Habitat:** Land
Location: Antarctica   **Animal type:** Dinosaur
Key species: Cryolophosaurus ellioti

Long arms with clawed hands for grabbing prey

This fossil clearly shows its sharp teeth, which were used to cut and tear through flesh.

Plesiosaurus

Plesiosaurus used its large flippers to push itself through water, like a sea turtle does. Its long neck meant that it would have made waves as it moved through the water, but it could move its neck surprisingly fast, so it was great at snatching prey. Its thin, sharp teeth were perfect for trapping small creatures, but not for biting larger animals.

Plesiosaurus grew to about 3.5 m (11.5 ft) in length, which is roughly the size of a large tiger.

Plesiosaurus lived entirely at sea and gave birth to live young.

Four paddle-like flippers powered Plesiosaurus through the sea.

Plesiosaurus: Swift and strong, this long-necked hunter is battle-ready!

Battle up!

These two creatures of the deep would have fought in fierce battles. Dolphin–like Temnodontosaurus was larger and faster, with strong jaws and big teeth, but Plesiosaurus's smaller, flexible body would have made it more agile.

Temnodontosaurus

Thanks to its narrow snout, streamlined shape, and powerful tail, Temnodontosaurus could speed through the water, keeping a lookout for prey with its huge eyes. It would approach quickly, with jaws wide open, ready to snap down on its target. Its cone-shaped teeth were strong and sharp, so once they took a bite, prey was unlikely to escape.

Nostrils on top of the snout allowed Temnodontosaurus to breathe at the water's surface.

Huge eyes measuring 25 cm (10 in) gave Temnodontosaurus great underwater eyesight.

Temnodontosaurus had the largest eyes of any vertebrate ever! Each was about the size of a football.

Temnodontosaurus: The Jurassic killer with an eye for spotting its next meal...

Who would win?

At three times the length of Plesiosaurus, Temnodontosaurus was a terrifying enemy. Plesiosaurus would try to swim away, but its speed was no match for its attacker. It may have fought back with its long, flexible neck, but this would be Plesiosaurus's downfall. Its neck was the perfect width for Temnodontosaurus to crush in its powerful jaws to win the battle.

Winner!

121

Pangaea

From around 300 to 230 million years ago, our planet was one giant land mass called Pangaea. Gradually, the land split apart to form the seven continents we know today. This is why fossils are found on every continent.

PANGAEA

Scientists have discovered that in the Triassic period many plant-eating dinosaurs travelled north to what is now Greenland. Plateosaurus fossils have been found there.

Allosaurus

Stegosaurus

England was home to the first discoveries of prehistoric fossils. It is also the place where the first dinosaurs were identified.

FOSSIL HOTSPOT
Hell Creek, USA

FOSSIL HOTSPOT
Isle of Wight, UK

ATLANTIC OCEAN

FOSSIL HOTSPOT
Sahara Desert

North America

During the 1880s, two American palaeontologists competed to find dinosaur bones. They ended up discovering almost 150 new types of dinosaur, including Allosaurus and Stegosaurus.

Argentinosaurus

PACIFIC OCEAN

Amazing fossilized finds in South America include some of the oldest dinosaurs, such as Eoraptor, and some of the largest titanosaurs, including Argentinosaurus.

South America

Eoraptor

ATLANTIC OCEAN

= top spot for finding dinosaur fossils

Dinosaur world

Dinosaurs lived all over the world during the Mesozoic Era. They stomped, sprinted, and scurried across every continent on Earth.

ARCTIC OCEAN

Researchers looking for evidence of early humans stumbled across dinosaur nests and eggs belonging to Oviraptor and other dinosaurs in the great Gobi Desert, in Mongolia and China. This led to more expeditions to Asia and the discovery of more fossils, including feathered Sinosauropteryx in China.

Diplodocus

Sinosauropteryx

Asia

Oviraptor

Europe

Megalosaurus

Carcharodontosaurus

Velociraptor

PACIFIC OCEAN

FOSSIL HOTSPOT ....
Sichuan, China

Spinosaurus

Africa

Africa's Sahara Desert has revealed many dinosaur fossils, including meat eater Spinosaurus. Morocco, in north Africa, was home to colossal Carcharodontosaurus.

Muttaburrasaurus

INDIAN OCEAN

Oceania

Fossils found on the Victoria coastline of Australia triggered a wave of dinosaur discoveries, including long-necked Austrosaurus, crested Muttaburrasaurus, and armoured Minmi.

Minmi

FOSSIL HOTSPOT ....
Dinosaur Cove, Australia

Cryolophosaurus

Until 1986, scientists thought that dinosaurs did not live in Antarctica, but this continent was much warmer in their time. Fossil finds, including meat eater Cryolophosaurus, proved it was home to dinosaurs.

SOUTHERN OCEAN

Antarctica

123

Camarasaurus

This peaceful plant eater is one of the most common dinosaur fossils found in Late Jurassic rocks in North America. Camarasaurus lived in herds for safety as it travelled across the Jurassic plains.

Extra-large cheeks gave Camarasaurus room to store leaves to eat later.

Very strong legs supported its typical, heavy sauropod body.

Weird but true!

Camarasaurus had large, spoon-shaped teeth for grasping leaves from trees.

Super stats

Name: Camarasaurus   **Pronunciation:** KAM-a-ra-SORE-us
Name meaning: Chambered lizard   **Period:** Jurassic
Length: 18 m (60 ft)   **Weight:** 20,000 kg (44,000 lb)
Diet: Herbivore   **Habitat:** Land   **Location:** North America
Animal type: Dinosaur   **Key species:** Camarasaurus supremus

Monolophosaurus

Meat–eating Monolophosaurus looked much like many other early, two–legged theropods, except for its striking head crest. This may have been used to attract a mate or to scare away predators in the Jurassic forests.

Large, hollow crest made its head appear much bigger than those of other theropods.

Teeth as sharp as knives sliced though prey in an instant

Weird but true!

Its head crest may have been brightly coloured so others of its kind could identify it, or to attract a mate.

Super stats

Name: Monolophosaurus
Pronunciation: MON-oh-LOAF-oh-SORE-rus
Name meaning: Single-crested lizard   **Period:** Jurassic
Length: 6 m (20 ft)   **Weight:** 680 kg (1,500 lb)
Diet: Carnivore   **Habitat:** Land   **Location:** Asia
Animal type: Dinosaur   **Key species:** Monolophosaurus jiangi

Liopleurodon

Liopleurodon was among the Jurassic ocean's top hunters. Rising up from the dark ocean depths, this powerful, four-flippered pliosaur shot through the water to seize fish and squid with its teeth.

Big nostrils detect the smell of prey over long distances

Strong flippers guided its enormous body through the Jurassic seas.

Weird but true!
Experts use a special swimming robot to study the way pliosaurs, such as Liopleurodon, moved.

Super stats

Name: Liopleurodon **Pronunciation:** LIE-oh-PLOOR-oh-don
Name meaning: Smooth-sided teeth **Period:** Jurassic
Length: 6.5 m (21 ft) **Weight:** 2,700 kg (6,000 lb)
Diet: Carnivore **Habitat:** Ocean **Location:** Europe
Animal type: Prehistoric creature **Key species:** Liopleurodon ferox

Lesothosaurus

Small and speedy, Lesothosaurus was one of the first plant eaters in Jurassic times. This long–legged dinosaur was always alert to danger and could easily outrun predators across the open plains.

Large eyes to keep a look out for enemies

Lesothosaurus's lightweight body made it easier to run fast.

Weird but true!

Just like humans, Lesothosaurus had five fingers on each hand.

Super stats

Name: Lesothosaurus **Pronunciation:** luh-SOO-too-SORE-us
Name meaning: Lizard from Lesotho
Period: Jurassic **Length:** 1 m (3 ft) **Weight:** 7 kg (15 lb)
Diet: Herbivore **Habitat:** Land **Location:** Africa
Animal type: Dinosaur **Key species:** Lesothosaurus diagnosticus

Massospondylus

Massospondylus was one of the earliest plant–eating Jurassic dinosaurs. Its strong hands and sharp thumb claws helped it to grip hold of trees while chewing on leaves. It swallowed small stones to help grind up the tough leaves it ate.

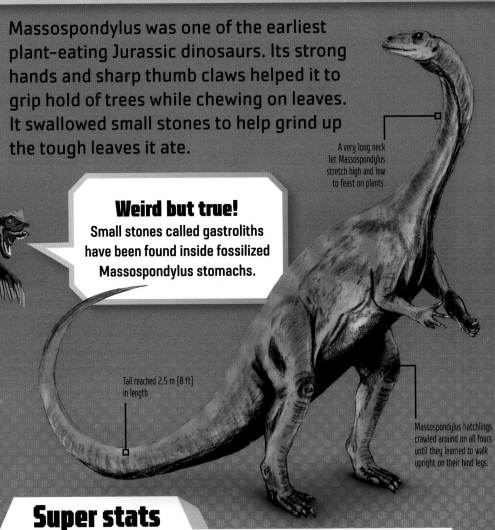

A very long neck let Massospondylus stretch high and low to feast on plants.

Weird but true!
Small stones called gastroliths have been found inside fossilized Massospondylus stomachs.

Tail reached 2.5 m (8 ft) in length

Massospondylus hatchlings crawled around on all fours until they learned to walk upright on their hind legs.

Super stats

Common name: Massospondylus
Pronunciation: MASS-oh-SPON-dill-us
Name meaning: Massive vertebra   **Period:** Jurassic
Length: 6 m (20 ft)   **Weight:** 1,000 kg (2,200 lb)
Diet: Herbivore   **Habitat:** Land   **Location:** Africa
Animal type: Dinosaur   **Key species:** Massospondylus carinatus

Epidexipteryx

Tiny theropod Epidexipteryx was a truly unique dinosaur. It is one of the smallest dinosaur species ever found and the first we know of with tail feathers used for showing off, instead of for flight.

Weird but true!
Epidexipteryx's thigh bone was only about half the size of a chicken's thigh bone.

Four fantastic feathers fanned out from the back to attract the attention of passing females.

Epidexipteryx had very long fingers and a strong grip for climbing trees in the Jurassic forests.

Super stats

Name: Epidexipteryx **Pronunciation:** ep-EE-dex-ip-TER-ix
Name meaning: Display feather **Period:** Jurassic
Length: 44.5 cm (17.5 in) **Weight:** 160 g (5.5 oz)
Diet: Carnivore **Habitat:** Land **Location:** Asia
Animal type: Dinosaur **Key species:** Epidexipteryx hui

Ichthyosaurus

Ichthyosaurus swam the Jurassic oceans, searching for fish, squid, and other marine animals to eat. This shark-shaped marine reptile had a streamlined body, a big dorsal fin, two pairs of flippers, and a forked tail. These all helped to make it a strong, speedy swimmer.

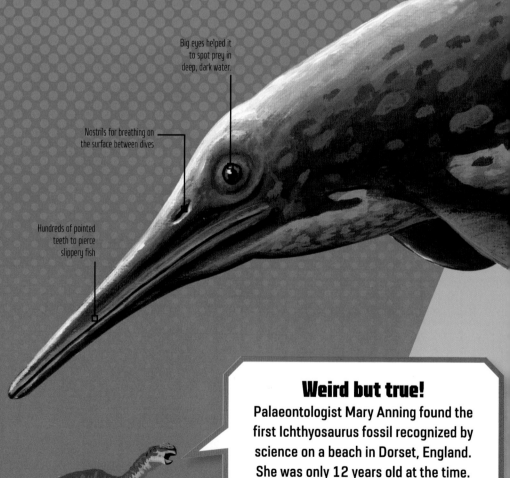

Big eyes helped it to spot prey in deep, dark water.

Nostrils for breathing on the surface between dives

Hundreds of pointed teeth to pierce slippery fish

Weird but true!

Palaeontologist Mary Anning found the first Ichthyosaurus fossil recognized by science on a beach in Dorset, England. She was only 12 years old at the time.

Super stats

Name: Ichthyosaurus
Pronunciation: ICK-thee-oh-SORE-us
Name meaning: Fish lizard   **Period:** Jurassic
Length: 3.3 m (11 ft)   **Weight:** 300 kg (660 lb)
Diet: Carnivore   **Habitat:** Ocean
Location: Europe and North America
Animal type: Prehistoric creature
Key species: Ichthyosaurus communis

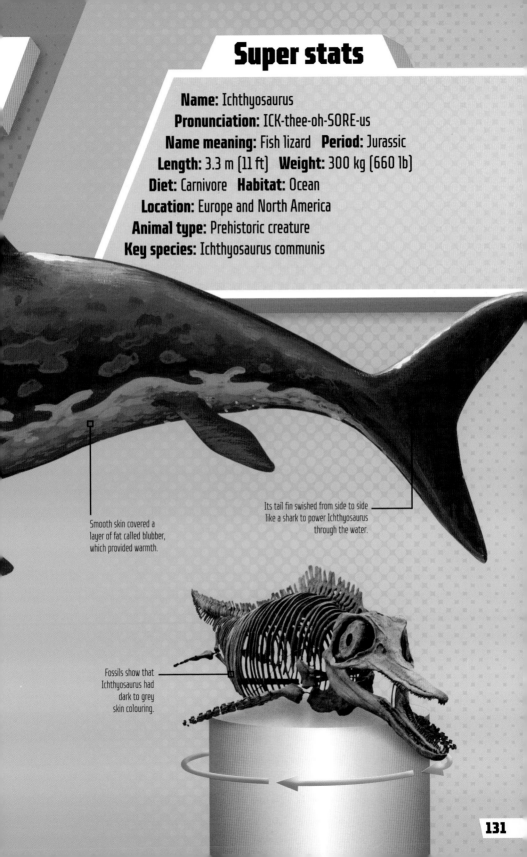

Smooth skin covered a layer of fat called blubber, which provided warmth.

Its tail fin swished from side to side like a shark to power Ichthyosaurus through the water.

Fossils show that Ichthyosaurus had dark to grey skin colouring.

Archaeopteryx

Even though Archaeopteryx was one of the first flying dinosaurs, its flying abilities were not fully developed. This means that it may have stayed on the ground to fight. Although Archaeopteryx was bird-like, it still had many dinosaur features, including sharp teeth and a raised claw on each foot. If a predator came too close, Archaeopteryx would lash out with its razor-sharp claws, causing serious damage.

Wing claws, probably used for gripping and climbing trees

One of the earliest relatives of modern birds, Archaeopteryx means "ancient wing".

Its bony jaws were filled with sharp, pointed teeth. These were perfect for catching small prey.

Archaeopteryx: This dangerous dinosaur decides between fight or flight.

Battle up!

Compsognathus was fast, but Archaeopteryx could fly! Would that ability have been enough for Archaeopteryx to be victorious? Or would Compsognathus's efficient hunting skills have given it the advantage?

Compsognathus

Compsognathus was a skilled predator. It shared many features with much larger theropod hunters, such as Tyrannosaurus and Allosaurus. It had good eyesight, sharp teeth and claws, and could run very fast. Small and quick, Compsognathus snatched tiny lizards with its claws, often swallowing them whole.

Compsognathus's strong, lightweight body and long back legs made it a speedy runner.

Lizard remains were found in the stomachs of the only two Compsognathus fossils ever found.

Each of its two fingers had a vicious hooked claw on the end.

Compsognathus: This feathery fiend has its eye on a meal... and hopes to have its claws on it, too!

Who would win?

Compsognathus relied on speed and good eyesight to sneak up on Archaeopteryx to then grab its enemy with its claws. Archaeopteryx fought back with its feet and flapped its wings to try to fly away. If Compsognathus managed to get a good grip, it could use its sharp claws to injure Archaeopteryx's wings, making escape impossible. Victory could go either way!

It's a draw!

Camptosaurus

This Jurassic herbivore walked on four legs to graze on plants, but could also move quickly on two legs to escape from predators. Camptosaurus travelled in herds for safety.

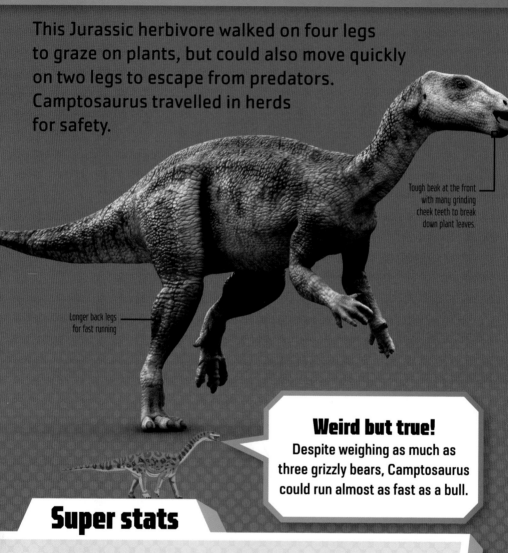

Tough beak at the front with many grinding cheek teeth to break down plant leaves.

Longer back legs for fast running

Weird but true!
Despite weighing as much as three grizzly bears, Camptosaurus could run almost as fast as a bull.

Super stats

Name: Camptosaurus **Pronunciation:** CAMP-toe-SORE-us
Name meaning: Flexible lizard **Period:** Jurassic
Length: 7 m (23 ft) **Weight:** 1,000 kg (2,200 lb)
Diet: Herbivore **Habitat:** Land **Location:** North America
Animal type: Dinosaur **Key species:** Camptosaurus dispar

Eurhinosaurus

Eurhinosaurus looked like an ancient swordfish, and was among the fastest marine reptiles in the Jurassic. It used its excellent eyesight and extended jaw to target and capture prey.

Weird but true!
Eurhinosaurus was the only ichthyosaur with a top jaw that was double the length of the lower jaw.

Front fins worked like giant flippers to help make sharp turns in the water

Big eyes to detect fish in the murky waters of the deep oceans

Super stats

Name: Eurhinosaurus **Pronunciation:** yoo-RYE-no-SORE-us
Name meaning: Well-nosed lizard **Period:** Jurassic
Length: 6 m (20 ft) **Weight:** 700 kg (1,500 lb) **Diet:** Carnivore
Habitat: Ocean **Location:** Europe **Animal type:** Prehistoric creature
Key species: Eurhinosaurus longirostris

Cylindroteuthis

This squid-like swimmer patrolled the Jurassic oceans, using its 10 wriggly arms to grab passing prey. Cylindroteuthis belonged to the belemnite family, a group of creatures known for their streamlined, bullet shape.

Flapping side fins could be tucked in for a speedy getaway

Hundreds of hooks on the arms were used to catch hold of prey.

Big eyes gave Cylindroteuthis clear vision for hunting in the deep, dark oceans.

Weird but true!
In the past, people mistook belemnite fossils for marks caused by lightning striking the ground.

Super stats

Name: Cylindroteuthis **Pronunciation:** SY-lin-DROW-too-thuss
Name meaning: Cylindrical squid **Period:** Jurassic to Cretaceous
Length: 22 cm (9 in) **Weight:** 1.5 kg (3 lb)
Diet: Carnivore **Habitat:** Ocean **Location:** Worldwide
Animal type: Prehistoric creature
Key species: Cylindroteuthis puzosiana

Miragaia

Plant eater Miragaia could stick its neck out further than any other stegosaur in the Jurassic world. It could reach the highest leaves.

Weird but true!
Miragaia had a total of 17 neck vertebrae. Most mammals today only have seven.

The extremely long neck was perfect for reaching plants to eat – it measured one third of the dinosaur's total body length.

Four stocky legs supported the heavy weight of Miragaia.

Super stats

Name: Miragaia   **Pronunciation:** MEE-rah-GUY-ah
Name meaning: Beautiful earth goddess   **Period:** Jurassic
Length: 6.5 m (21 ft)   **Weight:** 2,000 kg (4,400 lb)
Diet: Herbivore   **Habitat:** Land   **Location:** Europe
Animal type: Dinosaur   **Key species:** Miragaia longicollum

Europasaurus

One of the smallest sauropods, Europasaurus was only about the size of a bull. Despite being small, it still had the long neck needed to reach up to the tasty trees in the Jurassic world.

Its long neck was flexible enough to feed on both tall trees and low plants.

Smaller, stockier body than most of the sauropods

Super stats

Name: Europasaurus
Pronunciation: yoo-ROW-pa-SORE-us
Name meaning: Europe lizard
Period: Jurassic
Length: 6 m (20 ft)   **Weight:** 800 kg (1,750 lb)
Diet: Herbivore   **Habitat:** Land
Location: Europe   **Animal type:** Dinosaur
Key species: Europasaurus holgeri

Weird but true!
Studies of the bones of Europasaurus have shown that it was a type of mini sauropod.

Juravenator

At night, this speedy dinosaur hunted down lizards, fish, and insects in lagoons and swamps. Three claws on each hand and jagged teeth worked together to catch prey and tear it apart.

Weird but true!

The only known fossil of Juravenator is of a young one. The adults might have been a lot bigger.

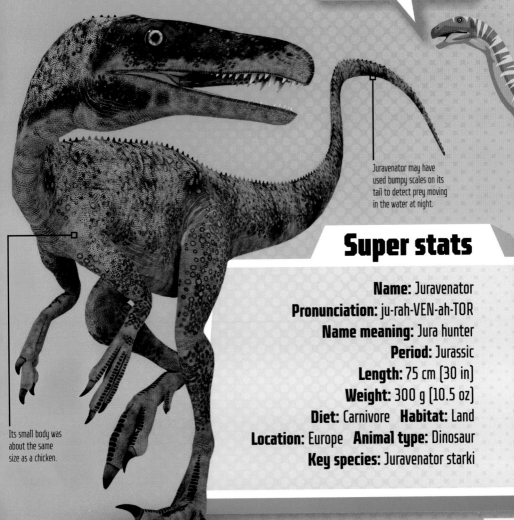

Juravenator may have used bumpy scales on its tail to detect prey moving in the water at night.

Its small body was about the same size as a chicken.

Super stats

Name: Juravenator
Pronunciation: ju-rah-VEN-ah-TOR
Name meaning: Jura hunter
Period: Jurassic
Length: 75 cm (30 in)
Weight: 300 g (10.5 oz)
Diet: Carnivore **Habitat:** Land
Location: Europe **Animal type:** Dinosaur
Key species: Juravenator starki

Megalosaurus

Record-breaking Megalosaurus was the first dinosaur to be given a scientific name. It was named in 1824, when a collection of bones was found inside underground mines near Oxford, in England. Whether munching on meat or chasing down prey, this fast-moving meat eater was a deadly hunter in its lush woodland home.

Meat-eating Megalosaurus regularly shed its big teeth but could grow new ones.

This powerful predator combined cutting claws, strong jaws, and sharp teeth to catch and eat prey.

Weird but true!
A thigh bone thought to have belonged to Megalosaurus was mistakenly believed to be from an elephant or a giant human.

Super stats

Name: Megalosaurus
Pronunciation: MEG-uh-lo-SORE-us
Name meaning: Great lizard **Period:** Jurassic
Length: 9 m (30 ft) **Weight:** 1,500 kg (3,300 lb)
Diet: Carnivore **Habitat:** Land **Location:** Europe
Animal type: Dinosaur
Key species: Megalosaurus bucklandii

Muscular body

Megalosaurus was one of the biggest predators on Earth when it was alive.

Built for speed, Megalosaurus moved quickly on two strong legs and used its long tail for balance.

Heavy tail

Watering hole

Herds of Miragaia roamed the Jurassic world, stopping to drink water and feed on leafy trees. These long-necked stegosaurs were named after the Miragaia area of Portugal where their fossilized remains were found.

Dinosaur diets

Dinosaurs ranged in size from miniature to mega, and their diets were just as varied. Some dinosaurs were fast hunters, taking down prey in seconds, while others spent the whole day eating ferns or munching on leaves.

Herbivores

Plant-eating dinosaurs, called herbivores, were the most common land animals. Many were tall sauropods with long necks, long tails, and massive bodies. Their necks towered into the trees to reach the best leaves. Other, smaller herbivores ate plants that grew close to the ground.

How do we know what dinosaurs ate?

The dinosaurs lived long ago, so it is amazing that we know so much about what they ate. Scientists can learn a lot from the size and shape of their teeth. Many carnivores had sharp, and sometimes pointed teeth, while many herbivores had peg-like teeth. Fossilized dinosaur poo, called coprolites, contain the remains of what they had eaten.

Carnivores

The mostly meat-eating dinosaurs, called carnivores, hunted other animals. Most sprinted on two strong legs, using their sharp claws and terrifying teeth to finish the kill. Some hunted alone, using their skills to capture prey, while others hunted in packs to take down the biggest animals. Hunting took time and effort, so some carnivores waited to feed on the leftovers of dead animals.

Omnivores

Very few species of dinosaur ate both meat and plants. These omnivores had to have flexible jaws and different types of teeth to tackle different types of food. If prey was in short supply, they could munch on fruit, seeds, eggs, and leaves so they did not go hungry.

Megazostrodon

Megazostrodon was one of the first mammals that scurried through the Jurassic forests. Despite being small and furry, this tiny predator came alive at night, using its strong senses to track down insects and worms.

A coat of fur kept Megazostrodon warm during cold nights spent hunting.

Clawed feet held down prey, while sharp teeth tore into the meal.

Weird but true!

Even though it was a mammal, Megazostrodon probably laid eggs, like those of modern platypuses.

Super stats

Name: Megazostrodon **Pronunciation:** MEG-ah-ZO-stroh-don
Name meaning: Large girdle tooth **Period:** Jurassic
Length: 10 cm (4 in) **Weight:** 25 g (1 oz)
Diet: Carnivore **Habitat:** Land **Location:** Europe and Africa
Animal type: Prehistoric creature
Key species: Megazostrodon rudnerae

Liparoceras

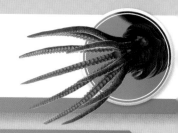

Liparoceras is a member of the ammonite group of extinct animals, who first appeared about 425 million years ago. They were closely related to octopuses and squid, but they lived inside a shell to protect their soft bodies.

Weird but true!
The ammonite shell was made from aragonite, the same mineral found in pearls.

Empty spaces inside the shell filled with gas or fluid to help the ammonite float.

Some ammonites have been found with squid or crustaceans caught in their arms.

The shell took on a spiral shape as the ammonite grew bigger.

Large eyes for sharp vision

Super stats

Name: Liparoceras   **Pronunciation:** LIP-ah-ro-SEH-russ
Name meaning: Fat head   **Period:** Jurassic
Diameter: 25 cm (10 in)   **Weight:** 1.5 kg (3 lb)   **Diet:** Carnivore
Habitat: Ocean   **Location:** Africa, Europe, and South America
Animal type: Prehistoric creature   **Key species:** Liparoceras cheltiense

Brontosaurus

Brontosaurus was a towering sauropod that roamed open plains. It had an extremely long neck which let it reach the tastiest leaves on the tallest trees. Some scientists believe it may have cracked its tail like a whip when threatened with attack.

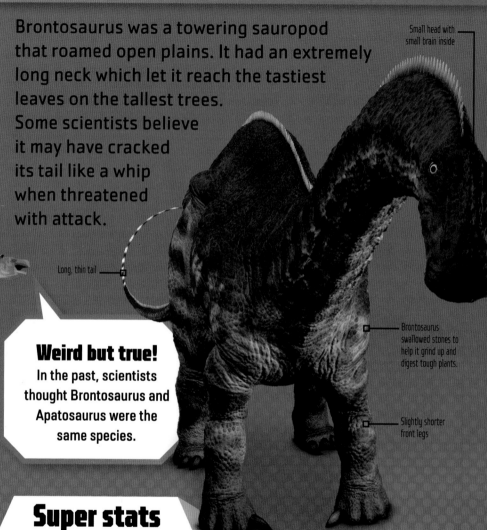

Small head with small brain inside

Long, thin tail

Brontosaurus swallowed stones to help it grind up and digest tough plants.

Slightly shorter front legs

Weird but true!
In the past, scientists thought Brontosaurus and Apatosaurus were the same species.

Super stats

Name: Brontosaurus   **Pronunciation:** bron-toe-SORE-us
Name meaning: Thunder lizard   **Period:** Jurassic
Length: 22 m (72 ft)   **Weight:** 1,500 kg (3,300 lb)
Diet: Herbivore   **Habitat:** Land   **Location:** North America
Animal type: Dinosaur   **Key species:** Brontosaurus excelsus

Temnodontosaurus

Marine reptile Temnodontosaurus lurked in the deepest, darkest oceans of the Jurassic period. Shaped like a dolphin, this skilled hunter swam at high speed, looking for prey to sink its teeth into.

The huge tail moved from side-to-side to propel Temnodontosaurus through the water.

Giant jaws full of sharp teeth cut through prey with ease.

Weird but true!
Temnodontosaurus could bite with twice the force of a crocodile.

Super stats

Name: Temnodontosaurus   **Pronunciation:** TEM-noe-DON-toe-SORE-us
Name meaning: Cutting-tooth lizard   **Period:** Jurassic
Length: 12 m (40 ft)   **Weight:** 6,500 kg (14,500 lb)   **Diet:** Carnivore
Habitat: Ocean   **Location:** Europe   **Animal type:** Prehistoric creature
Key species: Temnodontosaurus platyodon

Pterodactylus

Flying high over the Jurassic coastline was stork-sized Pterodactylus. Among the smallest pterosaurs, this expert hunter swooped down from the sky to snatch fish and insects in its long jaws.

Large wings were attached to extremely long fourth fingers.

Jaws packed with sharp teeth

The lightweight body and hollow bones made Pterodactylus a strong, skilled flier.

Weird but true!

Pterodactylus was the first creature to be named and identified as a flying reptile.

Super stats

Name: Pterodactylus   **Pronunciation:** TEH-roe-DACK-till-us
Name meaning: Winged finger   **Period:** Jurassic
Wingspan: 1 m (3 ft)   **Weight:** 4.5 kg (10 lb)
Diet: Carnivore   **Habitat:** Land / Sky   **Location:** Europe
Animal type: Prehistoric creature   **Key species:** Pterodactylus antiquus

Giraffatitan

This dinosaur lives up to its name, meaning "giant giraffe". Giraffatitan weighed the same as six elephants, and, at 12 m (40 ft) tall, was the height of a three-storey building. To maintain its size, the skyscraping sauropod chomped on leafy trees all day long in its woodland home.

Its enormous neck made up half of this dinosaur's total length.

Air spaces in neck bones kept the neck light and flexible.

Scaly skin

Weird but true!

Palaeontologists are not sure where Giraffatitan's nostrils sat, but used to think they were on its forehead.

Super stats

Name: Giraffatitan **Pronunciation:** ji-RAF-a-TIE-tan
Name meaning: Giraffe titan **Period:** Jurassic
Length: 22 m (72 ft) **Weight:** 25,000 kg (55,000 lb)
Diet: Herbivore **Habitat:** Land **Location:** Africa
Animal type: Dinosaur **Key species:** Giraffatitan brancai

Leedsichthys

Meet the biggest bony fish in history. Leedsichthys was an enormous creature, and had very few predators. However, it ate only the smallest marine life, such as zooplankton (tiny sea creatures).

Big fins helped with gentle floating and fast swimming

Powerful tail to push Leedsichthys through the water

Shunosaurus

Two pairs of short spikes at the end of an enormous tail

Most sauropods relied on their huge size to stay safe from predators, but Shunosaurus had a special weapon. Its tail had a bony club and sharp spikes that could deliver a deadly hit.

Weird but true!
Shunosaurus was one of the very few dinosaurs to have tail spikes.

Super stats

Name: Leedsichthys
Pronunciation: LEEDS-ick-thus
Name meaning: Leeds' fish **Period:** Jurassic
Length: 16 m (52 ft) **Weight:** 45,000 kg (99,000 lb)
Diet: Carnivore **Habitat:** Ocean
Location: Europe and South America
Animal type: Prehistoric creature
Key species: Leedsichthys problematicus

A mostly toothless mouth sieved water for tiny sealife to eat.

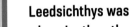

Weird but true!

Leedsichthys was 10 times heavier than the biggest bony fish alive today.

Strong, long neck stretched up to leafy treetops that smaller sauropods could not quite reach

Super stats

Name: Shunosaurus
Pronunciation: SHOE-noe-SORE-us
Name meaning: Shu lizard
Period: Jurassic
Length: 10 m (33 ft) **Weight:** 4,000 kg (8,800 lb)
Diet: Herbivore **Habitat:** Land
Location: Asia **Animal type:** Dinosaur
Key species: Shunosaurus lii

Stegosaurus

Meet the superstar of the supersized stegosaurs! Stegosaurus was roughly the size of a minibus, and had a huge appetite. This plant–eating powerhouse spent much of its time munching on low–lying plants in vast, Jurassic forests to maintain its bulky body.

Heavyweight Stegosaurus moved very slowly, so its size and spikes were useful to scare off enemies.

Sharp beak, with small peg-like teeth

Super stats

Name: Stegosaurus
Pronunciation: STEG-oh-SORE-us
Name meaning: Roof lizard   **Period:** Jurassic
Length: 9 m (30 ft)   **Weight:** 4,000 kg (8,800 lb)
Diet: Herbivore   **Habitat:** Land
Location: Europe and North America
Animal type: Dinosaur
Key species: Stegosaurus Marsh

Weird but true!

Despite the extraordinary size of Stegosaurus, its brain was only as big as a plum.

These big, bony plates may have helped Stegosaurus to control its temperature, helping it to warm up or cool down.

When under attack, Stegosaurus lashed out using its spiky tail as a weapon.

Dilophosaurus

Dilophosaurus's long claws were sharp and dangerous, but its teeth were even more deadly. They were serrated, or jagged, for sawing easily through meat. Dilophosaurus also had a pair of head crests that made it look even more threatening, but they were not used as weapons.

Head crests were most likely used to show off, as they were not strong weapons.

Small dinosaurs, such as Scutellosaurus, would have been high on Dilophosaurus's lunch menu!

Long, muscular hind legs helped Dilophosaurus to run at speeds of up to 32 kph (20 mph).

Dilophosaurus: This crested killer has a meal in sight and is ready to attack.

Battle up!

While ferocious Dilophosaurus stalked across the Jurassic plains hunting for food, small Scutellosaurus could not have been more different. A fifth of Dilophosaurus's height, and very light, Scutellosaurus dined on plants, not meat.

Scutellosaurus

One of the smallest dinosaurs, Scutellosaurus was quick and crafty. It had powerful thigh muscles and a lightweight body, which meant it could run fast. It was covered with bony spikes, called scutes, that protected it against attack.

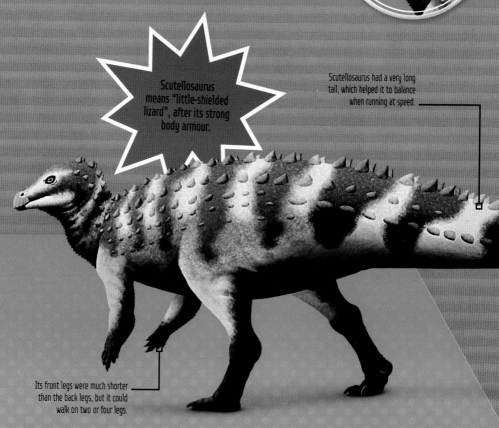

Scutellosaurus means "little-shielded lizard", after its strong body armour.

Scutellosaurus had a very long tail, which helped it to balance when running at speed.

Its front legs were much shorter than the back legs, but it could walk on two or four legs.

Scutellosaurus: Small but speedy, this little dinosaur has some fancy moves on its side.

Who would win?

Dilophosaurus had strength on its side, as well as teeth. There's no doubt that if it could trap Scutellosaurus, the battle would be over – despite its body armour. But Scutellosaurus was quick on its feet. It would be able to twist and scamper away from an attack. Dilophosaurus was nowhere near as speedy as its tiny foe. Most of the time, it could only watch as Scutellosaurus scurried off. Sharp teeth, slashing claws, and bigger size do not always win. Victory to the little one!

Winner!

Rhamphorhynchus

A fantastic flier, Rhamphorhynchus soared through the skies before swooping down to snap up fish from seas and rivers. It kept a tight hold on its food, then chowed down with its razor-sharp teeth.

Weird but true!
Bony rods in Rhamphorhynchus's long tail helped it to fly as straight as a dart.

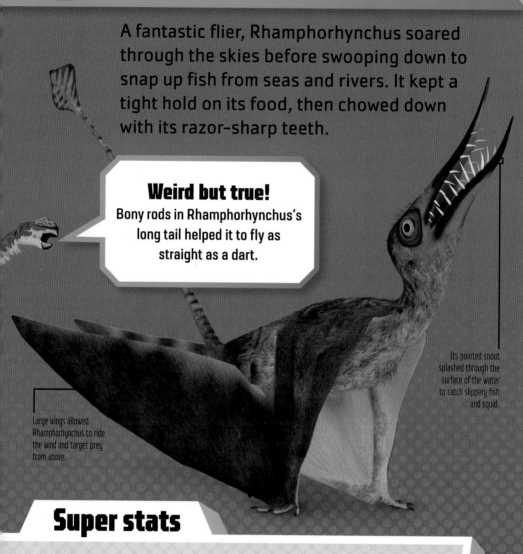

Its pointed snout splashed through the surface of the water to catch slippery fish and squid.

Large wings allowed Rhamphorhynchus to ride the wind and target prey from above.

Super stats

Name: Rhamphorhynchus   **Pronunciation:** ram-foe-RINK-us
Name meaning: Beak snout   **Period:** Jurassic
Wingspan: 2 m (6.5 ft)   **Weight:** 4.5 kg (10 lb)
Diet: Carnivore   **Habitat:** Land   **Location:** Europe
Animal type: Prehistoric creature
Species name: Rhamphorhynchus muensteri

Stenopterygius

This sleek, streamlined marine reptile pushed itself through the water at high speed, while on the lookout for fish and squid to eat. Its long snout opened to reveal sharp teeth that could tear through prey in seconds.

Weird but true!
Speedy Stenopterygius travelled through water at up to 40 kph (25 mph).

A dorsal fin kept Stenopterygius stable and balanced in the water, like modern-day dolphins and sharks.

Long, slender jaws, filled with sharp teeth

Smooth skin helped Stenopterygius slip through the water easily at high speed.

Super stats

Name: Stenopterygius
Pronunciation: sten-OP-terr-IDGE-ee-us
Name meaning: Narrow fin **Period:** Jurassic
Length: 4 m (13 ft) **Weight:** 750 kg (1,650 lb) **Diet:** Carnivore
Habitat: Ocean **Location:** Europe **Animal type:** Prehistoric creature
Species name: Stenopterygius quadriscissus

Scelidosaurus

Weighty body armour provided protection for Scelidosaurus. This slow–moving plant eater scared away predators with a tough covering of bony plates that ran from its tiny head to the tip of its long tail.

The heavyweight body plates, called scutes, served as protection, while horns on the back of its skull may have been used for display.

Its long tail may have been used to lash out at prey in defence.

Weird but true!

Its bony plates were covered in tough keratin, the same substance that our fingernails are made from.

Super stats

Name: Scelidosaurus **Pronunciation:** SKELL-ih-doe-SORE-us
Name meaning: Limb lizard **Period:** Jurassic
Length: 4 m (13 ft) **Weight:** 320 kg (700 lb) **Diet:** Herbivore
Habitat: Land **Location:** Europe **Animal type:** Dinosaur
Key species: Scelidosaurus harrisonii

Spinophorosaurus

Standing tall among the early sauropods was Spinophorosaurus. An almost complete skeleton was discovered in 2007 in Niger, in Africa. At first, palaeontologists thought that it had spikes at the end of its tail, but that turned out to be wrong.

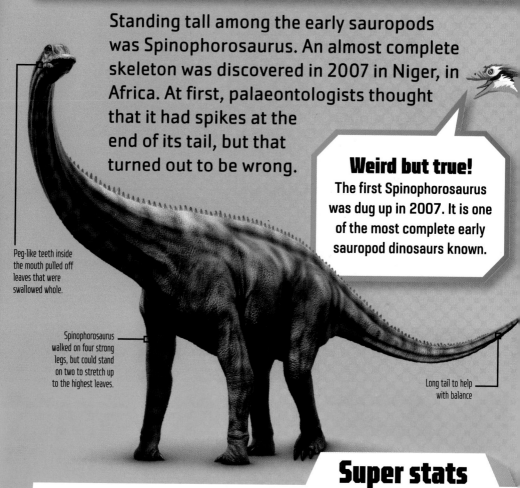

Weird but true!
The first Spinophorosaurus was dug up in 2007. It is one of the most complete early sauropod dinosaurs known.

Peg-like teeth inside the mouth pulled off leaves that were swallowed whole.

Spinophorosaurus walked on four strong legs, but could stand on two to stretch up to the highest leaves.

Long tail to help with balance

Super stats

Name: Spinophorosaurus
Pronunciation: SPINE-oh-fo-row-SORE-us
Name meaning: Spike lizard   **Period:** Jurassic
Length: 13 m (43 ft)   **Weight:** 6,350 kg (14,000 lb)   **Diet:** Herbivore
Habitat: Land   **Location:** Africa   **Animal type:** Dinosaur
Key species: Spinophorosaurus nigerensis

Yi

Somewhere between an early bird and an ancient bat, Yi was a unique dinosaur that lived in what is now China. Its dramatic, featherless wings led to its full name Yi qi, meaning "strange wing". It was only the size of a pigeon, but it could climb up trees and glide through the air.

Weird but true!

Only one fossil of Yi has ever been found. It was discovered by a farmer in China, and was then sold to a Chinese museum.

Thin layer of skin covering the wings, similar to modern bat wings

Clawed feet gripped hold of branches while Yi climbed trees.

Super stats

Name: Yi **Pronunciation:** yee
Name meaning: Strange wing
Period: Jurassic
Wingspan: 60 cm (2 ft) **Weight:** 380 g (13 oz)
Diet: Carnivore **Habitat:** Land **Location:** Asia
Animal type: Dinosaur
Species: Yi qi

The short feathers that covered the body were different from the flight feathers of modern birds.

Look closely and you can see some feathers on this fossil.

Long bone attached to each wrist helped Yi to spread its wings for gliding.

Lonely Stegosaurus

The biggest plated dinosaur of all, Stegosaurus was a tremendous sight – but, it was possibly a quiet dinosaur that lived on its own. Its huge body, bony plates, and spiky tail scared away predators as it searched for plants to eat.

Torvosaurus

Torvosaurus was one of the biggest predators to ever exist in Europe. This huge hunter dominated the Jurassic forests and floodplains. A killing machine, it had a powerful body, strong legs, long claws, and sharp teeth.

This dinosaur's big, sharp teeth could bite through prey, including slow-moving sauropods.

Large hand claws, perfect for slashing at prey

Weird but true!
The name Torvosaurus means "savage lizard" because of its angry and aggressive nature.

Super stats

Name: Torvosaurus   **Pronunciation:** tor-VOE-SORE-us
Name meaning: Savage lizard   **Period:** Jurassic
Length: 10 m (33 ft)   **Weight:** 3,000 kg (6,600 lb)
Diet: Carnivore   **Habitat:** Land
Location: North America and Europe   **Animal type:** Dinosaur
Key species: Torvosaurus tanneri

Gargoyleosaurus

Gargoyleosaurus was covered in bony plates and sharp spikes, giving it lots of protection against attack. This helped the small plant eater to graze in safety.

Weird but true!

Gargoyleosaurus was an unusual armoured dinosaur because its protective plates were hollow at the base.

Bony plates covered the back to scare away predators.

Four stocky legs supported the heavy body armour.

Super stats

Name: Gargoyleosaurus   **Pronunciation:** GAR-goy-LEE-oh-SORE-us
Name meaning: Gargoyle lizard   **Period:** Jurassic
Length: 3.5 m (11.5 ft)   **Weight:** 850 kg (1,900 lb)
Diet: Herbivore   **Habitat:** Land
Location: North America   **Animal type:** Dinosaur
Key species: Gargoyleosaurus parkpinorum

Yangchuanosaurus

Big and brainy, Yangchuanosaurus used lots of different methods to target prey. Possibly working in packs, hunting alone, or finding dead meat to eat, this fierce hunter posed a serious threat.

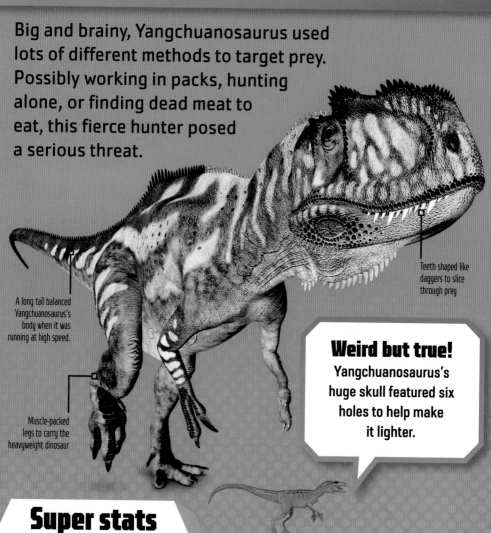

Teeth shaped like daggers to slice through prey

A long tail balanced Yangchuanosaurus's body when it was running at high speed.

Muscle-packed legs to carry the heavyweight dinosaur

Weird but true!
Yangchuanosaurus's huge skull featured six holes to help make it lighter.

Super stats

Name: Yangchuanosaurus **Pronunciation:** YANG-chwan-oh-SORE-us
Name meaning: Yangchuan lizard **Period:** Jurassic
Length: 11 m [36 ft] **Weight:** 3,300 kg [7,300 lb]
Diet: Carnivore **Habitat:** Land
Location: Asia **Animal type:** Dinosaur
Key species: Yangchuanosaurus shangyouensis

Plesiosaurus

Marine life had to watch out for Plesiosaurus, a deadly ocean predator. It could pop up suddenly from deep, dark waters, with its powerful biting jaws and pointy teeth ready to seize fish and molluscs.

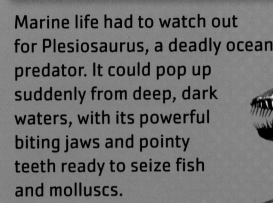

Its long, flexible neck could move in all directions to snatch prey.

Four paddle-like flippers pushed Plesiosaurus through the water like a marine turtle.

Weird but true!

In the past, some people claimed Scotland's famous Loch Ness "monster" looked like a plesiosaur.

Super stats

Name: Plesiosaurus   **Pronunciation:** PLEE-see-oh-SORE-us
Name meaning: Near to lizard   **Period:** Jurassic
Length: 3.5 m (11.5 ft)   **Weight:** 850 kg (1,900 lb)
Diet: Carnivore   **Habitat:** Ocean
Location: Europe   **Animal type:** Prehistoric creature
Key species: Plesiosaurus dolichodeirus

Heterodontosaurus

This small, speedy dinosaur searched scrublands for food to eat, from plants and trees to rodents and insects. Heterodontosaurus used its long arms to grasp plants and its sharp teeth to fight enemies.

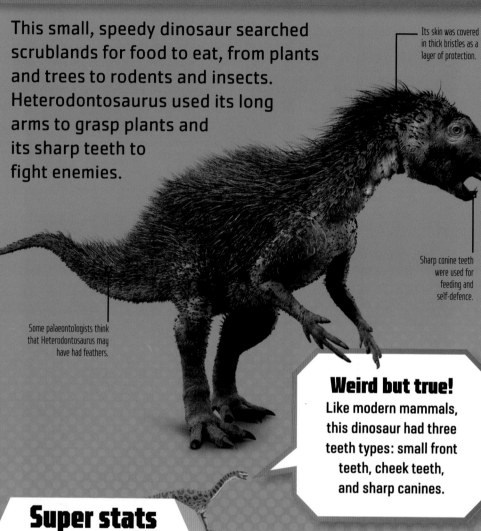

Its skin was covered in thick bristles as a layer of protection.

Sharp canine teeth were used for feeding and self-defence.

Some palaeontologists think that Heterodontosaurus may have had feathers.

Weird but true!
Like modern mammals, this dinosaur had three teeth types: small front teeth, cheek teeth, and sharp canines.

Super stats

Name: Heterodontosaurus
Pronunciation: HET-er-oh-DON-toe-SORE-us
Name meaning: Different-toothed lizard   **Period:** Jurassic
Length: 1.2 m (4 ft)   **Weight:** 10 kg (22 lb)   **Diet:** Omnivore
Habitat: Land   **Location:** North America
Animal type: Dinosaur   **Key species:** Heterodontosaurus tucki

Dakosaurus

Prehistoric predator Dakosaurus swam through the seas on the hunt for fish and other marine reptiles. Four flippers and a fish-like tail silently powered this creature towards its unsuspecting prey.

Weird but true!
Dakosaurus means "biter lizard" because it had very big teeth compared to most prehistoric creatures.

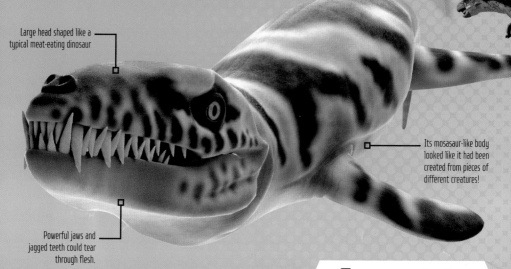

Large head shaped like a typical meat-eating dinosaur

Its mosasaur-like body looked like it had been created from pieces of different creatures!

Powerful jaws and jagged teeth could tear through flesh.

Super stats

Name: Dakosaurus **Pronunciation:** DACK-oh-SORE-us
Name meaning: Biter lizard **Period:** Jurassic to Cretaceous
Length: 5 m (16 ft) **Weight:** 900 kg (2,000 lb)
Diet: Carnivore **Habitat:** Ocean **Location:** Europe and South America
Animal type: Prehistoric creature **Key species:** Dakosaurus maximus

Diplodocus

This giant was one of the longest creatures to ever walk the Earth. Diplodocus was almost the same length as a blue whale! Its incredibly flexible, long neck towered in the treetops, allowing it to pick the highest, lushest leaves to fuel its enormous body.

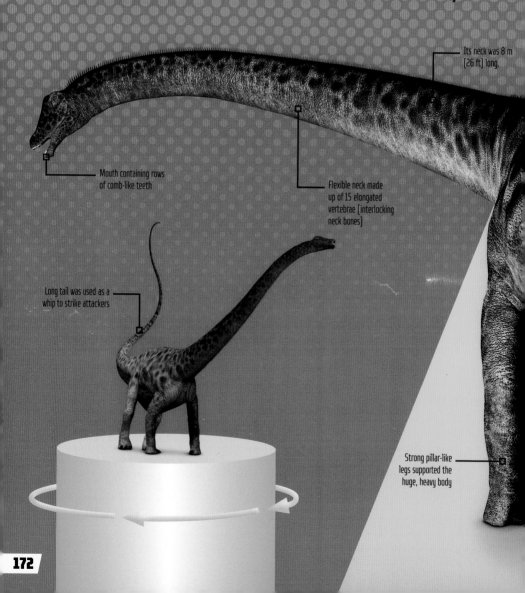

Its neck was 8 m (26 ft) long.

Mouth containing rows of comb-like teeth

Flexible neck made up of 15 elongated vertebrae (interlocking neck bones)

Long tail was used as a whip to strike attackers

Strong pillar-like legs supported the huge, heavy body

Super stats

Name: Diplodocus
Pronunciation: dip-LOD-o-kuss
Name meaning: Double beam   **Period:** Jurassic
Length: 26 m (85 ft)   **Weight:** 15,000 kg (33,000 lb)
Diet: Herbivore   **Habitat:** Land   **Location:** North America
Animal type: Dinosaur
Key species: Diplodocus carnegii

Weird but true!
Diplodocus could reach treetops twice the height that giraffes can reach today.

Diplodocus could also stand up on its two back legs to reach the tallest branches.

Flying reptiles

The first vertebrates to fly were the pterosaurs, who ruled the skies in the Mesozoic Era. They were not dinosaurs, although at first they did have some dinosaur-like features, such as long tails and short, rounded beaks. Pterosaurs developed to become better suited to life in the air, with shorter tails and smooth-shaped bodies.

Dimorphodon

Early pterosaurs, like Dimorphodon, had long tails, small wings, and strong bodies. Although they could fly, they spent most of their time on land.

Pteranodon

Pterosaurs had large head crests, which they used to show off. The male Pteranodon, a kite-shaped pterosaur, had a crest that grew up to 70 cm (28 in) long.

Quetzalcoatlus

Quetzalcoatlus had a massive wingspan of 10 m (33 ft). It was the size of a small plane! These large creatures could only fly because their bones were hollow and lightweight.

Pterodaustro

Pterosaur jaws were suited to their diet. Pterodaustro's lower jaw was filled with hundreds of thin teeth that helped to sieve small sea creatures from shallow waters.

Pterosaur egg

Scientists in China discovered hundreds of incredibly well-preserved pterosaur eggs in 2017.

Rhamphorhynchus

One of the best-preserved pterosaur fossils belongs to Rhamphorhynchus. The fossilized remains are so detailed, even the wings can be seen.

Pterodactylus

Although it was a later pterosaur, Pterodactylus was the first to be discovered. It had webbed feet and a shorter tail than other pterosaurs. Its webbed feet were better for walking on land.

Weird but true!

Remember, pterosaurs are not birds! Their wings were made of thin skin, not feathers.

Cretaceous

Dinosaurs still ruled the Earth in the Cretaceous period, but the world was changing. As sea levels rose, the huge continents continued to split apart, starting to look similar to the ones we know today. There were new creatures and environments. Flowering plants appeared with bees, as well as other insects. But, the biggest change of all came at the end of this period. A huge asteroid hit the Earth, leading to many species dying out.

Albertosaurus

Named after Alberta, a place in Canada, Albertosaurus was one of the most terrifying predators in North America. It weighed as much as three modern moose, but was still only about half the size of its cousin, Tyrannosaurus.

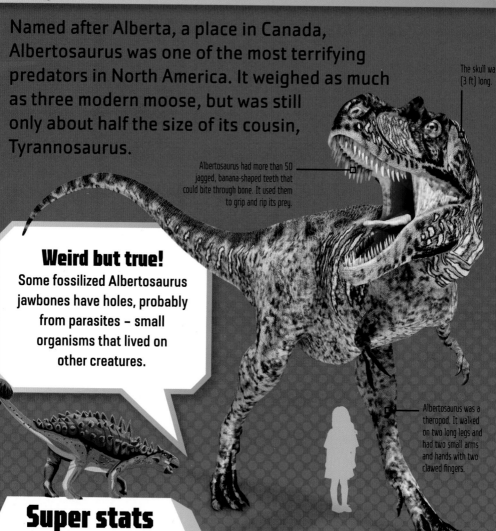

The skull wa [3 ft] long.

Albertosaurus had more than 50 jagged, banana-shaped teeth that could bite through bone. It used them to grip and rip its prey.

Weird but true!
Some fossilized Albertosaurus jawbones have holes, probably from parasites – small organisms that lived on other creatures.

Albertosaurus was a theropod. It walked on two long legs and had two small arms and hands with two clawed fingers.

Super stats

Name: Albertosaurus **Pronunciation:** al-BERT-oh-SORE-us
Name meaning: Alberta lizard **Period:** Cretaceous
Length: 9 m [30 ft] **Weight:** 2,000 kg [4,400 lb] **Diet:** Carnivore
Habitat: Land **Location:** North America **Animal type:** Dinosaur
Key species: Albertosaurus sarcophagus

Chasmosaurus

Chasmosaurus was a member of the ceratopsian dinosaur family, who all had parrot-like beaks, horns, and striking, bony neck frills. It was also discovered in Alberta, in Canada, and was about half the size of its relative Triceratops.

Weird but true!

Chasmosaurus's neck frill had holes in it, but they were covered with skin so the frill looked solid.

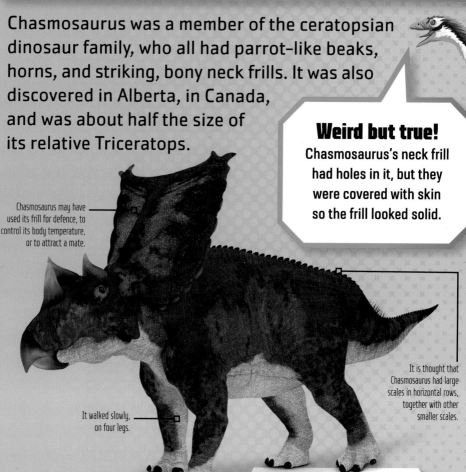

Chasmosaurus may have used its frill for defence, to control its body temperature, or to attract a mate.

It is thought that Chasmosaurus had large scales in horizontal rows, together with other smaller scales.

It walked slowly, on four legs.

Super stats

Name: Chasmosaurus   **Pronunciation:** KAZ-moe-SORE-us
Name meaning: Opening lizard   **Period:** Cretaceous
Length: 5 m (16.5 ft)   **Weight:** 3,000 kg (6,600 lb)   **Diet:** Herbivore
Habitat: Land   **Location:** North America
Animal type: Dinosaur   **Key species:** Chasmosaurus belli

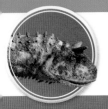

Carnotaurus

As fast as a leopard and as heavy as a rhino, Carnotaurus was a fearsome hunter. Its name means "meat–eating bull" and it was one of the top predators in the south of the world.

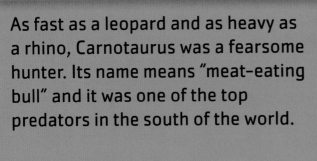

These two 15 cm (6 in) long horns may have been used in fights over territory or mates.

Compared to other theropods, Carnotaurus had a short skull – about one third the height of the average human male.

Tiny arms were not useful for hunting.

Strong leg muscles helped it to run at speeds of up to 56 kph (35 mph).

Weird but true!
Carnotaurus's huge tail muscles helped it to move fast, but it would not have been able to turn quickly.

Super stats

Name: Carnotaurus   **Pronunciation:** car-noe-TOR-us
Name meaning: Meat-eating bull   **Period:** Cretaceous
Length: 8 m (26 ft)   **Weight:** 2,000 kg (4,400 lb)   **Diet:** Carnivore
Habitat: Land   **Location:** South America   **Animal type:** Dinosaur
Key species: Carnotaurus sastrei

Deinonychus

This deadly dinosaur was from a family of mostly small, fast, and agile predators. It had a relatively large brain. Deinonychus used its intelligence to track and catch its prey, including other dinosaurs.

Its long tail helped Deinonychus balance when it ran or attacked prey.

Like other dromaeosaurs, Deinonychus almost certainly had feathers on parts of its body.

Long, curved "killing claws" on each foot could tear prey apart. Claws could be up to 13 cm (5 in) long.

Weird but true!

Deinonychus was the model for the "raptors" in the movie *Jurassic Park*.

Super stats

Name: Deinonychus   **Pronunciation:** dye-NON-ee-cus
Name meaning: Terrible claw   **Period:** Cretaceous
Length: 3.6 m (12 ft)   **Weight:** 100 kg (220 lb)   **Diet:** Carnivore
Habitat: Land   **Location:** North America   **Animal type:** Dinosaur
Key species: Deinonychus Ostrom

Malawisaurus

Malawisaurus is only known from part of one skeleton, including pieces of the skull and the brain case (the bone that holds the brain). It was named after Malawi, the country where it was discovered, and was about as tall as a giraffe.

Small skull

Long neck to reach high plants

Bony growths on the skin, called osteoderms, may have formed a protective armour.

Its tail was roughly 8 m (26 ft) long.

Weird but true!
Malawisaurus went through a few name changes before it was finally named after the place where it was found.

Super stats

Name: Malawisaurus
Pronunciation: ma-la-wee-SORE-us
Name meaning: Malawi lizard **Period:** Cretaceous
Height: 11 m (36 ft) **Weight:** 4,500 kg (10,000 lb)
Diet: Herbivore **Habitat:** Land **Location:** Africa
Animal type: Dinosaur **Key species:** Malawisaurus dixeyi

Microraptor

This small, winged carnivore was covered in feathers. Experts think that it glided from tree to tree, and may have been able to flap its wings and fly. Fossil evidence shows that it had shiny black feathers, like some modern birds.

Weird but true!

A new species of prehistoric lizard was found in the stomach of a Microraptor fossil discovered in China.

Teeth were jagged on one side, probably to help grip fish

Long tail feathers may have been used to attract mates.

Extra-long leg feathers

Microraptor had four wings and a wingspan of 70 cm (28 in).

Super stats

Name: Microraptor **Pronunciation:** MY-crow-RAP-tor
Name meaning: Small thief **Period:** Cretaceous
Length: 80 cm (2.5 ft) **Weight:** 1 kg (2 lb) **Diet:** Carnivore
Habitat: Land / Sky **Location:** Asia **Animal type:** Dinosaur
Key species: Microraptor zhaoianus

Triceratops

With its massive body, horns as long as broom handles, and a unique neck frill, Triceratops was an awesome sight. This mighty herbivore weighed four times as much as a rhinoceros, and it is among the very largest of the ceratopsian dinosaurs. Experts think that Triceratops travelled in herds to stay safe.

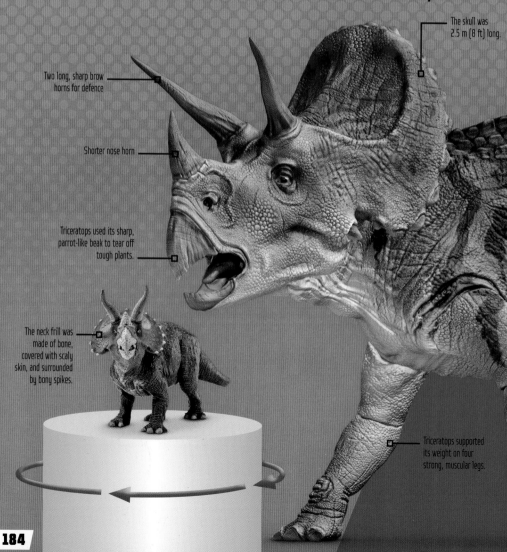

The skull was 2.5 m (8 ft) long.

Two long, sharp brow horns for defence

Shorter nose horn

Triceratops used its sharp, parrot-like beak to tear off tough plants.

The neck frill was made of bone, covered with scaly skin, and surrounded by bony spikes.

Triceratops supported its weight on four strong, muscular legs.

Super stats

Name: Triceratops
Pronunciation: try-SERRA-tops
Name meaning: Three-horned face   **Period:** Cretaceous
Height: 3.6 m (12 ft)   **Weight:** 8,000 kg (17,500 lb)
Diet: Herbivore   **Habitat:** Land   **Location:** North America
Animal type: Dinosaur   **Key species:** Triceratops horridus

Scaly skin

Weird but true!

Triceratops often damaged their horns during battles over territory or mates. Fossils show that this damage could heal over time.

Triceratops could outrun the average human child.

A long tail helped Triceratops to balance.

Ankylosaurus

The size of a tank and heavily armoured, Ankylosaurus was in no way a helpless herbivore – it was covered by a protective shield of bone. Predators would have had a very hard time finding a soft spot to take a bite. If that was not enough, at the end of Ankylosaurus's tail was a big, bony club, perfect for whacking predators.

A thump from Ankylosaurus's huge tail club was powerful enough to break an enemy's bones.

Four horns and a bony shield on top of its head provided even more protection.

Ankylosaurus: Armoured and dangerous, does this dinosaur look worried?

Battle up!

No dinosaur was scarier – or more dangerous – than Tyrannosaurus. Ankylosaurus's soft belly would be no match for the predator's teeth. But, if Ankylosaurus stayed on its feet, it could rely on its strong body armour for protection!

Tyrannosaurus

One of the largest meat-eating dinosaurs, Tyrannosaurus has a reputation as the most ferocious predator ever to exist. Everything about it was perfect for hunting and killing — it had strong muscles, powerful jaws, huge teeth, sharp claws, and excellent eyesight. Cunning Tyrannosaurus could even sneak up on its prey!

Tyrannosaurus had the strongest, most terrifying bite of any animal that ever lived.

Tyrannosaurus was not just scary, it was big, too. At 13 m (43 ft) long, and weighing as much as three hippopotamuses, no wonder it was the most fearsome predator!

Tyrannosaurus: This prime predator wants its dinner, and it wants it now!

Who would win?

Snapping its jaws down onto Ankylosaurus, Tyrannosaurus would be very frustrated - there was nowhere to sink its teeth into! Meanwhile, Ankylosaurus could whip its tail to deliver a bone-crushing blow with its bony club. The club was strong enough to shatter Tyrannosaurus's lower leg. Unless Tyrannosaurus could find a way to reach the lower, softer part of Ankylosaurus's body, it was victory to the not-so-helpless herbivore!

Winner!

Marine reptiles

Dinosaurs might have ruled on land, but the seas were ruled by giant marine reptiles. They swam and hunted in the water. From giant underwater killers and fierce sharks to graceful swimmers and tiny shell-covered creatures, life under the ocean was nothing like it is today.

Pliosaurus

This terrifying ocean killer had a really powerful bite. With a skull 2 m (6.5 ft) long, it could eat prey larger than a rhinoceros.

Ichthyosaurus

This super-fast marine reptile had a smooth body with a pointy snout – it was shaped a bit like a missile.

Shonisaurus

The largest known marine reptile of all time, Shonisaurus, was almost as long as a blue whale.

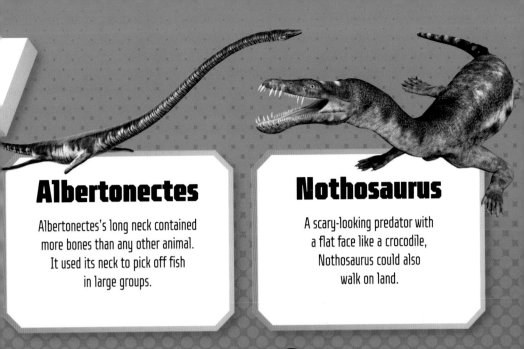

Albertonectes

Albertonectes's long neck contained more bones than any other animal. It used its neck to pick off fish in large groups.

Nothosaurus

A scary-looking predator with a flat face like a crocodile, Nothosaurus could also walk on land.

Hybodus

Reptiles were the top ocean predators, but they had competition from other swimming beasts, such as ferocious shark Hybodus.

Liopleurodon

Bigger than a great white shark, this marine reptile had huge, strong jaws and powerful flippers – it was a fearsome hunter.

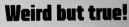

Weird but true!

The whales, dolphins, and seals of today did not appear until after the mighty marine reptiles died out.

Carcharodontosaurus

One of the largest meat eaters ever to stomp the Earth, Carcharodontosaurus could swallow small dinosaurs whole. It gets its name from its sharp teeth – "carcharodont" means having teeth like a great white shark.

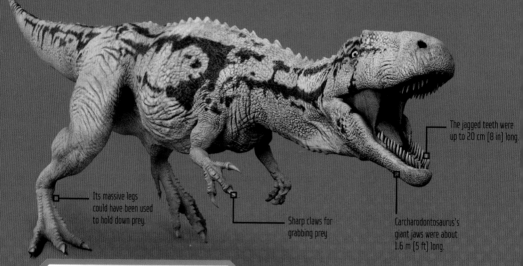

The jagged teeth were up to 20 cm (8 in) long.

Its massive legs could have been used to hold down prey.

Sharp claws for grabbing prey

Carcharodontosaurus's giant jaws were about 1.6 m (5 ft) long.

Weird but true!
Early Carcharodontosaurus fossils found in the 1930s were destroyed during World War II.

Super stats

Name: Carcharodontosaurus
Pronunciation: CAR-ka-roe-DON-toe-SORE-us
Name meaning: Shark-toothed lizard   **Period:** Cretaceous
Length: 13 m (43 ft)   **Weight:** 7,500 kg (16,500 lb)   **Diet:** Carnivore
Habitat: Land   **Location:** Africa   **Animal type:** Dinosaur
Key species: Carcharodontosaurus saharicus

Pentaceratops

It might not be as famous as its relative Triceratops, but Pentaceratops outdid it with its number of horns. Its name means "five-horned face" and Pentaceratops had two horns on its cheeks, plus three horns on its head.

Weird but true!
Pentaceratops had the largest skull of any living land animal ever. A skull found in the USA is 2.65 m (8.5 ft) high.

Pentaceratops also had a longer bony frill than Triceratops.

Short nose horn

Sharp, parrot-like beak

A human child is smaller than Pentaceratops's leg.

Super stats

Name: Pentaceratops   **Pronunciation:** PEN-ta-SERRA-tops
Name meaning: Five-horned face   **Period:** Cretaceous
Length: 8 m (26 ft)   **Weight:** 6,500 kg (14,500 lb)   **Diet:** Herbivore
Habitat: Land   **Location:** North America   **Animal type:** Dinosaur
Key species: Pentaceratops sternbergii

Zhenyuanopterus

This pterosaur was discovered in the early 21st century, in northeast China, and its fossils include a complete skeleton. It had a very long snout, which was lined with rows of long, needle-like teeth.

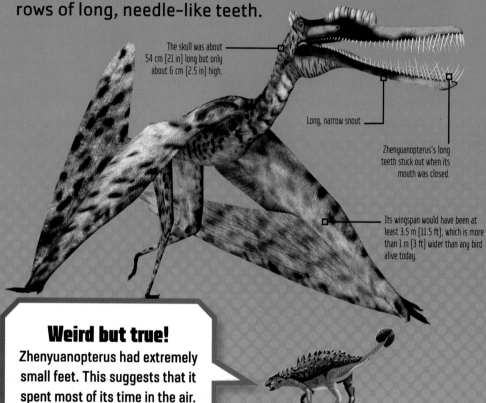

The skull was about 54 cm (21 in) long but only about 6 cm (2.5 in) high.

Long, narrow snout

Zhenyuanopterus's long teeth stuck out when its mouth was closed.

Its wingspan would have been at least 3.5 m (11.5 ft), which is more than 1 m (3 ft) wider than any bird alive today.

Weird but true!
Zhenyuanopterus had extremely small feet. This suggests that it spent most of its time in the air.

Super stats

Name: Zhenyuanopterus
Pronunciation: ZEN-yoo-an-OP-teh-rus
Name meaning: Zhenyuan wing   **Period:** Cretaceous
Wingspan: 3.5 m (11.5 ft)   **Weight:** 10 kg (22 lb)   **Diet:** Carnivore
Habitat: Land / Sky   **Location:** Asia   **Animal type:** Prehistoric creature
Key species: Zhenyuanopterus longirostris

Nasutoceratops

Like all ceratopsian dinosaurs, Nasutoceratops was a herbivore. It had a much larger nose than the rest of its family, and longer horns that pointed forwards, like a modern bull.

Weird but true!
Nasutoceratops had a big nose, but its sense of smell was poor because its smell receptors were far back in its skull.

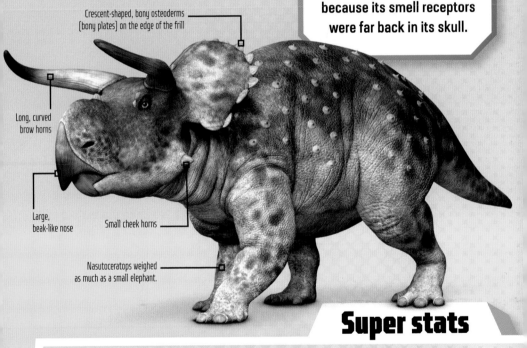

Crescent-shaped, bony osteoderms [bony plates] on the edge of the frill

Long, curved brow horns

Large, beak-like nose

Small cheek horns

Nasutoceratops weighed as much as a small elephant.

Super stats

Name: Nasutoceratops **Pronunciation:** NA-su-toe-SERRA-tops
Name meaning: Large-nosed horned-face **Period:** Cretaceous
Length: 5 m [16.5 ft] **Weight:** 2,000 kg [4,400 lb] **Diet:** Herbivore
Habitat: Land **Location:** North America
Animal type: Dinosaur **Key species:** Nasutoceratops titusi

Bistahieversor

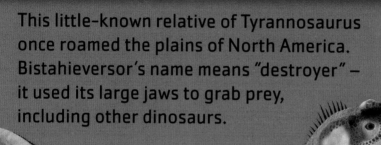

This little-known relative of Tyrannosaurus once roamed the plains of North America. Bistahieversor's name means "destroyer" — it used its large jaws to grab prey, including other dinosaurs.

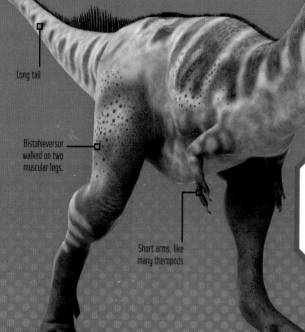

Long tail

Bistahieversor walked on two muscular legs.

Short arms, like many theropods

Bistahieversor had arou 64 teeth – that's me than Tyrannosaur

Weird but true!
Teenage and adult Bistahieversor fossils have been unearthed in New Mexico, in the USA.

Super stats

Name: Bistahieversor **Pronunciation:** BIS-tah-HE-ee-VER-sor
Name meaning: Bistahi destroyer **Period:** Cretaceous
Length: 9 m (30 ft) **Weight:** 3,800 kg (8,400 lb) **Diet:** Carnivore
Habitat: Land **Location:** North America **Animal type:** Dinosaur
Key species: Bistahieversor sealeyi

Sarcosuchus

Sarcosuchus was at least twice the size of a modern crocodile. It was only slightly smaller than the mighty Deinosuchus, making it one of the largest crocodile–like creatures to ever exist.

Sarcosuchus's strong, powerful tail would have been great for swimming.

Sarcosuchus weighed about as much as a small bulldozer.

Sarcosuchus had such strong jaws that no prey, not even small dinosaurs, could pry them open.

Short limbs allowed for limited movement on land.

Weird but true!
Sarcosuchus lived for 50–60 years and kept on growing throughout its life.

Super stats

Name: Sarcosuchus **Pronunciation:** SAR-ko-SU-KUS
Name meaning: Flesh crocodile
Period: Cretaceous **Length:** 9.5 m (30 ft)
Weight: 4,000 kg (8,800 lb) **Diet:** Carnivore **Habitat:** Ocean
Location: Africa and South America **Animal type:** Prehistoric creature
Key species: Sarcosuchus imperator

Tyrannosaurus

Probably the most famous dinosaur, Tyrannosaurus was also among the biggest and most powerful land predators. It sat at the top of the food chain, thanks to its huge jaws that could gobble up a massive 230 kg (500 lb) meal – about the same size as a big pig – in one bite. It could even chomp through solid bone.

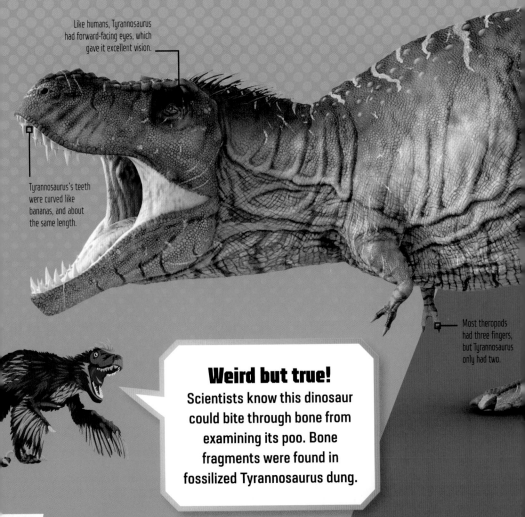

Like humans, Tyrannosaurus had forward-facing eyes, which gave it excellent vision.

Tyrannosaurus's teeth were curved like bananas, and about the same length.

Most theropods had three fingers, but Tyrannosaurus only had two.

Weird but true!
Scientists know this dinosaur could bite through bone from examining its poo. Bone fragments were found in fossilized Tyrannosaurus dung.

Super stats

Name: Tyrannosaurus
Pronunciation: TIE-ran-oh-SORE-us
Name meaning: Tyrant lizard king   **Period:** Cretaceous
Length: 13 m (43 ft)   **Weight:** 7,000 kg (14,800 lb)
Diet: Carnivore   **Habitat:** Land   **Location:** North America
Animal type: Dinosaur   **Key species:** Tyrannosaurus rex

Long, rigid tail helped to balance the heavy head

Tyrannosaurus had powerful leg muscles and may have been able to run up to 25 kph (15 mph).

Tyrannosaurus's mighty jaw muscles gave it a bite that was about 10 times more powerful than an alligator's.

Three strong, sharp claws on each foot kept Tyrannosaurus steady.

Carnivore cousins

Crunch! Tarbosaurus proved that small arms were
no problem if you had big, powerful jaws. This
enormous predator was busy terrifying prey a few
million years before its cousin, Tyrannosaurus.

Borealopelta

This armoured ankylosaur was one of the most exciting dinosaur discoveries of the 21st century. It was so well preserved that experts can tell what colour Borealopelta's skin was, and what type of plants it ate.

Long shoulder spikes may have been used for defence or to attract mates.

Rows of bony armoured plates protected Borealopelta from predators.

Spiky tail

Sturdy legs

Borealopelta had a beak, like many other herbivores.

Borealopelta's skin was reddish-brown on its back and lighter on its belly.

Weird but true!

When Borealopelta's skeleton was found by a miner, it took six years to extract it from the rock.

Super stats

Name: Borealopelta **Pronunciation:** BOR-e-al-OH-pel-tah
Name meaning: Northern shield **Period:** Cretaceous
Length: 5.5 m (18 ft) **Weight:** 1,360 kg (3,000 lb)
Diet: Herbivore **Habitat:** Land
Location: North America **Animal type:** Dinosaur
Key species: Borealopelta markmitchelli

Tarbosaurus

A few million years before its cousin Tyrannosaurus ruled North America, Tarbosaurus was stomping around Asia. It was top of the food chain and most likely hunted big sauropods, such as Nemegtosaurus.

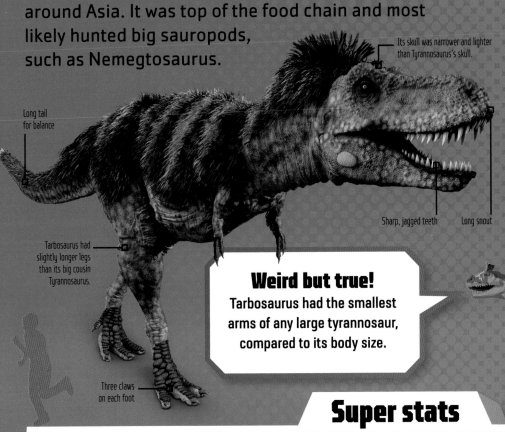

Its skull was narrower and lighter than Tyrannosaurus's skull.

Long tail for balance

Tarbosaurus had slightly longer legs than its big cousin Tyrannosaurus.

Three claws on each foot

Sharp, jagged teeth

Long snout

Weird but true!
Tarbosaurus had the smallest arms of any large tyrannosaur, compared to its body size.

Super stats

Name: Tarbosaurus   **Pronunciation:** TAR-bow-SORE-us
Name meaning: Alarming lizard   **Period:** Cretaceous
Length: 10 m (40 ft)   **Weight:** 5,000 kg (1,000 lb)
Diet: Carnivore   **Habitat:** Land   **Location:** Asia
Animal type: Dinosaur   **Key species:** Tarbosaurus bataar

Citipati

Citipati was a large, speedy oviraptorid. It ate small animals, seeds, and leaves, and was slightly bigger than a modern ostrich. Like an ostrich, it could not fly.

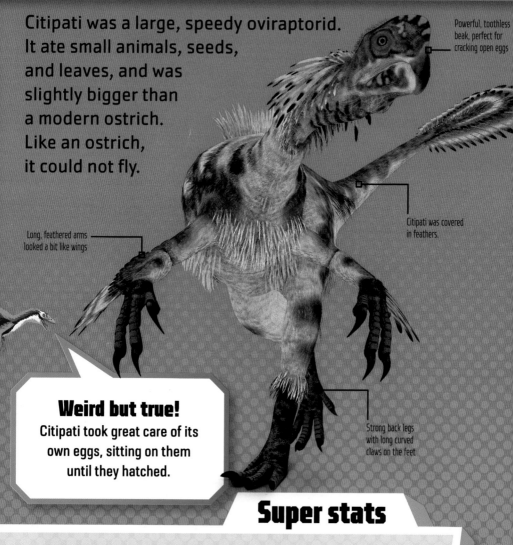

Powerful, toothless beak, perfect for cracking open eggs

Citipati was covered in feathers.

Long, feathered arms looked a bit like wings

Strong back legs with long curved claws on the feet

Weird but true!
Citipati took great care of its own eggs, sitting on them until they hatched.

Super stats

Name: Citipati **Pronunciation:** SIH-tee-PAH-tee
Name meaning: Funeral pyre lord **Period:** Cretaceous
Length: 3 m (10 ft) **Weight:** 80 kg (175 lb) **Diet:** Omnivore
Habitat: Land **Location:** Asia **Animal type:** Dinosaur
Key species: Citipati osmolskae

Hypsilophodon

This small ornithopod is a relative of the bigger Iguanodon. It once roamed the woodlands of southern England, where there were plenty of tasty plants to eat, and lots of trees and shrubs to hide in from predators.

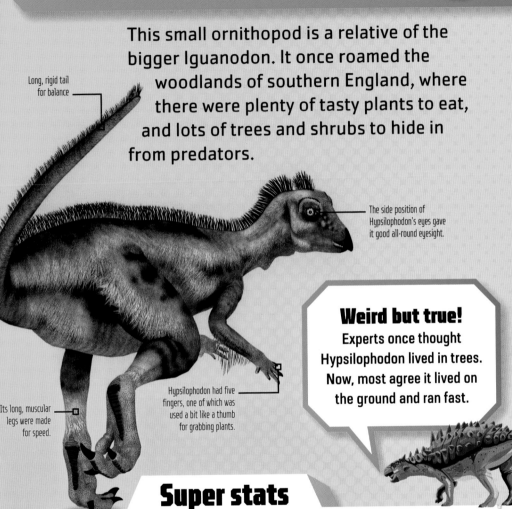

Long, rigid tail for balance

The side position of Hypsilophodon's eyes gave it good all-round eyesight.

Its long, muscular legs were made for speed.

Hypsilophodon had five fingers, one of which was used a bit like a thumb for grabbing plants.

Weird but true!

Experts once thought Hypsilophodon lived in trees. Now, most agree it lived on the ground and ran fast.

Super stats

Name: Hypsilophodon **Pronunciation:** HIP-sih-LOAF-oh-don
Name meaning: High-crested tooth **Period:** Cretaceous
Length: 2 m (6.5 ft) **Weight:** 25 kg (55 lb) **Diet:** Herbivore
Habitat: Land **Location:** Europe **Animal type:** Dinosaur
Key species: Hypsilophodon foxii

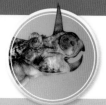

Styracosaurus

It is no wonder that Styracosaurus's name means "spiked lizard". It had a horn on its nose, one on each cheek, up to six long horns on its neck frill, and many more smaller spikes running from its frill to its tail.

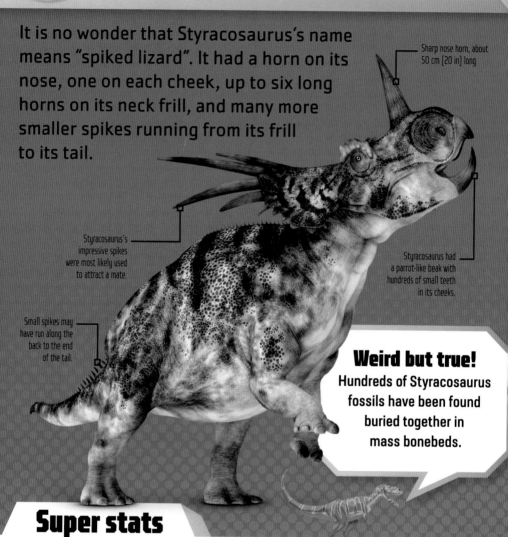

Sharp nose horn, about 50 cm (20 in) long

Styracosaurus's impressive spikes were most likely used to attract a mate.

Styracosaurus had a parrot-like beak with hundreds of small teeth in its cheeks.

Small spikes may have run along the back to the end of the tail.

Weird but true!
Hundreds of Styracosaurus fossils have been found buried together in mass bonebeds.

Super stats

Name: Styracosaurus **Pronunciation:** sty-RACK-oh-SORE-us
Name meaning: Spiked lizard **Period:** Cretaceous
Length: 5.5 m (18 ft) **Weight:** 2,700 kg (6,000 lb)
Diet: Herbivore **Habitat:** Land **Location:** North America
Animal type: Dinosaur **Key species:** Styracosaurus albertensis

Parasaurolophus

Many hadrosaurs had impressive head crests, but Parasaurolophus's crest was perhaps the most dramatic. At about 1 m (3 ft) long, it doubled the length of its skull.

Super stats

Name: Parasaurolophus
Pronunciation: PA-ra-SORE-oh-LOAF-us
Name meaning: Near crested lizard
Period: Cretaceous **Length:** 10 m (33 ft)
Weight: 3,250 kg (7,200 lb)
Diet: Herbivore **Habitat:** Land
Location: North America
Animal type: Dinosaur
Key species: Parasaurolophus walkeri

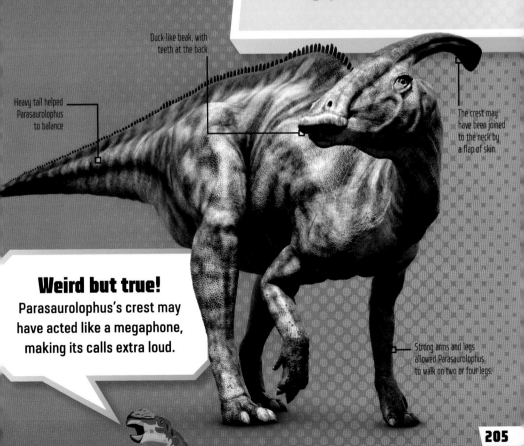

Duck-like beak, with teeth at the back

Heavy tail helped Parasaurolophus to balance

The crest may have been joined to the neck by a flap of skin.

Strong arms and legs allowed Parasaurolophus to walk on two or four legs.

Weird but true!

Parasaurolophus's crest may have acted like a megaphone, making its calls extra loud.

Muttaburrasaurus

Bony crest

This hefty herbivore was about the same length as two cars, and roamed what is now Australia. An ornithopod, like Iguanodon and Edmontosaurus, it had an unusual, rounded snout with a bony crest on top.

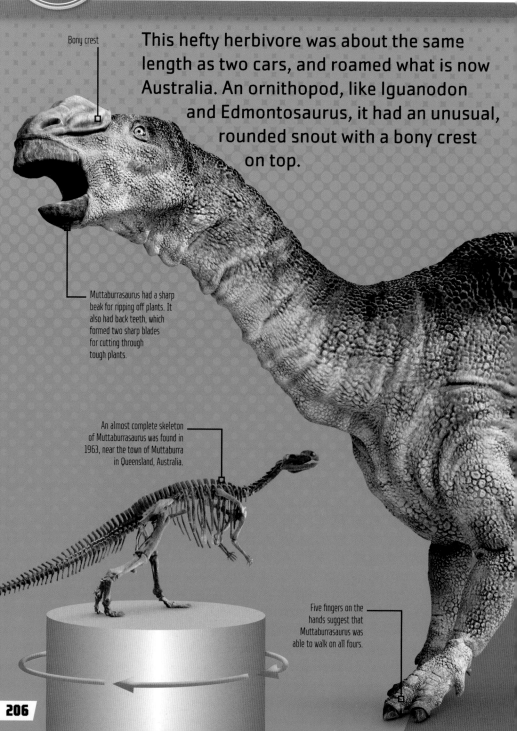

Muttaburrasaurus had a sharp beak for ripping off plants. It also had back teeth, which formed two sharp blades for cutting through tough plants.

An almost complete skeleton of Muttaburrasaurus was found in 1963, near the town of Muttaburra in Queensland, Australia.

Five fingers on the hands suggest that Muttaburrasaurus was able to walk on all fours.

Super stats

Name: Muttaburrasaurus
Pronunciation: MUH-tah-BUH-ruh-SORE-us
Name meaning: Muttaburra lizard
Period: Cretaceous   **Length:** 7 m (23 ft)
Weight: 2,800 kg (6,200 lb)   **Diet:** Herbivore
Habitat: Land   **Location:** Oceania   **Animal type:** Dinosaur
Key species: Muttaburrasaurus langdoni

Weird but true!

Muttaburrasaurus's crest may have had an inflatable sac on top to make its calls louder, like the throat sacs of some modern frogs.

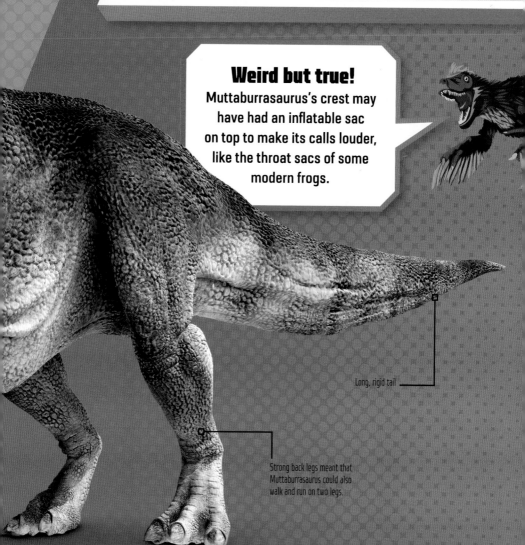

Long, rigid tail

Strong back legs meant that Muttaburrasaurus could also walk and run on two legs.

Deinonychus

Although it was not huge, Deinonychus was a fearsome predator. It was about the length of a rhinoceros, but only weighed as much as a cheetah. This meant that it was fast and agile. Deinonychus was also quite clever for a dinosaur, so it was very good at tracking prey. When it found its victim, Deinonychus could use its 13 cm (5 in) long claws to rip it apart.

Deinonychus would have hunted in packs, like modern wolves, to bring down large prey.

One slash from its clawed foot would rip through flesh with ease.

Deinonychus also had flexible wrists that helped it to grip prey.

Deinonychus: Will this clawed creature triumph in battle?

Battle up!

Scientists have fossil evidence to prove that Deinonychus definitely attacked Tenontosaurus. It would have been a classic match up of carnivore vs. herbivore and speed vs. size, but who would have won?

Tenontosaurus

Tenontosaurus was a big herbivore, up to 8 m (26 ft) long. That is about as long as a bus. It weighed about 1,350 kg (3,000 lb), which is about as heavy as a rhinoceros. It would have moved slowly, with its weight balanced by its very long tail. Although it mainly walked on four legs, Tenontosaurus could rear up onto two back legs to reach food, or to defend itself.

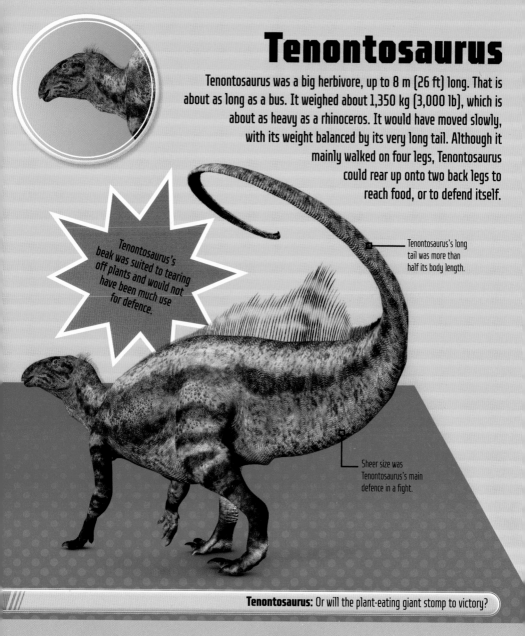

Tenontosaurus's beak was suited to tearing off plants and would not have been much use for defence.

Tenontosaurus's long tail was more than half its body length.

Sheer size was Tenontosaurus's main defence in a fight.

Tenontosaurus: Or will the plant-eating giant stomp to victory?

Who would win?

Tenontosaurus might have been much bigger, but Deinonychus would have won the fight. Deinonychus's killing claws would have inflicted serious damage on the herbivore. Then, it would use its powerful jaw muscles, which were strong enough to bite through bone. Tenontosaurus would not have stood a chance.

Winner!

Dracorex

This bone-headed dinosaur's unusual spikes and frills earned it a name that means "dragon king". However, some palaeontologists think that Dracorex is simply the teenage version of Pachycephalosaurus.

Long tail for balance

Weird but true!

This dinosaur's full name is Dracorex hogwartsia, in honour of Hogwarts School in J. K. Rowling's *Harry Potter* books.

Repenomamus

Repenomamus was a meat-eating mammal about the size of a badger. It was much bigger than most other mammals from the time of the dinosaurs, and had very sharp teeth.

Its jaw had sharp teeth at the front and smaller teeth for chewing at the sides.

Like a cat, Repenomamus probably had whiskers, and would have used them to sense prey, or to warn it of danger.

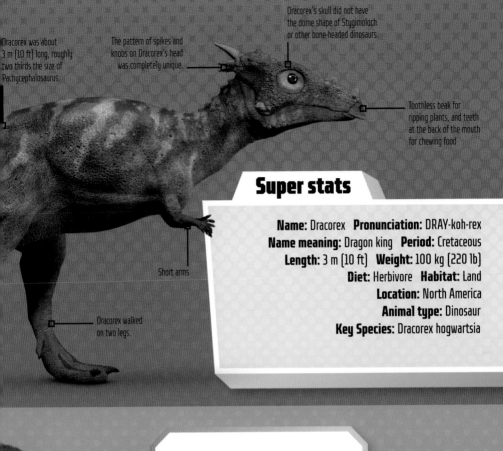

Dracorex was about 3 m (10 ft) long, roughly two thirds the size of Pachycephalosaurus.

The pattern of spikes and knobs on Dracorex's head was completely unique.

Dracorex's skull did not have the dome shape of Stygimoloch or other bone-headed dinosaurs.

Toothless beak for ripping plants, and teeth at the back of the mouth for chewing food

Short arms

Dracorex walked on two legs.

Super stats

Name: Dracorex **Pronunciation:** DRAY-koh-rex
Name meaning: Dragon king **Period:** Cretaceous
Length: 3 m (10 ft) **Weight:** 100 kg (220 lb)
Diet: Herbivore **Habitat:** Land
Location: North America
Animal type: Dinosaur
Key Species: Dracorex hogwartsia

Furry tail

Weird but true!

A Repenomamus fossil was found with a baby Psittacosaurus in its stomach.

Repenomamus walked on four wide feet.

Super stats

Name: Repenomamus
Pronunciation: REP-en-OH-ma-MUSS
Name meaning: Reptile mammal **Period:** Cretaceous
Length: 1 m (3 ft) **Weight:** 14 kg (30 lb)
Diet: Carnivore **Habitat:** Land **Location:** Asia
Animal type: Prehistoric creature
Key species: Repenomamus robustus

Archaeoceratops

This was one of the first ceratopsian dinosaurs in the Cretaceous period, and was one of the smallest of this group. It was discovered in China, and probably walked on two legs, rather than four.

Weird but true!
Archaeoceratops means "ancient horned face" but it did not even have horns.

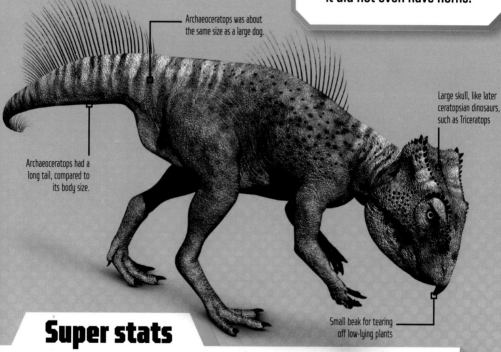

Archaeoceratops was about the same size as a large dog.

Large skull, like later ceratopsian dinosaurs, such as Triceratops

Archaeoceratops had a long tail, compared to its body size.

Small beak for tearing off low-lying plants

Super stats

Name: Archaeoceratops **Pronunciation:** AR-kay-OH-seh-RAH-tops
Name meaning: Ancient horned face **Period:** Cretaceous
Length: 1 m (3 ft) **Weight:** 10 kg (22 lb) **Diet:** Herbivore
Habitat: Land **Location:** Asia
Animal type: Dinosaur **Key species:** Archaeoceratops oshimai

Nigersaurus

Nigersaurus was a small sauropod that weighed about as much as an elephant, and once plodded around Africa. Its unusual, wide, straight-edged snout looks a little like a vacuum cleaner.

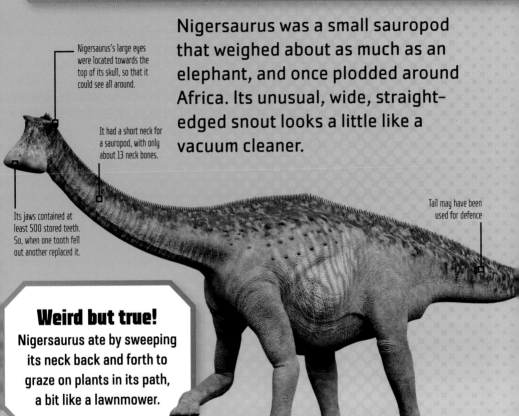

Nigersaurus's large eyes were located towards the top of its skull, so that it could see all around.

It had a short neck for a sauropod, with only about 13 neck bones.

Its jaws contained at least 500 stored teeth. So, when one tooth fell out another replaced it.

Tail may have been used for defence

Weird but true!

Nigersaurus ate by sweeping its neck back and forth to graze on plants in its path, a bit like a lawnmower.

Super stats

Name: Nigersaurus **Pronunciation:** NAI-juh-SAW-russ
Name meaning: Niger reptile **Period:** Cretaceous
Length: 9 m (30 ft) **Weight:** 4,000 kg (8,800 lb) **Diet:** Herbivore
Habitat: Land **Location:** Africa **Animal type:** Dinosaur
Key species: Nigersaurus taqueti

Altirhinus

Altirhinus was an ornithopod that once roamed around Mongolia. It was related to other dinosaurs, such as Iguanodon, and was around the same length as a large minibus.

Its long tail may have helped it balance when it stood up to feed on high-growing plants.

Altirhinus probably ran on two legs to escape predators.

Neovenator

This predator likely preyed on Iguanodon and possibly even sauropods. Neovenator weighed about the same as two male polar bears.

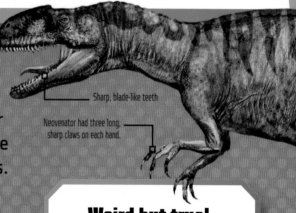

Sharp, blade-like teeth

Neovenator had three long, sharp claws on each hand.

Weird but true!
Neovenator was first discovered when fossils fell from cliffs during a storm in the Isle of Wight, UK.

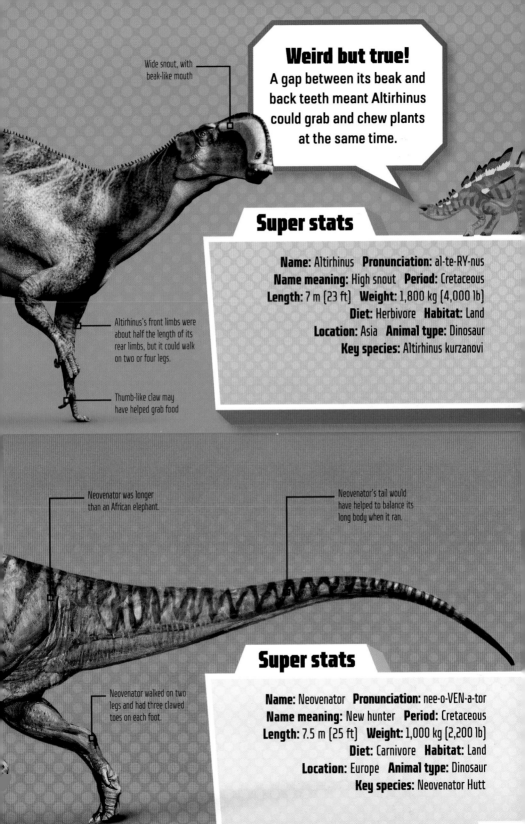

Wide snout, with beak-like mouth

Weird but true!

A gap between its beak and back teeth meant Altirhinus could grab and chew plants at the same time.

Altirhinus's front limbs were about half the length of its rear limbs, but it could walk on two or four legs.

Thumb-like claw may have helped grab food

Super stats

Name: Altirhinus **Pronunciation:** al-te-RY-nus
Name meaning: High snout **Period:** Cretaceous
Length: 7 m (23 ft) **Weight:** 1,800 kg (4,000 lb)
Diet: Herbivore **Habitat:** Land
Location: Asia **Animal type:** Dinosaur
Key species: Altirhinus kurzanovi

Neovenator was longer than an African elephant.

Neovenator's tail would have helped to balance its long body when it ran.

Neovenator walked on two legs and had three clawed toes on each foot.

Super stats

Name: Neovenator **Pronunciation:** nee-o-VEN-a-tor
Name meaning: New hunter **Period:** Cretaceous
Length: 7.5 m (25 ft) **Weight:** 1,000 kg (2,200 lb)
Diet: Carnivore **Habitat:** Land
Location: Europe **Animal type:** Dinosaur
Key species: Neovenator Hutt

Ankylosaurus

The dinosaur equivalent of an armoured tank, Ankylosaurus was incredibly hard to defeat. Its huge body was covered from head to tail with tough, bony armour. Just in case that was not enough to put off predators, it also had a deadly bony club at the end of its tail.

Bony plates were fused together on the head to protect the skull.

Ankylosaurus's beak-like mouth was designed for tearing off plants.

Four horns on its face provided extra protection for Ankylosaurus.

Ankylosaurus moved slowly on four short, sturdy legs.

Super stats

Name: Ankylosaurus
Pronunciation: an-KIE-loh-SAW-russ
Name meaning: Fused lizard   **Period:** Cretaceous
Length: 9 m (30 ft)   **Weight:** 6,000 kg (13,200 lb)
Diet: Herbivore   **Habitat:** Land
Location: North America   **Animal type:** Dinosaur
Key species: Ankylosaurus magniventris

Like all armoured dinosaurs, Ankylosaurus was covered in bony plates called osteoderms.

Weird but true

Ankylosaurus's tail had a club-like tip made from bony plates joined together. If it was swung, it could shatter another dinosaur's bones!

Ankylosaurus's large gut could digest massive amounts of plant material.

The tail club was used to defend Ankylosaurus, and perhaps its young, from predators.

Prehistoric plants

Plants were around long before the dinosaurs. The first plants lived in water, but began to grow on land about 500 million years ago. The Carboniferous period, around 358–298 million years ago, was known as the "Age of Plants". Dense, swampy forests flourished, creating perfect conditions for ferns, mosses, and horsetails to grow.

Mosses

These would have been among the first plants to move from water to land. Most fossil mosses are tiny and need to be looked at using a microscope.

Ferns

These low-lying plants were one of the most common plants of the Carboniferous period. They would have been chomped on by herbivores.

Cycads

Found on every continent, cycads made up about 20 per cent of all land plants. Larger herbivores, such as Muttaburrasaurus, would have eaten their tough leaves.

Weird but true!
The remains of Carboniferous forests formed the coal that is burnt today to make electricity.

Conifers

Large conifers first appeared during the Triassic period. They grew in thick forests and could be up to 30 m (100 ft) tall.

Horsetails

These simple plants still exist today. They were ideal for shorter herbivores, such as Polacanthus, although some of the now extinct species were 50 m (165 ft) tall!

Ginkgos

These trees were common from the Triassic period onwards. Only one type has survived until today, and it has changed very little over millions of years.

Grasses

Today, grass is the main diet for many herbivores. Grasses only appeared in the Cretaceous period, so many prehistoric herbivores never got to try it.

Elasmosaurus

Elasmosaurus was a plesiosaur, a long-necked reptile that lived in the sea. Its neck was great for helping it to sneak up on prey. Elasmosaurus would flick its neck quickly to grab unsuspecting fish.

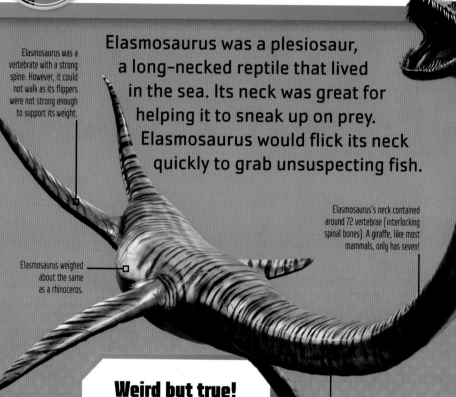

Elasmosaurus was a vertebrate with a strong spine. However, it could not walk as its flippers were not strong enough to support its weight.

Elasmosaurus's neck contained around 72 vertebrae (interlocking spinal bones). A giraffe, like most mammals, only has seven!

Elasmosaurus weighed about the same as a rhinoceros.

It was twice as long as a shark, but at least half of its length was its neck.

Weird but true!

When Elasmosaurus's skeleton was first reconstructed, the head was attached to the wrong end.

Super stats

Name: Elasmosaurus **Pronunciation:** el-LAZZ-moe-SORE-us
Name meaning: Thin plated lizard **Period:** Cretaceous
Length: 12 m (40 ft) **Weight:** 8,500 kg (19,000 lb)
Diet: Carnivore **Habitat:** Ocean **Location:** North America
Animal type: Prehistoric creature
Key species: Elasmosaurus platyurus

Albertaceratops

This unusual–looking ceratopsian had long brow horns, but no nose horn. Instead, Albertaceratops had a bony, banana–shaped ridge on its nose. It also had two large, curved hooks on its spiky frill.

Weird but true!

Albertaceratops's brow horns grew up to 60 cm (24 in) long, about half the length of Triceratops horns.

Super stats

Name: Albertaceratops
Pronunciation: al-BURT-a-sera-tops
Name meaning: Alberta horned face
Period: Cretaceous
Length: 6 m (20 ft)
Weight: 3,500 kg (7,700 lb)
Diet: Herbivore   **Habitat:** Land
Location: North America
Animal type: Dinosaur
Key species: Albertaceratops nesmoi

Neck frill

Large, beak-like snout for tearing off plants

Its tail may have had quill-like feathers at the end.

Albertaceratops walked on four sturdy legs.

Amargasaurus

Amargasaurus might have been small for a sauropod, but it was one of the most unique-looking. It had a shorter neck than other sauropods, and a double row of spikes running along its neck and back.

Weird but true!
This dinosaur could only have reached plants up to about 3 m (10 ft) high.

Cronopio

New discoveries are beginning to help us understand what prehistoric mammals were doing in South America when dinosaurs ruled the Earth. Fossils of a sabre-tooth, squirrel-like mammal named Cronopio, found in Argentina, give us some fresh clues.

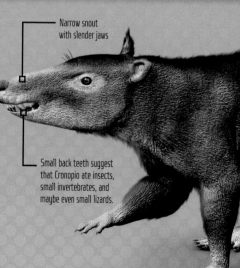

Narrow snout with slender jaws

Small back teeth suggest that Cronopio ate insects, small invertebrates, and maybe even small lizards.

It weighed about the same as a rhinoceros. Like all sauropods, its bones were light, but strong.

Amargasaurus's spikes were most likely used to scare off predators, or to attract a mate.

Pencil-like teeth

Amargasaurus walked on four legs.

Super stats

Name: Amargasaurus
Pronunciation: ah-MAR-gah-SORE-us
Name meaning: Amarga lizard **Period:** Cretaceous
Length: 9.5 m (31 ft) **Weight:** 2,700 kg (6,000 lb)
Diet: Herbivore **Habitat:** Land
Location: South America
Animal type: Dinosaur
Key species: Amargasaurus cazaui

Weird but true!

Cronopio's teeth and jaws were so fine and slender that if it had bitten down hard with its teeth, it would have injured itself.

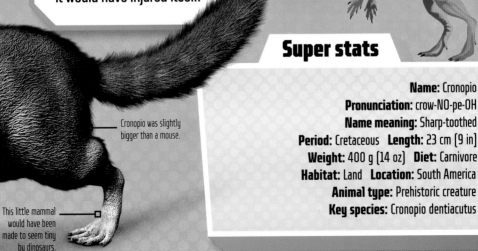

Cronopio was slightly bigger than a mouse.

This little mammal would have been made to seem tiny by dinosaurs.

Super stats

Name: Cronopio
Pronunciation: crow-NO-pe-OH
Name meaning: Sharp-toothed
Period: Cretaceous **Length:** 23 cm (9 in)
Weight: 400 g (14 oz) **Diet:** Carnivore
Habitat: Land **Location:** South America
Animal type: Prehistoric creature
Key species: Cronopio dentiacutus

Ouranosaurus

Palaeontologists cannot agree why Ouranosaurus had a large, sail–like hump on its back. The sail grew bigger as the dinosaur got older, so it seems likely that it was used to attract a mate.

Weird but true!

Ouranosaurus lived near river mouths and may have been hunted by Sarcosuchus, nicknamed "Supercroc".

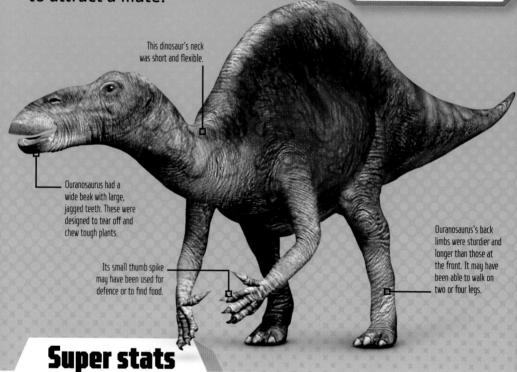

This dinosaur's neck was short and flexible.

Ouranosaurus had a wide beak with large, jagged teeth. These were designed to tear off and chew tough plants.

Its small thumb spike may have been used for defence or to find food.

Ouranosaurus's back limbs were sturdier and longer than those at the front. It may have been able to walk on two or four legs.

Super stats

Name: Ouranosaurus **Pronunciation:** oo-RAN-oh-SORE-us
Name meaning: Brave lizard **Period:** Cretaceous
Length: 8 m (26 ft) **Weight:** 3,000 kg (6,600 lb)
Diet: Herbivore **Habitat:** Land **Location:** Africa
Animal type: Dinosaur **Key species:** Ouranosaurus nigeriensis

Dolichorhynchops

Large eyes were ideal for spotting small prey.

This short-necked plesiosaur's flippers were perfect for swimming, but not great for moving on land. So, Dolichorhynchops spent its entire life in the ocean. It hunted small fish — and tried to avoid huge mosasaurs, such as Tylosaurus.

These wing-like flippers allowed Dolichorhynchops to "fly" through the water.

Smooth skin

Its long, narrow jaws captured fish, which were swallowed whole.

Weird but true!
Dolichorhynchops may have swallowed small rocks to help it break up food inside its stomach.

Super stats

Name: Dolichorhynchops   **Pronunciation:** DOL-ee-kor-RIN-chops
Name meaning: Long-nosed face   **Period:** Cretaceous
Length: 4 m (13 ft)   **Weight:** 1,500 kg (3,300 lb)
Diet: Carnivore   **Habitat:** Ocean
Location: North America   **Animal type:** Prehistoric creature
Key species: Dolichorhynchops osborni

Quetzalcoatlus

A pterosaur, not a dinosaur, Quetzalcoatlus is possibly the largest flying animal that has ever lived. Quetzalcoatlus stood as tall as a giraffe, and had a wingspan as big as a small aircraft. Amazingly though, this heavy beast could fly, covering huge distances without stopping.

Powerful wings meant that it could fly at speeds of up to 130 kph (80 mph).

Quetzalcoatlus did not have teeth and would have had to swallow its prey whole.

Small, padded feet meant that Quetzalcoatlus could also move fast on land.

Long limbs

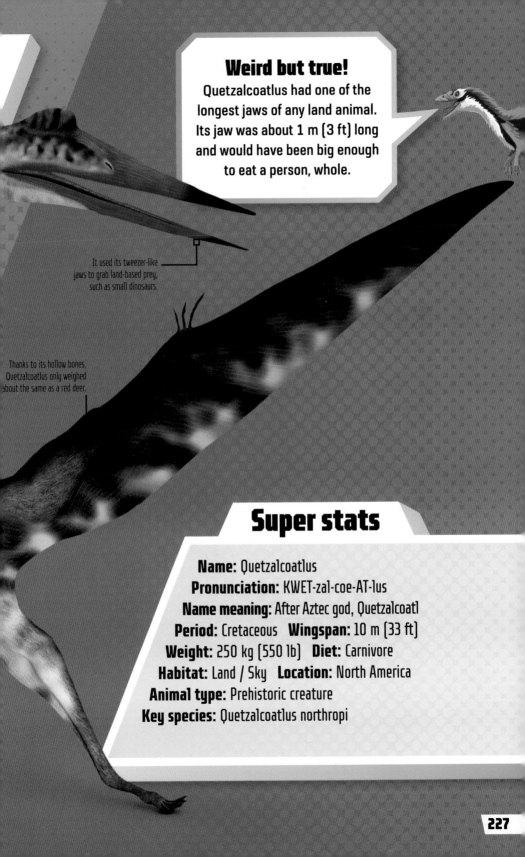

Weird but true!
Quetzalcoatlus had one of the longest jaws of any land animal. Its jaw was about 1 m (3 ft) long and would have been big enough to eat a person, whole.

It used its tweezer-like jaws to grab land-based prey, such as small dinosaurs.

Thanks to its hollow bones, Quetzalcoatlus only weighed about the same as a red deer.

Super stats

Name: Quetzalcoatlus
Pronunciation: KWET-zal-coe-AT-lus
Name meaning: After Aztec god, Quetzalcoatl
Period: Cretaceous   **Wingspan:** 10 m (33 ft)
Weight: 250 kg (550 lb)   **Diet:** Carnivore
Habitat: Land / Sky   **Location:** North America
Animal type: Prehistoric creature
Key species: Quetzalcoatlus northropi

Psittacosaurus

This small ceratopsian dinosaur was bigger than Repenomamus, but nowhere near the size of its relative, Triceratops. However, what it lacked in size, Psittacosaurus made up for with intelligence. Its larger-than-average brain meant that it was smart enough to form herds with other Psittacosauruses to stay safe from predators. It was also really good at hiding, thanks to its skin that could blend in with its surroundings.

Psittacosaurus would have used its beak and its arms to defend itself in a fight.

Its cheek horns were too small to do much damage in a battle.

Psittacosaurus could run as fast as 40 kph (25 mph).

Psittacosaurus: This bristle-tailed beast had a talent for hiding!

Battle up!

Fossils of Repenomamus have been found with the bones of baby Psittacosauruses in its stomach. But, battling babies is hardly a fair fight! Did mighty Repenomamus really have the strength to take down a fully grown Psittacosaurus?

Repenomamus

It might have looked soft and furry, but Repenomamus was a deadly hunter. It was much larger than most other mammals at the time — about the size of a modern badger — and had wide jaws filled with extremely sharp teeth. A meat eater, Repenomamus was big enough and strong enough to prey on small dinosaurs.

Its sturdy, long body was covered in a coat of fur.

Repenomamus's whiskers helped it to sense when its prey was close.

Repenomamus lived alongside dinosaurs – and was bigger than some of them.

Repenomamus: A furry hunter with food on its mind!

Who would win?

It would be a close call. A baby Psittacosaurus was easy prey, but an adult would have been more of a challenge. First, Repenomamus had to find Psittacosaurus, which was not easy, thanks to its camouflage, which kept it hidden. Even if it did spot one, Psittacosaurus would probably have been protected as part of a herd. But, in a one-on-one contest, Repenomamus would triumph over Psittacosaurus.

Winner!

Tyrannotitan

Despite its name, Tyrannotitan is more closely related to Carcharodontosaurus and Giganotosaurus than Tyrannosaurus. Tyrannotitan had a set of 60 terrifying, shark–like teeth, capable of ripping apart any dinosaur.

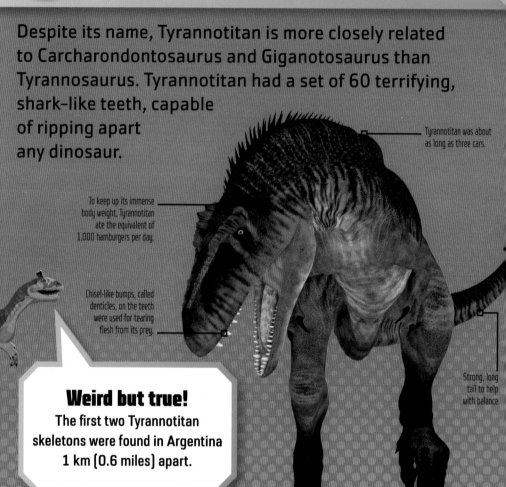

Tyrannotitan was about as long as three cars.

To keep up its immense body weight, Tyrannotitan ate the equivalent of 1,000 hamburgers per day.

Chisel-like bumps, called denticles, on the teeth were used for tearing flesh from its prey.

Strong, long tail to help with balance

Weird but true!
The first two Tyrannotitan skeletons were found in Argentina 1 km (0.6 miles) apart.

Super stats

Name: Tyrannotitan
Pronunciation: TIE-ran-no-TIE-tan
Name meaning: Tyrant giant   **Period:** Cretaceous
Length: 12 m (40 ft)   **Weight:** 5,200 kg (11,500 lb)
Diet: Carnivore   **Habitat:** Land   **Location:** South America
Animal type: Dinosaur   **Key species:** Tyrannotitan chubutensis

Tenontosaurus

Tenontosaurus was a plant–eating ornithopod, and was related to Iguanodon. Its name means "sinew lizard" because it had a network of tendons to support its super–long tail. This kept its tail from dragging along the ground.

Super stats

Name: Tenontosaurus
Pronunciation: ten-NON-toe-SORE-us
Name meaning: Sinew lizard
Period: Cretaceous
Length: 8 m (26 ft)
Weight: 1,350 kg (3,000 lb)
Diet: Herbivore **Habitat:** Land
Location: North America
Animal type: Dinosaur
Key species: Tenontosaurus tilletti

U-shaped beak helped Tenontosaurus bite through plants

Tenontosaurus was about as long as two white rhinoceroses.

Tenontosaurus's tail was as long as the rest of its body.

Weird but true!

A Tenontosaurus fossil was found with bite marks from Deinonychus — a much smaller and lighter dinosaur.

It weighed about as much as 42 10-year-old children.

Centrosaurus

Centrosaurus was quite small for a ceratopsian dinosaur. It looked a bit like a rhinoceros, but was longer and had a horny frill that it probably used to attract a mate.

Weird but true!

Thousands of Centrosaurus bones were found in Canada in a giant bonebed — a herd may have drowned while crossing a flooded river.

Its spiked frill had two hooks that curved forwards.

Muscles attached to its frill would have given Centrosaurus a strong bite so it could eat tough plants.

Centrosaurus had sturdy legs with four toes on each foot.

Super stats

Name: Centrosaurus   **Pronunciation:** SEN-tro-SORE-russ
Name meaning: Pointed lizard   **Period:** Cretaceous
Length: 6 m (20 ft)   **Weight:** 1,180 kg (2,600 lb)
Diet: Herbivore   **Habitat:** Land
Location: North America   **Animal type:** Dinosaur
Key species: Centrosaurus apertus

Struthiomimus

Struthiomimus means "ostrich mimic" because it was tall and feathered like a modern ostrich. One of the fastest dinosaurs, it could run up to 65 kph (40 mph), which is similar to an ostrich.

Big eyes gave Struthiomimus good all-round vision.

Toothless beak

Its long, slim neck helped Struthiomimus reach high plants.

A rigid tail helped Struthiomimus balance when running.

Weird but true!
A nearly complete Struthiomimus skeleton was found by the Red Deer River, in Canada, in 1914.

It had arms covered in feathers, but could not fly.

Super stats

Name: Struthiomimus
Pronunciation: STROO-thee-oh-MIME-us
Name meaning: Ostrich mimic   **Period:** Cretaceous
Length: 5.5 m (18 ft)   **Weight:** 420 kg (925 lb)
Diet: Omnivore   **Habitat:** Land   **Location:** North America
Animal type: Dinosaur   **Key species:** Struthiomimus altus

Gallimimus

Its name means "chicken mimic", but Gallimimus was much heavier than a chicken. It was probably more similar to an ostrich. Like an ostrich, Gallimimus could run very fast, up to 65 kph (40 mph).

The long tail helped Gallimimus with balance when running.

Weird but true!
Gallimimus was almost twice as tall as the average adult human, and could run faster than a horse.

Kunbarrasaurus

Discovered in Australia and named as recently as 2015, Kunbarrasaurus means "shield lizard". It gets its name from the bony armour on its back that is typical of all ankylosaurs.

Kunbarrasaurus used teeth in its cheeks for chewing food.

Its parrot-like beak tore leaves, fruit, and seeds from plants.

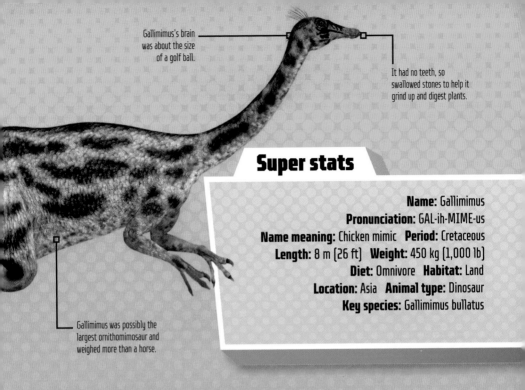

Gallimimus's brain was about the size of a golf ball.

It had no teeth, so swallowed stones to help it grind up and digest plants.

Gallimimus was possibly the largest ornithomimosaur and weighed more than a horse.

Super stats

Name: Gallimimus
Pronunciation: GAL-ih-MIME-us
Name meaning: Chicken mimic   **Period:** Cretaceous
Length: 8 m (26 ft)   **Weight:** 450 kg (1,000 lb)
Diet: Omnivore   **Habitat:** Land
Location: Asia   **Animal type:** Dinosaur
Key species: Gallimimus bullatus

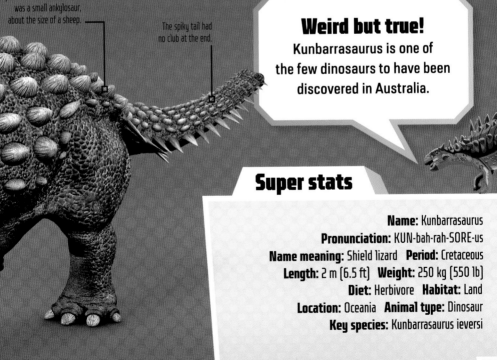

Experts think Kunbarrasaurus was a small ankylosaur, about the size of a sheep.

The spiky tail had no club at the end.

Weird but true!

Kunbarrasaurus is one of the few dinosaurs to have been discovered in Australia.

Super stats

Name: Kunbarrasaurus
Pronunciation: KUN-bah-rah-SORE-us
Name meaning: Shield lizard   **Period:** Cretaceous
Length: 2 m (6.5 ft)   **Weight:** 250 kg (550 lb)
Diet: Herbivore   **Habitat:** Land
Location: Oceania   **Animal type:** Dinosaur
Key species: Kunbarrasaurus ieversi

Baryonyx

With its long snout and sharp teeth, Baryonyx had a head that looked a bit like a crocodile. It hunted in water and along lakes and rivers, using its mighty jaws to catch fish. However, Baryonyx also hunted on land and dined on dinosaurs, including adults and their young.

At 10 m (33 ft) long, Baryonyx was twice as long as a modern saltwater crocodile.

Baryonyx used its long, muscular tail for balance.

Super stats

Name: Baryonyx
Pronunciation: bah-ree-ON-ix
Name meaning: Heavy claw   **Period:** Cretaceous
Length: 10 m (33 ft)   **Weight:** 2,000 kg (4,400 lb)
Diet: Carnivore   **Habitat:** Land
Location: Europe   **Animal type:** Dinosaur
Key species: Baryonyx walkeri

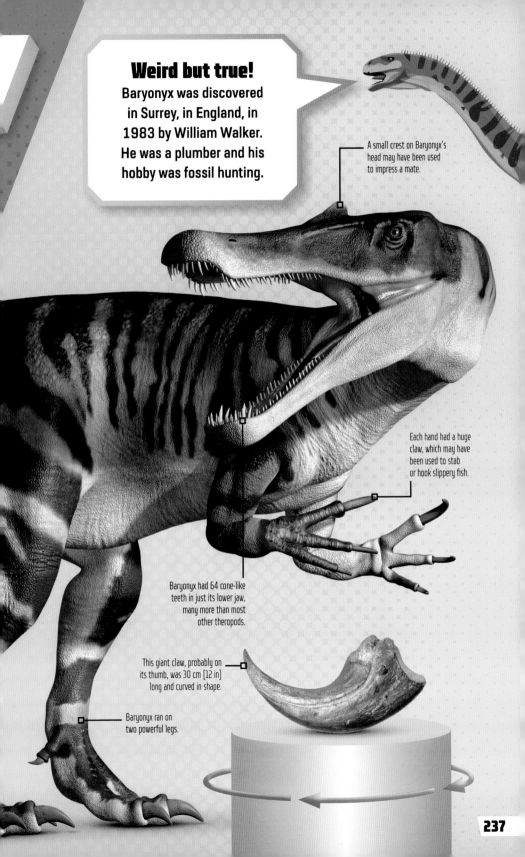

Weird but true!
Baryonyx was discovered in Surrey, in England, in 1983 by William Walker. He was a plumber and his hobby was fossil hunting.

A small crest on Baryonyx's head may have been used to impress a mate.

Each hand had a huge claw, which may have been used to stab or hook slippery fish.

Baryonyx had 64 cone-like teeth in just its lower jaw, many more than most other theropods.

This giant claw, probably on its thumb, was 30 cm (12 in) long and curved in shape.

Baryonyx ran on two powerful legs.

Showy Styracosaurus

Scientists think that Styracosaurus might have been a bit of a show-off. Its fearsome horns and spikes might have scared away some predators, but it is more likely that Styracosaurus used them to impress members of its own species and attract a mate.

Insects

Most insects and other creepy crawlies, such as spiders, appeared around the time that plants were beginning to bloom, about 350 million years ago. We know a lot about prehistoric insects because their fossils have been found around the world. Many were trapped in sticky tree resin that hardened to form amber. Lots of species grew much bigger than those around today.

Arthropleura

(arth-row-PLOO-ra) This millipede was about 2.5 m (8 ft) long – about six times longer than the longest modern millipede. It shed its hard outer skeleton when it grew new legs.

Meganeura

(MEG-ah-new-ra) This relative of the dragonfly was the largest flying insect. It had a wingspan of 75 cm (30 in), which is twice as big as many modern bats.

Cockroach

It turns out that cockroaches are nothing new. The early relatives of this tough bug were crawling around more than 300 million years ago.

Jaekelopterus

[JAY-kel-OP-ter-us] This sea scorpion
was 2.6 m [9 ft] long. It was an arthropod –
the family that includes spiders and
scorpions. It may also have been
able to walk on land.

Bedbugs

Bedbugs are thought to have
been around for 100 million years.
They probably annoyed small mammals
rather than bothering big dinosaurs.

Rhyniognatha

[RY-nee-oh-NATH-uh] One of the
oldest insect fossils found so far
belonged to Rhyniognatha, which
lived in Scotland, in the UK,
around 410 million years ago.

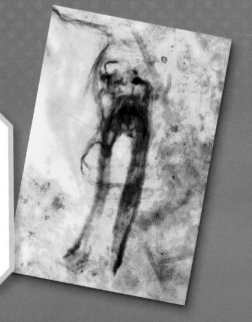

Saurolophus

Saurolophus was a duck-billed dinosaur, or hadrosaur, and its name means "lizard crest". Unusually, Saurolophus's crest was largely made of solid bone. It pointed backwards and grew bigger as the dinosaur got older.

Spikes ran from the neck to the end of the tail.

It weighed about 3,000 kg (6,600 lb), which is about the same as a female African elephant.

Weird but true!
Saurolophus had hundreds of cheek teeth and cheek pouches in its beak to help it grind and chew its food.

Saurolophus had a wide bill.

It is likely that Saurolophus could walk on two or four legs.

Super stats

Name: Saurolophus   **Pronunciation:** sore-roh-LOAF-uss
Name meaning: Lizard crest   **Period:** Cretaceous
Length: 9 m (30 ft)   **Weight:** 3,000 kg (6,600 lb)
Diet: Herbivore   **Habitat:** Land
Location: North America and Asia
Animal type: Dinosaur   **Key species:** Saurolophus osborni

Suchomimus

This large theropod was related to Spinosaurus and Baryonyx. Its name means "crocodile mimic" because, like a crocodile, Suchomimus had long, narrow jaws. These were perfect for catching fish and other sea creatures.

Super stats

Name: Suchomimus
Pronunciation: soo-ko-MIME-us
Name meaning: Crocodile mimic
Period: Cretaceous
Length: 10.5 m (34.5 ft)
Weight: 2,500 kg (5,500 lb)
Diet: Carnivore
Habitat: Land   **Location:** Africa
Animal type: Dinosaur
Key species: Suchomimus tenerensis

Long, narrow nostrils near the end of the snout

Suchomimus had wide jaws with more than 120 long, cone-shaped teeth.

Weird but true!
Though it looked a bit like a crocodile, Suchomimus was not suited to life in water. Its body was about four times heavier than a crocodile's.

Suchomimus weighed about as much as a large car.

Long, sharp hand claws would have been used to snatch prey or slash enemies.

Deinosuchus

Deinosuchus was slow and clumsy on land, but in the water it was a fast and dangerous predator. It mostly ate sea creatures, as well as any dinosaurs that ventured into the water.

Sharp pointed teeth were ideal for grabbing onto slippery prey.

Like an alligator, Deinosuchus could poke its snout and eyes out of the water to hunt for food.

This strong, muscular tail was great for swimming and helped Deinosuchus to lunge at prey.

Deinosuchus's bite was twice as powerful as Tyrannosaurus's.

Small, slightly webbed feet stopped Deinosuchus from sinking into muddy riverbanks.

Weird but true!
After grabbing its prey, Deinosuchus would roll over onto it and use its weight to overpower its food.

Super stats

Name: Deinosuchus **Pronunciation:** DIE-no-SOO-kuss
Name meaning: Terrible crocodile **Period:** Cretaceous
Length: 12 m (40 ft) **Weight:** 5,000 kg (11,000 lb)
Diet: Carnivore **Habitat:** Water
Location: North America **Animal type:** Prehistoric creature
Key species: Deinosuchus hatcheri

Beelzebufo

Its name means "devil toad", and Beelzebufo could be the largest ever frog. It lived in Madagascar, in Africa, and was about as big as a beach ball. It may have eaten young or small dinosaurs.

Weird but true!
Beelzebufo's armoured body protection included a bony head shield.

Beelzebufo's head was gigantic compared to its body.

It may also have had a long, sticky tongue, like modern frogs, to grab its prey.

It had many sharp teeth and a powerful bite.

Beelzebufo weighed about 4.5 kg (10 lb), which is heavier than most newborn babies.

Super stats

Name: Beelzebufo   **Pronunciation:** bee-EL-zeh-BOO-fo
Name meaning: Devil toad   **Period:** Cretaceous
Length: 41 cm (16 in)   **Weight:** 4.5 kg (10 lb)
Diet: Carnivore   **Habitat:** Land
Location: Africa   **Animal type:** Prehistoric creature
Key species: Beelzebufo ampinga

Ichthyovenator

A member of the spinosaur family, Ichthyovenator was only discovered in 2010. It was very unusual–looking, with two sails on its back. Its name means "fish hunter", although it probably also ate small dinosaurs.

This double sail may have been to attract mates, maintain bod temperature, or to store energy.

Tail spines might have helped Ichthyovenator to swim.

Its tail would also have helped to propel it through water.

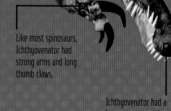

Like most spinosaurs, Ichthyovenator had strong arms and long thumb claws.

Ichthyovenator had a long snout containing cone-shaped teeth.

Weird but true!

So far, no Ichthyovenator skulls or limbs have been found. Scientists use what they know about other spinosaurs to work out what it looked like.

Super stats

Name: Ichthyovenator **Pronunciation:** IK-fee-o-ven-ah-tor
Name meaning: Fish hunter **Period:** Cretaceous
Length: 9 m (30 ft) **Weight:** 2,200 kg (4,850 lb)
Diet: Carnivore **Habitat:** Land
Location: Asia **Animal type:** Dinosaur
Key species: Ichthyovenator laosensis

Kaprosuchus

Kaprosuchus had large tusk-like teeth in its top and bottom jaws. These stuck out like a boar's tusks when its mouth was closed. This is why its name means "boar crocodile".

Weird but true!
Kaprosuchus may have used its long tusks to crack open dinosaur eggs to feed on.

The front of Kaprosuchus's snout may have been used to ram prey.

Kaprosuchus had slightly forward-facing eyes, which suggest that it was mostly a land predator.

Kaprosuchus had longer legs than most modern crocodiles, which also indicates that it might have hunted on land.

It is likely that Kaprosuchus used its "tusks" to stab its prey and then its large jaws to hold it.

Super stats

Name: Kaprosuchus   **Pronunciation:** KAP-roe-SOO-kuss
Name meaning: Boar crocodile   **Period:** Cretaceous
Length: 6 m (20 ft)   **Weight:** 900 kg (2,000 lb)
Diet: Carnivore   **Habitat:** Land
Location: Africa   **Animal type:** Prehistoric creature
Key species: Kaprosuchus saharicus

Argentinosaurus

Argentinosaurus is quite possibly the largest land animal that has ever lived. Enormous, even for a titanosaur, it was nearly seven times as large as an African elephant, and 12 times heavier. However, its size meant that it could only plod along at about 8 kph (5 mph).

Argentinosaurus's long neck allowed it to eat plants that other dinosaurs could not reach.

Argentinosaurus had a big appetite and may have eaten up to 850 kg (1,900 lb) of plants every day. That's about the same weight as 300 bricks!

Peg-like teeth

Super stats

Name: Argentinosaurus
Pronunciation: ARE-jen-TEEN-oh-SORE-us
Name meaning: Argentine lizard   **Period:** Cretaceous
Length: 35 m (115 ft)   **Weight:** 70,000 kg (155,000 lb)
Diet: Herbivore   **Habitat:** Land
Location: South America
Animal type: Dinosaur
Key species: Argentinosaurus huinculensis

Weird but true!

Argentinosaurus babies had to look after themselves as soon as they hatched. One immediate danger was being trampled on by their enormous parents.

Long, heavy tail

Strong legs and massive feet supported Argentinosaurus's huge body.

Argentinosaurus's footprint would have been more than 1.5 m (5 ft) long. That's bigger than the height of most 12-year-olds.

Spinosaurus

Spinosaurus definitely had size on its side, but it also had special features to help it hunt for fish. Its long, thin snout moved easily through water, and its paddle-shaped feet helped it to swim fast. Most important of all was its thick, deep, paddle-shaped tail, which pushed its body along when swimming.

Scientists worked out that Spinosaurus lived partly in water by studying chemicals in its teeth!

Long fingers and claws, including an extra-long claw on the first finger of each hand, gave Spinosaurus a huge advantage over fish.

It may even have had webbed feet to help it swim faster.

Spinosaurus: This floodplain fiend gets ready to rumble.

Battle up!

Spinosaurus hunted in swampy floodplains and swam in lakes and rivers. Its feet were designed to walk in mud, and its crocodile-like skull was perfect for snatching fish. Massive Mawsonia would easily have caught its attention!

Mawsonia

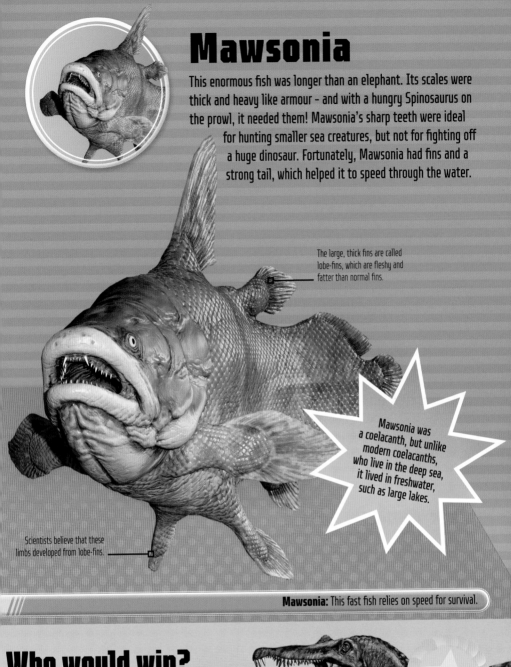

This enormous fish was longer than an elephant. Its scales were thick and heavy like armour – and with a hungry Spinosaurus on the prowl, it needed them! Mawsonia's sharp teeth were ideal for hunting smaller sea creatures, but not for fighting off a huge dinosaur. Fortunately, Mawsonia had fins and a strong tail, which helped it to speed through the water.

The large, thick fins are called lobe-fins, which are fleshy and fatter than normal fins.

Mawsonia was a coelacanth, but unlike modern coelacanths, who live in the deep sea, it lived in freshwater, such as large lakes.

Scientists believe that these limbs developed from lobe-fins.

Mawsonia: This fast fish relies on speed for survival.

Who would win?

Mawsonia was an expert swimmer, but Spinosaurus was one of the only dinosaurs who could hope to catch it. Mawsonia's thick, armour-like scales might have offered enough protection against most predators, but they were no match for the sharp claws and deadly bite of Spinosaurus. Once Spinosaurus managed to trap Mawsonia with its teeth, the battle was already won.

Winner!

Agujaceratops

Super stats

Name: Agujaceratops
Pronunciation: A-gu-ha-SERRA-tops
Name meaning: Horned face of Aguja
Period: Cretaceous   **Length:** 5.2 m [17 ft]
Weight: 2,000 kg (4,400 lb)
Diet: Herbivore   **Habitat:** Land
Location: North America
Animal type: Dinosaur
Key species: Agujaceratops
mariscalensis

It was originally thought to be a Chasmosaurus, but Agujaceratops is instead a close relative. It probably looked more like Pentaceratops, though, with a short nose horn, long brow horns, and a large frill.

Weird but true!

If Agujaceratops strayed too close to water, it would have been in danger from the marine predator Deinosuchus.

Large frill, probably for display

Long brow horns for defence

Typical ceratopsian beak

It weighed about the same as a rhinoceros.

Agujaceratops walked on four legs.

Kosmoceratops

Kosmoceratops had more horns than any other ceratopsian – 15 in total. It had one nose horn, two cheek horns, two brow horns, and 10 horns on its frill.

Kosmoceratops's skull was almost 2 m (6.5 ft) long. That's about the same length as a leatherback sea turtle.

Scientists think that Kosmoceratops used its horns to show off or to fight its own species.

This herbivore used its parrot-like beak to tear off plants.

Weird but true!
Kosmoceratops was about half the size of Triceratops, but had many more horns.

Its body was about as long as the average car.

It walked on four sturdy legs.

Super stats

Name: Kosmoceratops   **Pronunciation:** KOS-moe-SERRA-tops
Name meaning: Ornamented horned face   **Period:** Cretaceous
Length: 4.5 m (15 ft)   **Weight:** 1,300 kg (2,900 lb)
Diet: Herbivore   **Habitat:** Land
Location: North America   **Animal type:** Dinosaur
Key species: Kosmoceratops richardsoni

Leaellynasaura

This small ornithopod lived in what is now Australia. In the Cretaceous period, this area was close to the South Pole, so Leaellynasaura would have had to live during long months with little sunlight.

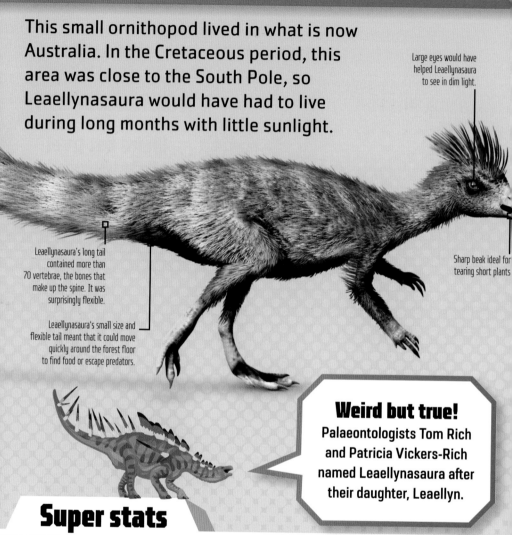

Large eyes would have helped Leaellynasaura to see in dim light.

Leaellynasaura's long tail contained more than 70 vertebrae, the bones that make up the spine. It was surprisingly flexible.

Leaellynasaura's small size and flexible tail meant that it could move quickly around the forest floor to find food or escape predators.

Sharp beak ideal for tearing short plants

Weird but true!
Palaeontologists Tom Rich and Patricia Vickers-Rich named Leaellynasaura after their daughter, Leaellyn.

Super stats

Name: Leaellynasaura   **Pronunciation:** lee-ELL-in-uh-SORE-ah
Name meaning: Leaellyn's lizard   **Period:** Cretaceous
Length: 1.2 m (4 ft)   **Weight:** 8 kg (18 lb)
Diet: Herbivore   **Habitat:** Land
Location: Oceania   **Animal type:** Dinosaur
Key species: Leaellynasaura amicagraphica

Mapusaurus

Mapusaurus's head was flatter, wider, and lighter than Giganotosaurus's.

Mapusaurus was a close relative of Giganotosaurus, and was around the same size as its cousin. It is one of the biggest carnivorous dinosaurs discovered so far.

Razor-sharp teeth for tearing flesh

Mapusaurus weighed almost twice as much as a hippopotamus.

Weird but true!
Mapusaurus may have preyed on young sauropods. It would also have been in danger of being trampled by adult sauropods!

Mapusaurus walked on two legs.

Super stats

Name: Mapusaurus   **Pronunciation:** mah-puh-SORE-us
Name meaning: Earth lizard   **Period:** Cretaceous
Length: 11 m (36 ft)   **Weight:** 3,000 kg (6,600 lb)
Diet: Carnivore   **Habitat:** Land   **Location:** South America
Animal type: Dinosaur   **Key species:** Mapusaurus roseae

Najash

The discovery of this prehistoric snake has helped scientists to understand a lot more about how modern snakes are formed. Najash not only had legs, but it also had a cheekbone.

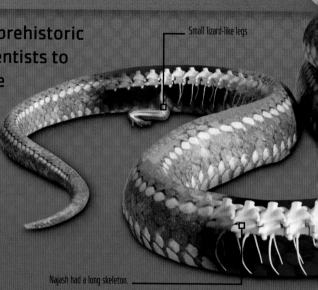

Small lizard-like legs

Najash had a long skeleton.

Wintonotitan

Despite its name, Wintonotitan was not actually a titanosaur. It was huge, though – about the same length as eight beds laid end to end.

Long neck

Weird but true!
Wintonotitan is nicknamed "Clancy" at the Australian Age of Dinosaurs Museum, in Queensland, Australia, where its fossils are on display.

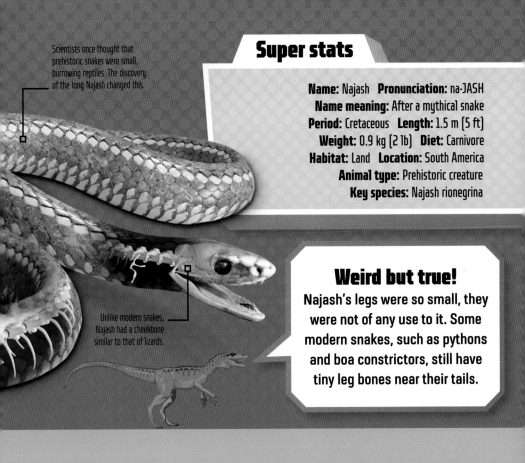

Scientists once thought that prehistoric snakes were small, burrowing reptiles. The discovery of the long Najash changed this.

Unlike modern snakes, Najash had a cheekbone similar to that of lizards.

Super stats

Name: Najash **Pronunciation:** na-JASH
Name meaning: After a mythical snake
Period: Cretaceous **Length:** 1.5 m (5 ft)
Weight: 0.9 kg (2 lb) **Diet:** Carnivore
Habitat: Land **Location:** South America
Animal type: Prehistoric creature
Key species: Najash rionegrina

Weird but true!

Najash's legs were so small, they were not of any use to it. Some modern snakes, such as pythons and boa constrictors, still have tiny leg bones near their tails.

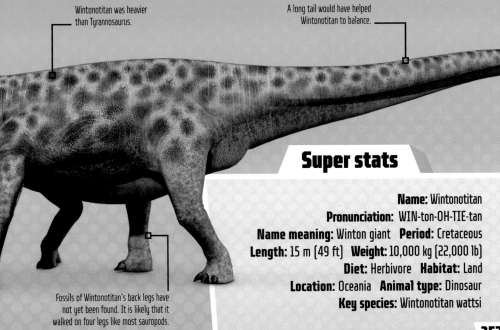

Wintonotitan was heavier than Tyrannosaurus.

A long tail would have helped Wintonotitan to balance.

Fossils of Wintonotitan's back legs have not yet been found. It is likely that it walked on four legs like most sauropods.

Super stats

Name: Wintonotitan
Pronunciation: WIN-ton-OH-TIE-tan
Name meaning: Winton giant **Period:** Cretaceous
Length: 15 m (49 ft) **Weight:** 10,000 kg (22,000 lb)
Diet: Herbivore **Habitat:** Land
Location: Oceania **Animal type:** Dinosaur
Key species: Wintonotitan wattsi

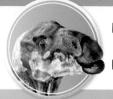

Iguanodon

In 1825, Iguanodon was one of the first dinosaurs to be officially named. At that time, experts were only just working out that dinosaurs had existed. Scientists spent a long time piecing together fossil clues. They discovered that Iguanodon was a herbivore, and larger than a modern elephant.

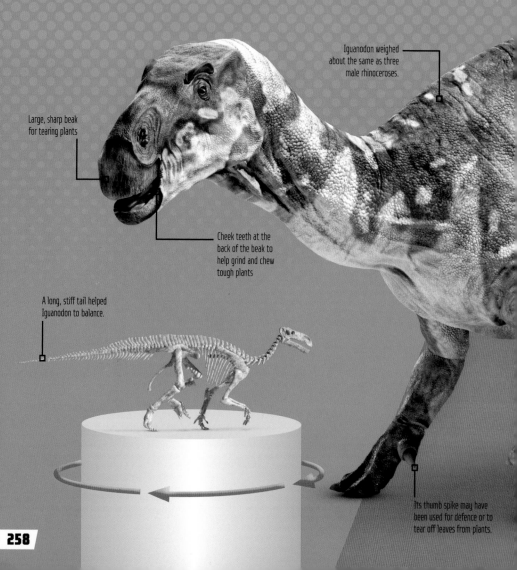

Iguanodon weighed about the same as three male rhinoceroses.

Large, sharp beak for tearing plants

Cheek teeth at the back of the beak to help grind and chew tough plants

A long, stiff tail helped Iguanodon to balance.

Its thumb spike may have been used for defence or to tear off leaves from plants.

Super stats

Name: Iguanodon
Pronunciation: ig-WAH-no-don
Name meaning: Iguana tooth   **Period:** Cretaceous
Length: 12 m (39 ft)   **Weight:** 7,000 kg (15,500 lb)
Diet: Herbivore   **Habitat:** Land
Location: Europe   **Animal type:** Dinosaur
Key species: Iguanodon bernissartensis

Weird but true!

At first, scientists thought that Iguanodon had a spike on its nose. Later, they worked out the spike was from its thumb.

Iguanodon's back legs were strong enough to support its weight, so it could walk on two legs when it needed.

Tyrannosaurus alert!

Edmontosaurus was a tasty meal for Tyrannosaurus. Although Edmontosaurus was faster and travelled in herds, Tyrannosaurus was probably more crafty. There might have been safety in numbers here, but the only sensible thing to do was run away!

Armour and weapons

There were many ferocious battles in the age of the dinosaurs. Predators used every weapon they had to hunt for food, but their prey had some mighty armour to defend themselves. Here are some ways dinosaurs used their bodies to attack and for protection.

Horns

Triceratops had three horns on its head. The two big brow horns were used to fight over territory, and to scare away predators. The nose horn may have been used to show off and to attract a mate.

Bony skull

Pachycephalosaurus had a thick skull with horns sticking out of it. These were short, so they would not break off during battle when Pachycephalosaurus butted into predators or other members of the same species.

Flexible fingers

Coelophysis developed three flexible fingers at the end of each of its long arms. These were perfect for catching and holding on to wriggling prey.

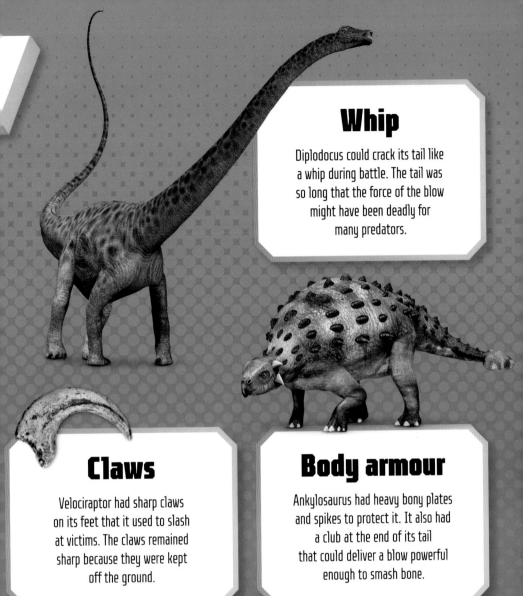

Whip

Diplodocus could crack its tail like a whip during battle. The tail was so long that the force of the blow might have been deadly for many predators.

Claws

Velociraptor had sharp claws on its feet that it used to slash at victims. The claws remained sharp because they were kept off the ground.

Body armour

Ankylosaurus had heavy bony plates and spikes to protect it. It also had a club at the end of its tail that could deliver a blow powerful enough to smash bone.

Predators vs. prey

Eyesight: Predators had eyes at the front of their heads to focus on chasing prey.

Brains: Predators had larger brains, so they could work out how to catch prey.

Speed: Predators needed to be fast to hunt, so they were not slowed down by heavy armour.

Eyesight: Prey had eyes on the sides of their heads, so they could see predators approaching from all directions.

Brains: Prey often had smaller brains, because they did not need to think about hunting.

Speed: Prey were often slow and heavy, relying on armour for protection.

Edmontosaurus

Edmontosaurus was one of the largest hadrosaurs, which are often called duck–billed dinosaurs. It used its beak to grab as many plants as it could.

Weird but true!
Edmontosaurus could run faster than Tyrannosaurus, but could not always escape predators.

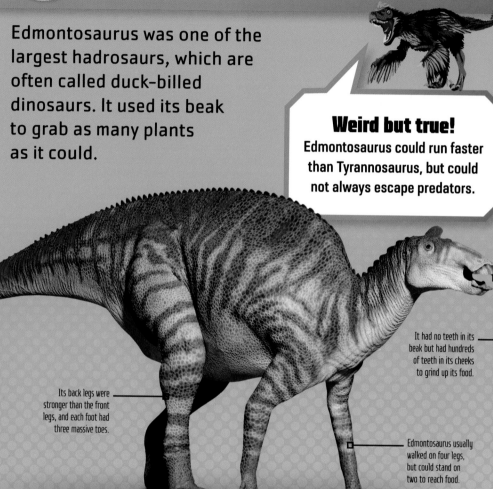

It had no teeth in its beak but had hundreds of teeth in its cheeks to grind up its food.

Its back legs were stronger than the front legs, and each foot had three massive toes.

Edmontosaurus usually walked on four legs, but could stand on two to reach food.

Super stats

Name: Edmontosaurus **Pronunciation:** ed-MONT-oh-SORE-us
Name meaning: Edmonton lizard **Period:** Cretaceous
Length: 12 m (39 ft) **Weight:** 5,500 kg (12,000 lb)
Diet: Herbivore **Habitat:** Land
Location: North America **Animal type:** Dinosaur
Key species: Edmontosaurus regalis

Hesperornis

Hesperornis was a giant prehistoric bird. It was similar to a penguin because it was a great swimmer, unsteady on land, and could not fly. It was hunted by dinosaurs on land and mosasaurs in the ocean.

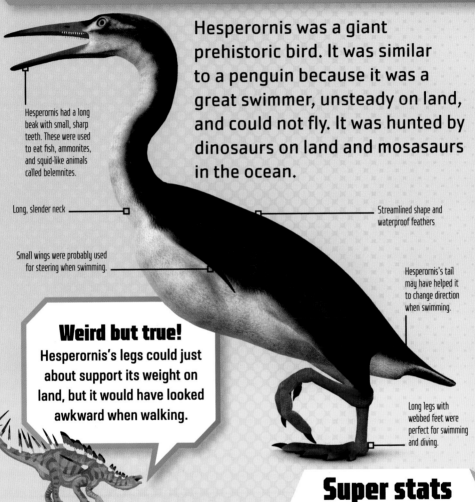

Hesperornis had a long beak with small, sharp teeth. These were used to eat fish, ammonites, and squid-like animals called belemnites.

Long, slender neck

Small wings were probably used for steering when swimming.

Streamlined shape and waterproof feathers

Hesperornis's tail may have helped it to change direction when swimming.

Long legs with webbed feet were perfect for swimming and diving.

Weird but true!

Hesperornis's legs could just about support its weight on land, but it would have looked awkward when walking.

Super stats

Name: Hesperornis   **Pronunciation:** HESS-per-ORE-niss
Name meaning: Western bird   **Period:** Cretaceous
Length: 2 m (6.5 ft)   **Weight:** 23 kg (51 lb)
Diet: Carnivore   **Habitat:** Ocean / Land   **Location:** North America
Animal type: Dinosaur   **Key species:** Hesperornis regalis

Concavenator

Concavenator was a medium–sized theropod, about as long as a large car. It had some unusual features, including a sail, or hump, near its hips.

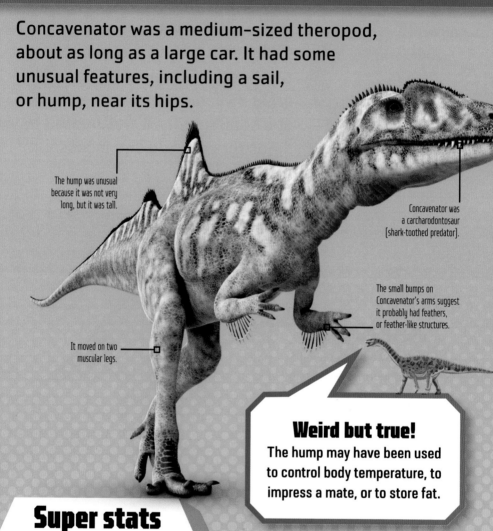

The hump was unusual because it was not very long, but it was tall.

Concavenator was a carcharodontosaur (shark-toothed predator).

The small bumps on Concavenator's arms suggest it probably had feathers, or feather-like structures.

It moved on two muscular legs.

Weird but true!
The hump may have been used to control body temperature, to impress a mate, or to store fat.

Super stats

Name: Concavenator **Pronunciation:** KON-ca-VEN-a-tour
Name meaning: Hunter from Cuenca **Period:** Cretaceous
Length: 6 m (20 ft) **Weight:** 980 kg (2,150 lb)
Diet: Carnivore **Habitat:** Land **Location:** Europe
Animal type: Dinosaur **Key species:** Concavenator corcovatus

Torosaurus

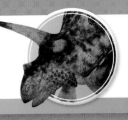

Torosaurus was related to Triceratops, but it had a much larger frill. Some scientists thought that Torosaurus was the adult version of Triceratops. Most scientists now accept that Torosaurus was a different dinosaur.

Super stats

Name: Torosaurus
Pronunciation: TOH-row-SAW-russ
Name meaning: Perforated lizard
Period: Cretaceous
Length: 8 m (26 ft)
Weight: 4,500 kg (10,000 lb)
Diet: Herbivore   **Habitat:** Land
Location: North America
Animal type: Dinosaur
Key species: Torosaurus latus

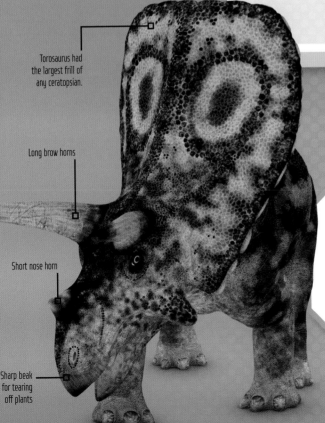

Torosaurus had the largest frill of any ceratopsian.

Long brow horns

Short nose horn

Sharp beak for tearing off plants

Weird but true!
Torosaurus's skull measured 2.6 m (8.5 ft) long, including the frill. It was as big as a car.

Olorotitan

Super stats

Name: Olorotitan
Pronunciation: oh-low-ROW-TI-tan
Name meaning: Gigantic swan
Period: Cretaceous
Length: 8 m (26 ft)
Weight: 3,200 kg (7,000 lb)
Diet: Herbivore **Habitat:** Land
Location: Asia **Animal type:** Dinosaur
Key species: Olorotitan arharensis

This hadrosaur's name means "gigantic swan". This is due to its long neck, as the rest of it was not very swan-like! Olorotitan also had a unique hollow crest on its head, similar to Parasaurolophus.

Olorotitan's fan-shaped crest pointed backwards.

Olorotitan ground up its food using hundreds of teeth. These were continuously replaced as they wore out.

Its long neck contained 18 vertebrae, and was probably the longest of any hadrosaur.

Olorotitan could walk on two or four legs.

Weird but true!
The air passages in Olorotitan's crest might have made its calls sound louder.

Xiphactinus

This ocean predator was bigger than most great white sharks, and faster, too! It could reach top speeds of 60 kph (37 mph). Some rare Xiphactinus fossils have their last meals inside their bellies.

Weird but true!
Xiphactinus may have swum to the surface of the water to attack seabirds, such as Hesperornis.

Xiphactinus's large jaws were lined with fang-like teeth.

This strong tail helped Xiphactinus to swim faster than most other ocean creatures.

It could swallow prey whole, up to 2 m (6.5 ft) long.

Xiphactinus might have had a dark blue back and a light silver belly, making it hard to spot from above or below.

Super stats

Name: Xiphactinus **Pronunciation:** zye-FAC-tee-nus
Name meaning: Sword ray **Period:** Cretaceous
Length: 6 m (20 ft) **Weight:** 2,800 kg (6,200 lb) **Diet:** Carnivore
Habitat: Ocean **Location:** North America
Animal type: Prehistoric creature **Key species:** Xiphactinus audax

Gigantoraptor

Gigantoraptor was by far the biggest member of the oviraptor family. It was about three times as long, and 30 times heavier, than Citipati, and was thought to have laid eggs the size of rugby balls. It is likely that Gigantoraptor had short feathers, but was unable to fly.

Gigantoraptor was nearly as tall as a giraffe and as long as two cars.

Short tail, mainly for balance

Gigantoraptor walked on two legs. It is likely that it could have run quite fast to avoid predators.

Weird but true!

When palaeontologists first found Gigantoraptor, they thought it was a tyrannosaur because it was so big.

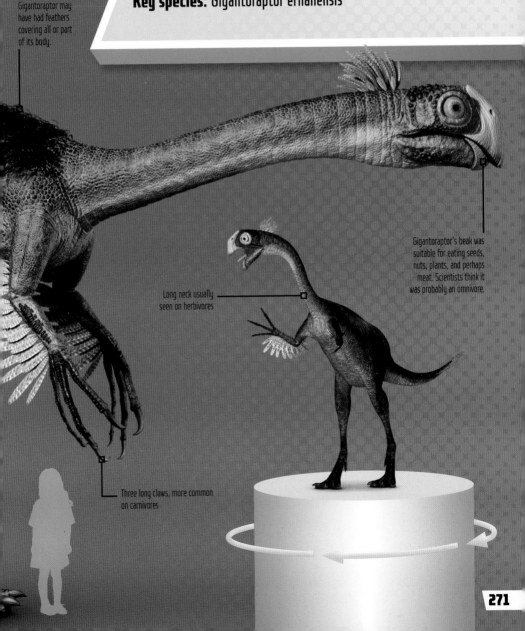

Name: Gigantoraptor
Pronunciation: JIG-an-toe-rap-tor
Name meaning: Giant seizer **Period:** Cretaceous
Length: 8.5 m (28 ft) **Weight:** 2,200 kg (4,850 lb)
Diet: Omnivore **Habitat:** Land
Location: Asia **Animal type:** Dinosaur
Key species: Gigantoraptor erlianensis

Gigantoraptor may have had feathers covering all or part of its body.

Gigantoraptor's beak was suitable for eating seeds, nuts, plants, and perhaps meat. Scientists think it was probably an omnivore.

Long neck usually seen on herbivores

Three long claws, more common on carnivores

Baryonyx

Baryonyx looked a bit like a crocodile, but was even more deadly. Its huge jaws were not only filled with rows of sharp teeth, but it also had a sharp 30 cm (12 in) curved thumb claw on each hand. Baryonyx was well suited to catching slippery fish, but it seems to have liked a varied diet and hunted some land animals, too.

Huge, slashing teeth to rip through flesh

Baryonyx had almost twice as many teeth as Tyrannosaurus.

Baryonyx could move swiftly on two legs to chase prey.

Baryonyx: This beast is hungry for dinosaurs and has spotted its prey!

Battle up!

Baryonyx and Iguanodon lived in the Cretaceous period. The first fossil of Baryonyx was found with the bones of a baby Iguanodon–like dinosaur inside. Was this just a snack before chomping on an adult Iguanodon?

Iguanodon

Larger than an elephant and weighing as much as five cars, Iguanodon was a huge herbivore. It moved around on two or four legs, and reared up to reach food and possibly to defend itself. Iguanodon had great all-round vision, which would have been useful for spotting predators. If one did happen to get too close, Iguanodon had two deadly weapons – a sharp spike on each thumb.

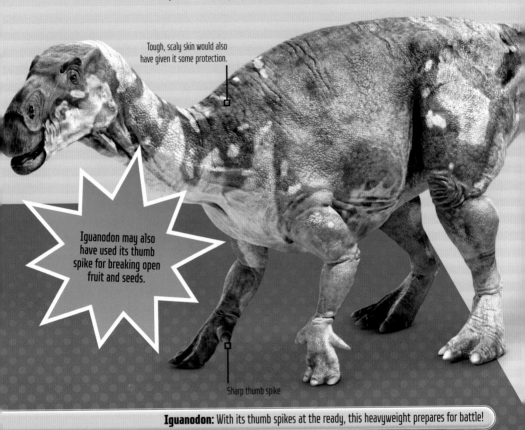

Tough, scaly skin would also have given it some protection.

Iguanodon may also have used its thumb spike for breaking open fruit and seeds.

Sharp thumb spike

Iguanodon: With its thumb spikes at the ready, this heavyweight prepares for battle!

Who would win?

This is a tough battle to call. Although Baryonyx was smaller and much lighter than Iguanodon, it was faster and more dangerous. But, Iguanodon was around three times heavier than its opponent and would not have been easily overpowered. There would have been easier prey for Baryonyx to feast on, but if it continued its attack, Iguanodon's slashing thumb spikes would have settled the contest.

Winner!

Kronosaurus

Kronosaurus was a pliosaur, a short-necked marine carnivore with a large head. It was discovered in Australia. Kronosaurus probably ate turtles and squid, as well as some of its longer-necked relatives, plesiosaurs.

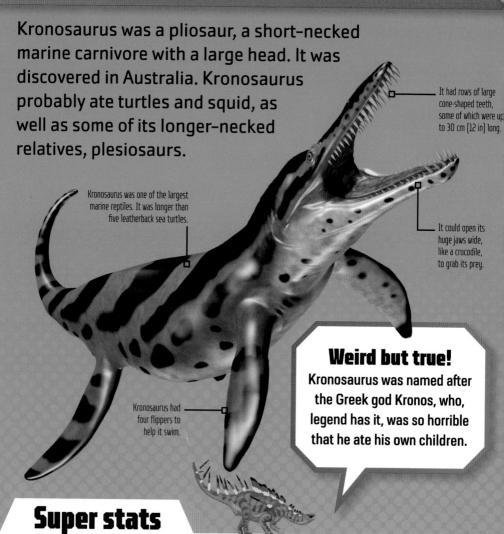

It had rows of large cone-shaped teeth, some of which were up to 30 cm (12 in) long.

Kronosaurus was one of the largest marine reptiles. It was longer than five leatherback sea turtles.

It could open its huge jaws wide, like a crocodile, to grab its prey.

Kronosaurus had four flippers to help it swim.

Weird but true!
Kronosaurus was named after the Greek god Kronos, who, legend has it, was so horrible that he ate his own children.

Super stats

Name: Kronosaurus   **Pronunciation:** KROW-no-SORE-us
Name meaning: Lizard of Kronos   **Period:** Cretaceous
Length: 10 m (33 ft)   **Weight:** 12,000 kg (26,500 lb)
Diet: Carnivore   **Habitat:** Ocean   **Location:** Oceania
Animal type: Prehistoric creature
Key species: Kronosaurus queenslandicus

Alxasaurus

Its small skull, leaf–shaped teeth, and long claws mean that Alxasaurus is a member of the therizinosaur family. These dinosaurs were theropods, but were mostly herbivores.

Super stats

Name: Alxasaurus
Pronunciation: ALKS-ah-SORE-us
Name meaning: Alxa lizard
Period: Cretaceous
Length: 4 m (13 ft)
Weight: 400 kg (880 lb)
Diet: Herbivore
Habitat: Land   **Location:** Asia
Animal type: Dinosaur
Key species: Alxasaurus elesitaiensis

Alxasaurus's beak-like mouth suggests that it did not eat meat.

Its long neck would have helped it to reach taller plants.

Its large claws would have been ideal for grabbing food from higher branches.

Alxasaurus's body was light and agile and it walked on two feet, similar to many carnivores.

Weird but true!

Scientists are not sure if Alxasaurus had feathers, but as other therizinosaurs had them, it is likely it did, too.

Coahuilaceratops

Coahuilaceratops had many recognizable skull features, like all ceratopsians. It had two large horns above its eyes and a shorter horn above its beak. It also had a head frill that was taller and narrower than that of Triceratops.

Thick skin to protect against predators

Sturdy legs to support large body weight

Lurdusaurus

Lurdusaurus had a strange shape for a member of the iguanodon family. It had shorter legs and a longer neck than others of its kind. Scientists think it may have spent a lot of time in water, a bit like a hippopotamus.

Weird but true!
Lurdusaurus's bones are big and heavy, which is why its name means "heavy lizard".

The enlarged thumb-claws on its hands may have been used as weapons.

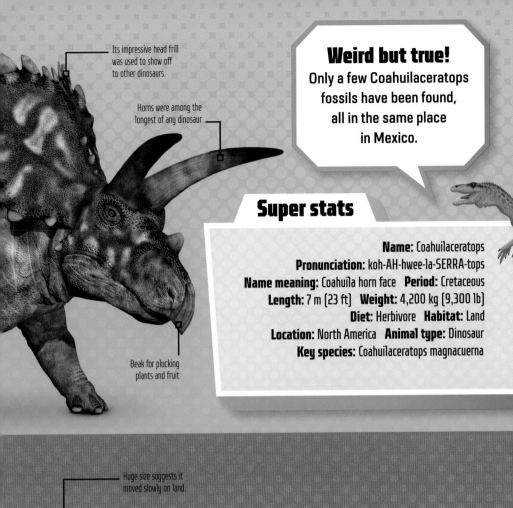

Its impressive head frill was used to show off to other dinosaurs.

Horns were among the longest of any dinosaur

Beak for plucking plants and fruit

Weird but true!
Only a few Coahuilaceratops fossils have been found, all in the same place in Mexico.

Super stats

Name: Coahuilaceratops
Pronunciation: koh-AH-hwee-la-SERRA-tops
Name meaning: Coahuila horn face   **Period:** Cretaceous
Length: 7 m (23 ft)   **Weight:** 4,200 kg (9,300 lb)
Diet: Herbivore   **Habitat:** Land
Location: North America   **Animal type:** Dinosaur
Key species: Coahuilaceratops magnacuerna

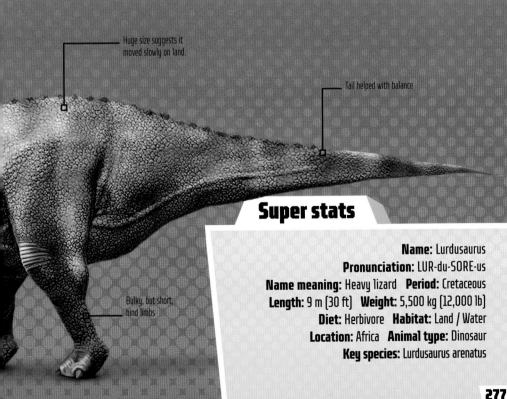

Huge size suggests it moved slowly on land.

Tail helped with balance

Bulky, but short, hind limbs

Super stats

Name: Lurdusaurus
Pronunciation: LUR-du-SORE-us
Name meaning: Heavy lizard   **Period:** Cretaceous
Length: 9 m (30 ft)   **Weight:** 5,500 kg (12,000 lb)
Diet: Herbivore   **Habitat:** Land / Water
Location: Africa   **Animal type:** Dinosaur
Key species: Lurdusaurus arenatus

Tethyshadros

Tethyshadros was a relative of the hadrosaurs and had long legs and a short neck and tail. It also had an unusual mix of features from both early and late hadrosaurs, plus an oddly shaped beak.

Weird but true!
This dinosaur was found at a site in Italy where a mostly complete skeleton was dug up.

Its beak was shaped like a shovel. Other hadrosaurs had duck-like beaks.

Masiakasaurus

This small theropod had very unusual front teeth. They stuck out from its mouth, instead of pointing up or down. Teeth like this would be no good at tearing meat. This tells us that Masiakasaurus ate fish and smaller animals.

It had spoon-shaped teeth with hooked edges for getting a really good grip on prey.

The stiff, straight neck is different from the S-shaped neck of many theropods.

The same length as an African elephant, Tethyshadros was small for a hadrosaur.

With its long legs, Tethyshadros was probably a fast runner.

Super stats

Name: Tethyshadros
Pronunciation: tef-iss-HAD-ross
Name meaning: Tethys hadrosaur   **Period:** Cretaceous
Length: 4 m (13 ft)   **Weight:** 350 kg (770 lb)
Diet: Herbivore   **Habitat:** Land
Location: Europe   **Animal type:** Dinosaur
Key species: Tethyshadros insularis

The tail made up almost half its length.

Weird but true!

Masiakasaurus was roughly the size of a very big dog.

There may have been two types of Masiakasaurus, with one being lighter and speedier than the other.

Super stats

Name: Masiakasaurus
Pronunciation: mah-SHE-ah-KAH-sore-us
Name meaning: Vicious lizard   **Period:** Cretaceous
Length: 2 m (6.5 ft)   **Weight:** 35 kg (80 lb)
Diet: Carnivore   **Habitat:** Land
Location: Africa   **Animal type:** Dinosaur
Key species: Masiakasaurus knopfleri

Euoplocephalus

Hefty Euoplocephalus was built like a tank. Its body was layered with thick bony studs, and the impressive bony club at the end of its tail could possibly be swung at attackers at speeds of up to 111 kph (69 mph).

Weird but true!
Euoplocephalus's skull was so heavily armoured that even its eyelids contained bone.

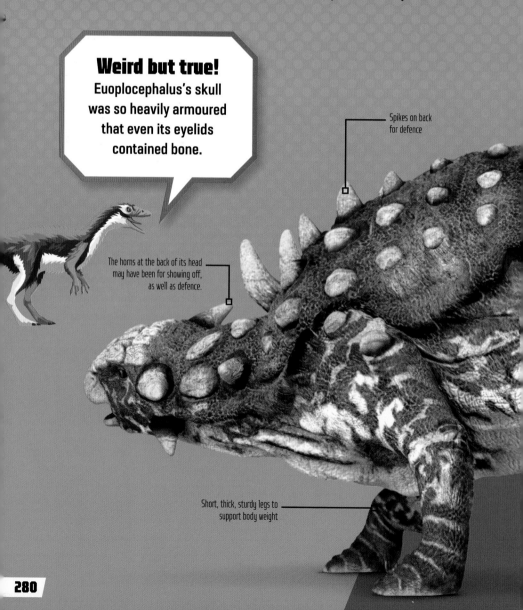

Spikes on back for defence

The horns at the back of its head may have been for showing off, as well as defence.

Short, thick, sturdy legs to support body weight

Super stats

Common name: Euoplocephalus
Pronunciation: YOU-owe-plo-SEFF-ah-lus
Name meaning: Well-armoured head
Period: Cretaceous   **Length:** 6 m (20 ft)
Weight: 2,000 kg (4,400 lb)   **Diet:** Herbivore
Habitat: Land   **Location:** North America
Animal type: Dinosaur
Key species: Euoplocephalus tutus

Back armour, made of many small, bony lumps called osteoderms

The heavy, rounded bone club at the end of its tail was strong enough to break an attacker's leg.

Well-armoured skull, covered with bony interlocking plates

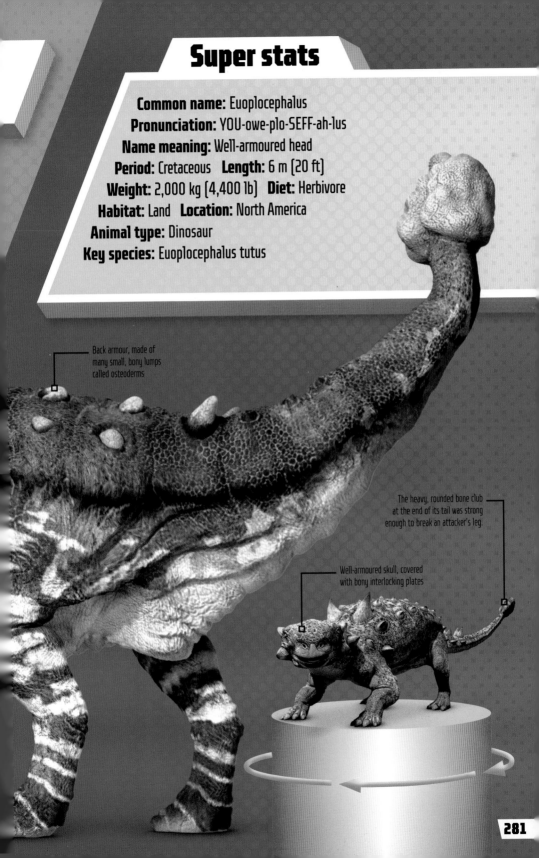

Protoceratops

This stocky ceratopsian was about the size of a sheep. Other than its frill, it was not well-armoured. Its main form of defence was to live in big herds, which would have been hard for predators to hunt. We know that its beak could give a powerful bite if a predator got close, but by that point it was probably already too late for Protoceratops.

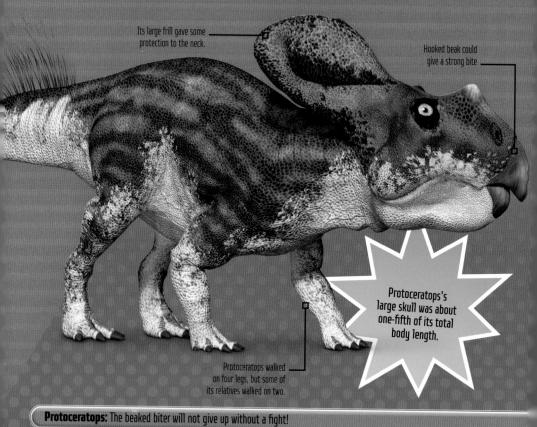

Its large frill gave some protection to the neck.

Hooked beak could give a strong bite

Protoceratops's large skull was about one-fifth of its total body length.

Protoceratops walked on four legs, but some of its relatives walked on two.

Protoceratops: The beaked biter will not give up without a fight!

Battle up!

A famous fossil shows these two Cretaceous dinosaurs locked in combat. Velociraptor had clawed at Protoceratops's throat, and Protoceratops had bitten and broken Velociraptor's arm.

Velociraptor

Sharp-toothed and killer-clawed, this predator was designed to hunt. The extra-long claw on its feet was perfect for pinning down smaller animals, ready for dinner. Velociraptor ran on two legs to chase its prey, reaching top speeds of over 40 kph (25 mph).

Razor-sharp teeth, for slicing through flesh

Velociraptor is unlikely to have fought adult Protoceratops often. It was easier and safer for it to hunt smaller prey.

Long claws, perfect for slashing at prey

Velociraptor: The turkey-sized terror gets ready for combat!

Who would win?

A Protoceratops separated from its herd was at risk to attack. Velociraptor was the perfect dinosaur to make that attack, and would probably have won the battle. However, Protoceratops was much bulkier than Velociraptor, so the fight would not have been one-sided. Velociraptor might have received some serious injuries, which could have proved deadly.

It's a draw!

283

Dinosaur teeth

Dinosaur teeth can tell us a lot, from how much time a dinosaur spent underwater, to whether a creature could produce poison. The shape of a tooth also tells a story. Cone-shaped teeth were good for catching fish. Serrated teeth could cut through meat. Spoon-shaped teeth helped strip leaves from branches. Teeth rot slower than bone, which means that many dinosaur teeth have survived, giving scientists lots to study.

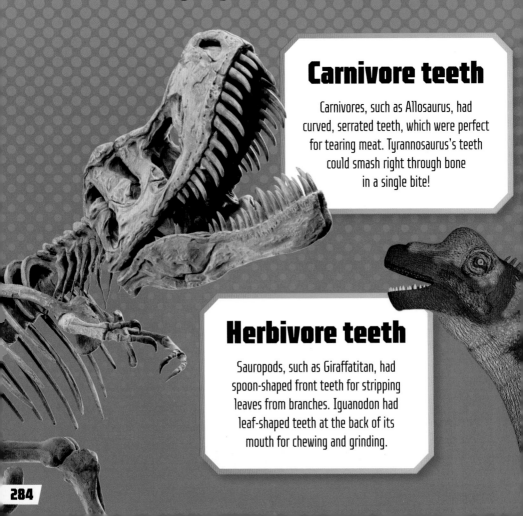

Carnivore teeth

Carnivores, such as Allosaurus, had curved, serrated teeth, which were perfect for tearing meat. Tyrannosaurus's teeth could smash right through bone in a single bite!

Herbivore teeth

Sauropods, such as Giraffatitan, had spoon-shaped front teeth for stripping leaves from branches. Iguanodon had leaf-shaped teeth at the back of its mouth for chewing and grinding.

Super-specialized

Some pterosaurs developed specialized teeth to help hunt for food. Pterodaustro's lower jaw was filled with hundreds of tall, thin teeth for filtering small fish and sea creatures out of the water.

Battery power

Some ceratopsians and hadrosaurs had "tooth batteries". These contained rows of new teeth waiting to grow up into the jaw to replace any lost or worn out teeth.

Weird but true!

Dinosaur teeth were used a lot, so they wore down quickly. If a tooth fell out, it was replaced by a new one.

To chew or not to chew?

Carnivores often ate quickly during or after a hunt. Slicing and tearing were more important to them than chewing – some meat eaters were even happy to swallow their food whole. Herbivores dined at their own, relaxed pace. Plants can be hard to digest, so the broad, flat teeth of herbivores were useful for chewing and grinding up their food.

Lambeosaurus

This duck-billed dinosaur was able to walk on either two or four legs. Its double-pronged head crest made it unique among hadrosaurs – the others only had one prong.

The oddly shaped head crest may have been brightly coloured, for attracting a mate.

Duck-like bill

Weird but true!
Lambeosaurus had hundreds of teeth stored in rows along its jaw. These replaced any lost or worn out teeth.

Pterodaustro

This strange-looking pterosaur was a filter feeder – it ate like a duck. To feed, it dipped its head down and used its teeth to sieve tiny animals out of the water.

Weird but true!
Pterodaustro eggs were soft, like modern reptile eggs, not hard like birds' eggs.

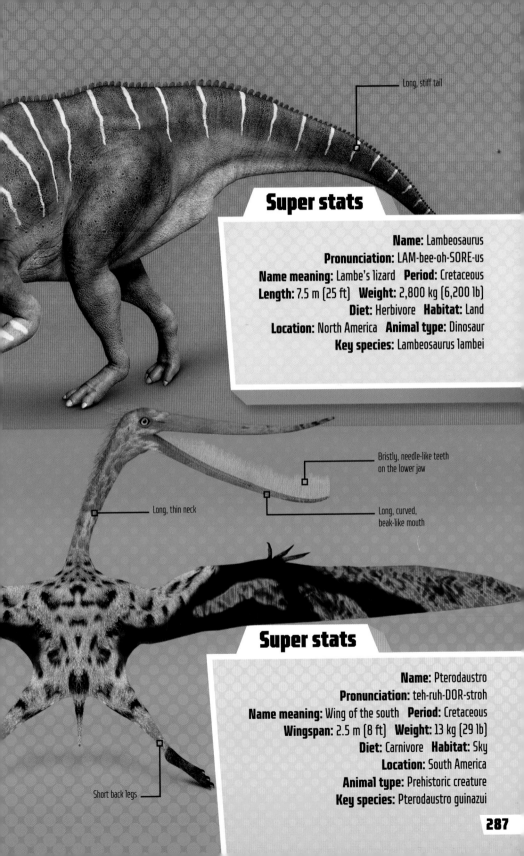

Long, stiff tail

Super stats

Name: Lambeosaurus
Pronunciation: LAM-bee-oh-SORE-us
Name meaning: Lambe's lizard   **Period:** Cretaceous
Length: 7.5 m (25 ft)   **Weight:** 2,800 kg (6,200 lb)
Diet: Herbivore   **Habitat:** Land
Location: North America   **Animal type:** Dinosaur
Key species: Lambeosaurus lambei

Bristly, needle-like teeth
on the lower jaw

Long, thin neck

Long, curved,
beak-like mouth

Super stats

Name: Pterodaustro
Pronunciation: teh-ruh-DOR-stroh
Name meaning: Wing of the south   **Period:** Cretaceous
Wingspan: 2.5 m (8 ft)   **Weight:** 13 kg (29 lb)
Diet: Carnivore   **Habitat:** Sky
Location: South America
Animal type: Prehistoric creature
Key species: Pterodaustro guinazui

Short back legs

Talarurus

Heavy and slow-moving, Talarurus was an impressive ankylosaur. Its whole body was designed for defence. Armour plates protected its back, and its clubbed tail could be used to swipe at hungry predators.

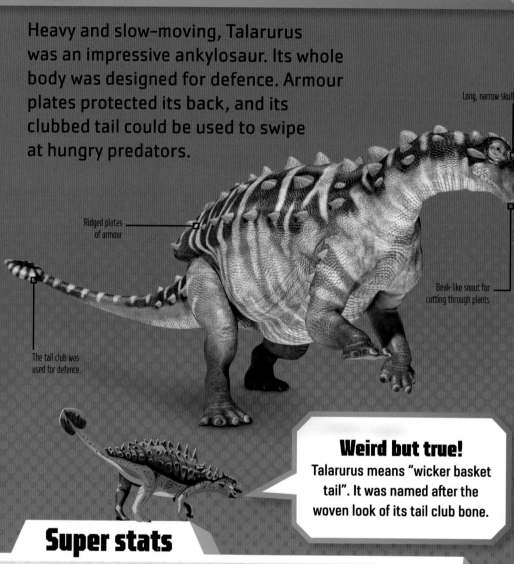

Long, narrow skull

Ridged plates of armour

Beak-like snout for cutting through plants

The tail club was used for defence.

Weird but true!
Talarurus means "wicker basket tail". It was named after the woven look of its tail club bone.

Super stats

Name: Talarurus   **Pronunciation:** tal-uh-ROOR-us
Name meaning: Wicker basket tail   **Period:** Cretaceous
Length: 5 m (16.5 ft)   **Weight:** 1,300 kg (2,900 lb)
Diet: Herbivore   **Habitat:** Land   **Location:** Asia
Animal type: Dinosaur   **Key species:** Talarurus plicatospineus

Archelon

This gigantic turtle used its sharp beak to scoop up jellyfish, squid, and fish. It could not pull its head and flippers inside its shell for safety. That meant it was a tasty meal for passing mosasaurs, despite its size.

Weird but true!
Archelon had a long life. One Archelon fossil suggests that it may have lived for 100 years.

Huge flippers

Wide, leathery shell on back

Powerful, sharp beak

Super stats

Name: Archelon   **Pronunciation:** ARE-kell-on
Name meaning: Ruler turtle   **Period:** Cretaceous
Length: 4.6 m (15 ft)   **Weight:** 2,200 kg (4,850 lb)
Diet: Carnivore   **Habitat:** Ocean   **Location:** North America
Animal type: Prehistoric creature   **Key species:** Archelon ischyros

Stegoceras

This goat–sized dinosaur had a thick dome on its head made of solid bone. Stegoceras lived in herds, and roamed around on legs three times longer than its short arms. It fed on leaves, roots, and insects.

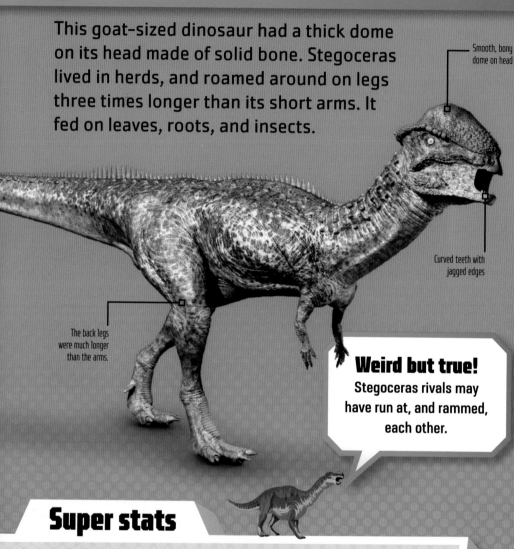

Smooth, bony dome on head

Curved teeth with jagged edges

The back legs were much longer than the arms.

Weird but true!
Stegoceras rivals may have run at, and rammed, each other.

Super stats

Name: Stegoceras **Pronunciation:** STEG-oh-SEH-russ
Name meaning: Roof horn **Period:** Cretaceous
Length: 2.2 m (7 ft) **Weight:** 45 kg (100 lb)
Diet: Omnivore **Habitat:** Land
Location: North America **Animal type:** Dinosaur
Key species: Stegoceras validum

Majungasaurus

The horn on this theropod's skull was probably too weak to be used in combat. Majungasaurus would have relied on its sharp teeth to bring down prey.

The skull contained pockets of air to make it lighter.

Weird but true!
Majungasaurus's diet is known to have included other Majungasaurus.

Tiny, almost useless arms

Long tail, for balance when running

Super stats

Name: Majungasaurus **Pronunciation:** mah-JUNG-ah-SORE-us
Name meaning: Mahajanga lizard **Period:** Cretaceous
Length: 6 m (20 ft) **Weight:** 1,300 kg (2,850 lb)
Diet: Carnivore **Habitat:** Land
Location: Africa **Animal type:** Dinosaur
Key species: Majungasaurus crenatissimus

Deinocheirus

This bizarre-looking ornithomimosaur had a humped back, a duck-like beak, and gigantic arms. Each arm was about 2.4 m (8 ft) long and ended in three 20 cm (8 in) long claws.

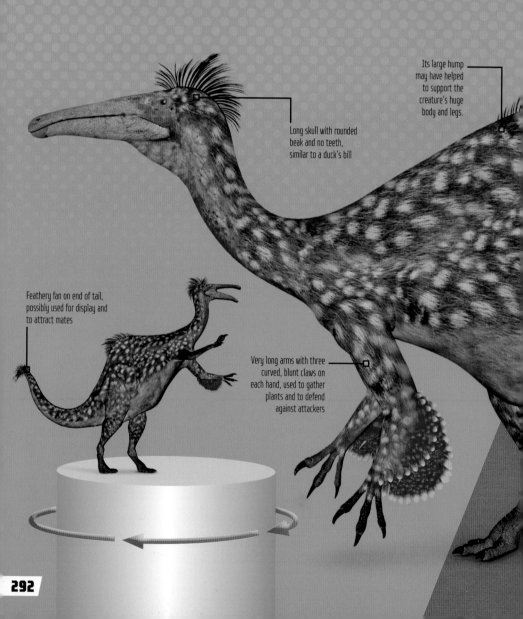

Its large hump may have helped to support the creature's huge body and legs.

Long skull with rounded beak and no teeth, similar to a duck's bill

Feathery fan on end of tail, possibly used for display and to attract mates

Very long arms with three curved, blunt claws on each hand, used to gather plants and to defend against attackers

Name: Deinocheirus
Pronunciation: DINO-ky-russ
Name meaning: Terrible hand   **Period:** Cretaceous
Length: 11 m [36 ft]   **Weight:** 6,000 kg [13,500 lb]
Diet: Omnivore   **Habitat:** Land   **Location:** Asia
Animal type: Dinosaur
Key species: Deinocheirus mirificus

Body covered in feathers

Weird but true!

For 50 years, the only known Deinocheirus fossil was a single pair of enormous arms.

Beelzebufo

A huge, round frog, Beelzebufo was a predator that hunted small animals, possibly even young dinosaurs. It had an enormous skull for its body size, and could open its jaws really wide. This helped Beelzebufo to eat fairly large prey. Fossils suggest there may have been small, bony lumps, called scutes, on top of its head. These would have given it some protection against larger predators.

Scientists believe Beelzebufo is related to modern horned frogs that live in South America.

Its large mouth could bite into much bigger animals than flies.

Beelzebufo probably could not use its short legs to hop because it was heavy.

Beelzebufo: The devilish frog with a massive mouth!

Battle up!

In Late-Cretaceous Africa, one predator was feared above all others – Majungasaurus. Beelzebufo was used to having its pick of small prey, but would the beach ball-sized frog make a tasty meal for the hungry theropod?

Majungasaurus

Majungasaurus was the top predator of its day. It may have had a row of small spikes down its back that was most likely used for showing off. Its tiny arms had clawed fingers, but these were too small to be of much use in battle. Majungasaurus's main weapons were its serrated teeth. These could slice through meat with ease, before swallowing the piece whole.

Majungasaurus's head horn was probably for show and would not be used in battle.

A complete skull of Majungasaurus has been pieced together. That is quite rare in palaeontology.

Very bulky hind legs gave it power and speed when chasing prey.

Majungasaurus: This horned predator had a big appetite!

Who would win?

Beelzebufo usually sat and waited for prey to pass by, but it would have had a nasty surprise if Majungasaurus turned up! The frog's head shield was no match for the predator's jaws, so the frog's only hope would be to flee to safety. But Majungasaurus's strong thighs helped it run fast. Sharp teeth and a few strong bites meant the unlucky frog would be no more.

Winner!

Babysitting duties

Many Psittacosaurus may have shared care of the herd's young. The adults and teenagers would have taken turns to look after the babies. Some modern birds, such as flamingos, still do this today.

Giganotosaurus

A massive meat eater, this predator was at the very top of the food chain. It was one of the largest carnivores to walk the Earth, and could hunt super–sized prey.

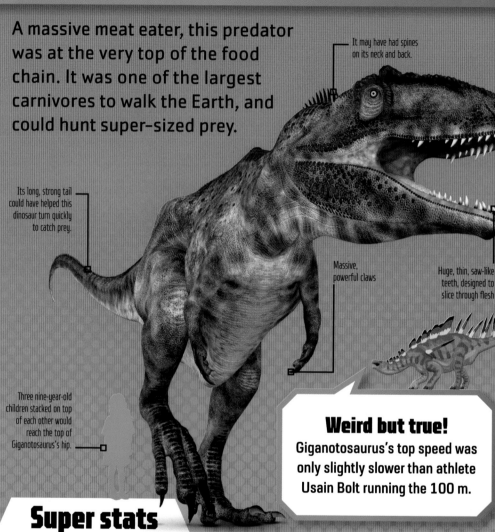

It may have had spines on its neck and back.

Its long, strong tail could have helped this dinosaur turn quickly to catch prey.

Massive, powerful claws

Huge, thin, saw-like teeth, designed to slice through flesh

Three nine-year-old children stacked on top of each other would reach the top of Giganotosaurus's hip.

Weird but true!
Giganotosaurus's top speed was only slightly slower than athlete Usain Bolt running the 100 m.

Super stats

Name: Giganotosaurus **Pronunciation:** jig-AN-oh-toe-SORE-us
Name meaning: Giant lizard **Period:** Cretaceous
Length: 12.5 m (41 ft) **Weight:** 8,000 kg (17,500 lb)
Diet: Carnivore **Habitat:** Land
Location: South America **Animal type:** Dinosaur
Key species: Giganotosaurus carolinii

Mosasaurus

This terror of the deep was one of the last giant ocean–living reptiles. It used its paddle–like flippers to turn and steer in the water, hunting down anything it could snap up in its powerful jaws.

Weird but true!
Mosasaurus could expand its jaw if it needed to swallow large prey, like snakes do today.

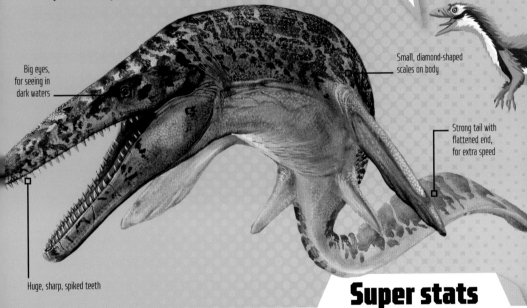

Big eyes, for seeing in dark waters

Small, diamond-shaped scales on body

Strong tail with flattened end, for extra speed

Huge, sharp, spiked teeth

Super stats

Name: Mosasaurus **Pronunciation:** MOSE-ah-SORE-us
Name meaning: Lizard of the Meuse River **Period:** Cretaceous
Length: 15 m (50 ft) **Weight:** 13,000 kg (29,000 lb)
Diet: Carnivore **Habitat:** Ocean
Location: Europe **Animal type:** Prehistoric creature
Key species: Mosasaurus hoffmannii

Puertasaurus

An immense titanosaur, Puertasaurus is only known from a handful of bones from the spine, called vertebrae. Studies of these vertebrae have shown that it is one of the biggest dinosaurs known to science. The largest vertebra is around 1 m (3 ft) tall and 1.7 m (5.5 ft) wide.

Long, flexible neck

Weird but true!
Puertasaurus may have used its incredible neck to reach many different plants, while keeping its body in one place.

Sinosauropteryx

A layer of fuzzy feathers covered the body of this theropod, keeping it warm as it hunted in ancient forests. It was the first dinosaur to be found that showed evidence of feathers, which was a scientific sensation.

Long tail made up half of whole body length

Strong legs with long, clawed toes

Super stats

Scientists think Puertasaurus had a very wide body with a huge rib cage.

Name: Puertasaurus
Pronunciation: PWER-tah-SORE-us
Name meaning: Puerta's lizard   **Period:** Cretaceous
Length: 28 m (92 ft)   **Weight:** 60,000 kg (132,000 lb)
Diet: Herbivore   **Habitat:** Land
Location: South America   **Animal type:** Dinosaur
Key species: Puertasaurus reuili

The long tail helped Puertasaurus balance.

Strong legs for carrying its enormous weight

Weird but true!

A Sinosauropteryx fossil showed it had brown feathers with an orange-and-white striped tail.

Soft layer of simple feathers covered the whole body

Super stats

Name: Sinosauropteryx
Pronunciation: SIGH-no-sore-OP-ter-ix
Name meaning: Chinese lizard wing   **Period:** Cretaceous
Length: 1 m (3 ft)   **Weight:** 0.5 kg (1 lb)
Diet: Carnivore   **Habitat:** Land
Location: Asia   **Animal type:** Dinosaur
Key species: Sinosauropteryx prima

Acrocanthosaurus

One of the largest ever theropods, Acrocanthosaurus was one of the main predators of its time. It grabbed prey in its jaws, then used its claws to tear its victim.

Weird but true!
One Acrocanthosaurus skeleton was found with black bones. This was caused by minerals in the ground.

Spines along the neck and down to the tip of the tail may have supported a hump or short sail

The tail helped with balance when it ran.

Short but powerful arms with three hooked claws

Muscular jaw with sharp, curved teeth

Super stats

Name: Acrocanthosaurus
Pronunciation: ak-row-KAN-fo-SORE-us
Name meaning: High-spined lizard **Period:** Cretaceous
Length: 11.5 m (38 ft) **Weight:** 6,200 kg (13,700 lb)
Diet: Carnivore **Habitat:** Land **Location:** North America
Animal type: Dinosaur **Key species:** Acrocanthosaurus atokensis

Polacanthus

Big spikes and bony armour made Polacanthus one of the best-defended dinosaurs of its time. Its low, heavy body meant it ate plants like ferns and horsetails, which grew on the ground.

Weird but true!

Fossils show blood vessels in Polacanthus's plates and spikes. These vessels may have supplied the plates with blood as they grew.

Strong beak for tearing up plants

A huge, single plate of bone protected its hips.

Small spikes along the tail

Super stats

Name: Polacanthus **Pronunciation:** pohl-la-CAN-thus
Name meaning: Many thorns **Period:** Cretaceous
Length: 5 m (16 ft) **Weight:** 2,000 kg (4,400 lb)
Diet: Herbivore **Habitat:** Land
Location: Europe **Animal type:** Dinosaur
Key species: Polacanthus foxii

Maiasaura

These duck–billed dinosaurs lived together in huge herds. They travelled long distances and returned to the same nesting sites each year, where adult Maiasaura cared for the babies until they could walk around and search for their own food.

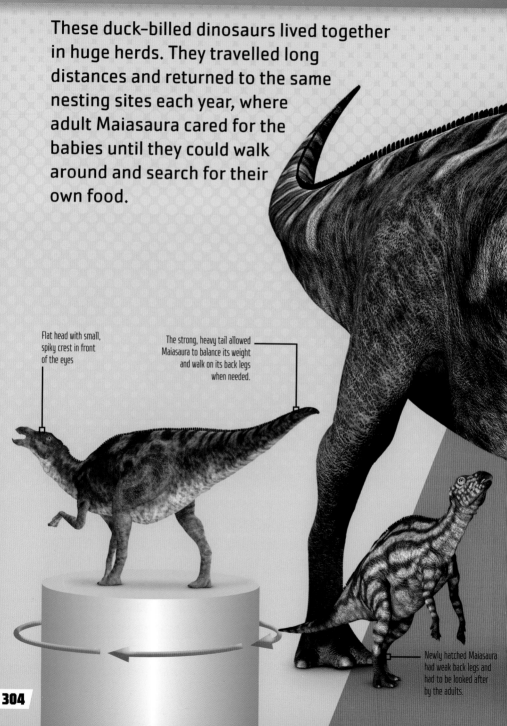

Flat head with small, spiky crest in front of the eyes

The strong, heavy tail allowed Maiasaura to balance its weight and walk on its back legs when needed.

Newly hatched Maiasaura had weak back legs and had to be looked after by the adults.

Super stats

Name: Maiasaura   **Pronunciation:** MY-a-SORE-a
Name meaning: Good mother lizard   **Period:** Cretaceous
Length: 9 m (30 ft)   **Weight:** 4,000 kg (8,800 lb)
Diet: Herbivore   **Habitat:** Land   **Location:** North America
Animal type: Dinosaur
Key species: Maiasaura peeblesorum

Flat beak, used for picking plants

Weird but true!
Maiasaura eggs were the same size as modern ostrich eggs. They were kept warm under a nice cosy layer of rotting plants.

Mapusaurus

One of the largest carnivores ever, Mapusaurus was a prime predator. Its huge, muscly thighs made it a fast runner, and its long tail helped balance out the weight of its large skull. Palaeontologists think that Mapusaurus had enough brainpower to hunt in packs when targeting large prey, such as sauropods.

At 11 m (36 ft) long – about as long as a truck – Mapusaurus was twice the size of Skorpiovenator.

Its serrated teeth were perfect for cutting and slicing through meat, just like a steak knife.

Mapusaurus walked on its two powerful legs.

Mapusaurus: The big-brained beast with an appetite to match!

Battle up!

Mapusaurus was one of the largest predators of all time, while Skorpiovenator was a medium–sized hunter. These two dinosaurs would have existed side-by-side and most likely battled often over food and territory.

Skorpiovenator

Despite its name, Skorpiovenator did not have the deadly sting of a scorpion! Its main weapons were sharp teeth and a strong, bony skull. When attacking, Skorpiovenator would overcome its prey with a few bashes of the head, then inflict extra damage with its sharp teeth.

Skorpiovenator was a successful hunter, but it lived alongside several larger predatory dinosaurs. This pushed it much lower down the food chain.

Skorpiovenator's tiny arms may not have been any use in battle.

Its strong legs would have been an advantage when rushing in to raid nests, looking for dinosaur babies to eat.

Skorpiovenator: This tiny-armed terror uses its head!

Who would win?

Whether hunting alone or in a pack, Mapusaurus was a terrifying foe. Skorpiovenator, with its strong skull and short snout would have used its head as a weapon against its attacker. These blows may have caused some damage to Mapusaurus, but not enough to stop it. Mapusaurus was bigger, stronger, faster, smarter, and had a more powerful bite! All it took was one or two snaps of its jaws to end the battle for good.

Winner!

Caudipteryx

The feathery, bird-like Caudipteryx was about the same size as a chicken. Its wings could be flapped up and down for display and to scare away predators.

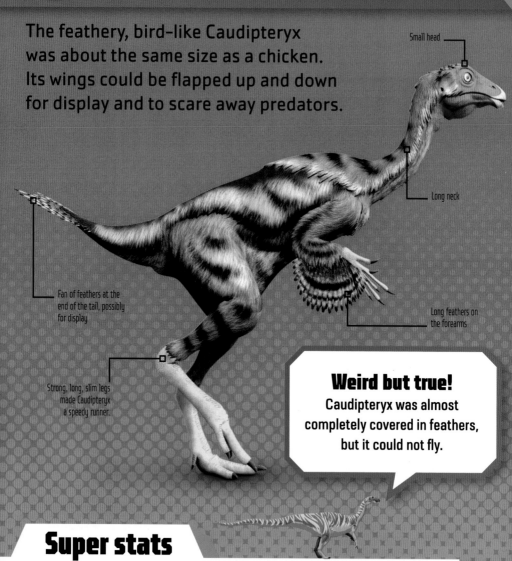

Small head

Long neck

Long feathers on the forearms

Fan of feathers at the end of the tail, possibly for display

Strong, long, slim legs made Caudipteryx a speedy runner.

Weird but true!
Caudipteryx was almost completely covered in feathers, but it could not fly.

Super stats

Name: Caudipteryx   **Pronunciation:** caw-DIP-ter-ix
Name meaning: Tail feather   **Period:** Cretaceous   **Length:** 1 m (3 ft)
Weight: 5 kg (11 lb)   **Diet:** Omnivore   **Habitat:** Land
Location: Asia   **Animal type:** Dinosaur
Key species: Caudipteryx zoui

Einiosaurus

This impressively frilled ceratopsian lived in herds, like modern cows do. If threatened, the whole herd would stampede. Einiosaurus had huge horns that looked very intimidating!

Bony ridges over the eyes

Large bony frill with wavy edges, and two long spikes at the top

Large downward curving horn on the nose

Weird but true!
Lots of specimens of both adult and young Einiosaurus have been found together in bonebeds.

Super stats

Name: Einiosaurus   **Pronunciation:** EYE-nee-o-SORE-us
Name meaning: Buffalo lizard   **Period:** Cretaceous
Length: 4.5 m (15 ft)   **Weight:** 1,500 kg (3,300 lb)   **Diet:** Herbivore
Habitat: Land   **Location:** North America   **Animal type:** Dinosaur
Key species: Einiosaurus procurvicornis

Shantungosaurus

This huge, plant-munching ornithopod roamed open plains and swamps in large herds. There was safety in numbers – living together in a herd made it harder for hungry predators to attack.

Weird but true!

Shantungosaurus had more than 1,500 teeth packed into its jaws. Most sat in wait ready to replace any lost or worn out teeth.

Sauropelta

Covered in spines, this ankylosaur would have been a challenge for hungry predators.
As well as its spines, it was protected by rows of hard studs.
Even the areas between its studs were defended by a flexible layer of small, bony bumps.

Its rear legs were longer than its front pair, making it easier to eat from the ground.

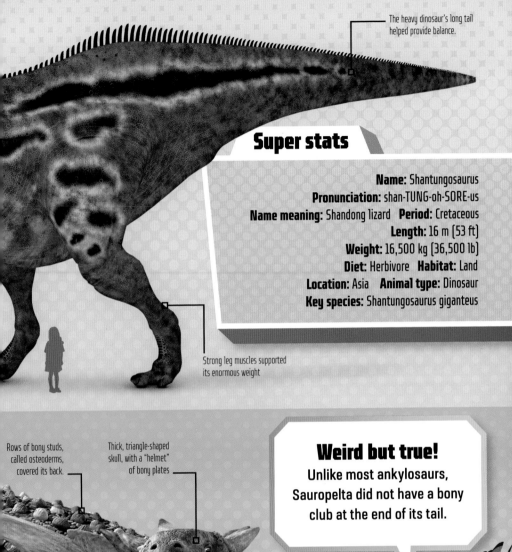

The heavy dinosaur's long tail helped provide balance.

Super stats

Name: Shantungosaurus
Pronunciation: shan-TUNG-oh-SORE-us
Name meaning: Shandong lizard   **Period:** Cretaceous
Length: 16 m (53 ft)
Weight: 16,500 kg (36,500 lb)
Diet: Herbivore   **Habitat:** Land
Location: Asia   **Animal type:** Dinosaur
Key species: Shantungosaurus giganteus

Strong leg muscles supported its enormous weight

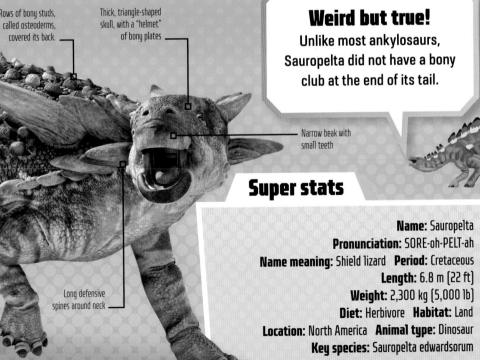

Rows of bony studs, called osteoderms, covered its back.

Thick, triangle-shaped skull, with a "helmet" of bony plates

Narrow beak with small teeth

Long defensive spines around neck

Weird but true!

Unlike most ankylosaurs, Sauropelta did not have a bony club at the end of its tail.

Super stats

Name: Sauropelta
Pronunciation: SORE-oh-PELT-ah
Name meaning: Shield lizard   **Period:** Cretaceous
Length: 6.8 m (22 ft)
Weight: 2,300 kg (5,000 lb)
Diet: Herbivore   **Habitat:** Land
Location: North America   **Animal type:** Dinosaur
Key species: Sauropelta edwardsorum

Mawsonia

This enormous coelacanth was a hunter, searching the sea floor for fish and invertebrates. It may have been nocturnal, sleeping in the day and looking for food at night.

Mawsonia had fleshy fins on top of its body, at its sides, underneath, and at the end of its tail.

Weird but true!

There are two species of coelacanth still alive today, but they live deep in the ocean and are rarely seen.

Thick, heavy scales

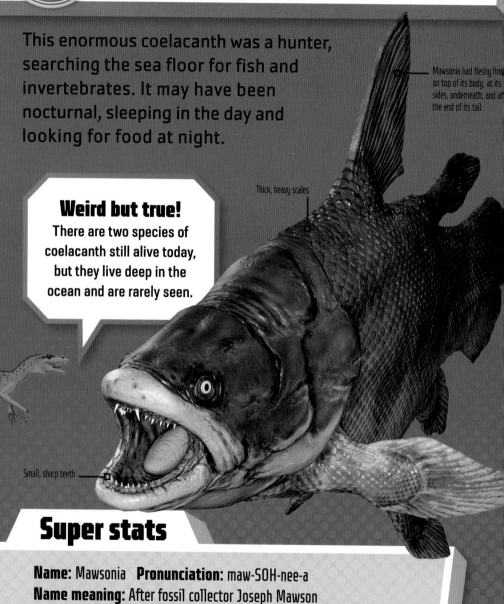

Small, sharp teeth

Super stats

Name: Mawsonia **Pronunciation:** maw-SOH-nee-a
Name meaning: After fossil collector Joseph Mawson
Period: Cretaceous **Length:** 6 m (20 ft) **Weight:** 300 kg (660 lb)
Diet: Carnivore **Habitat:** Ocean **Location:** South America and Africa
Animal type: Prehistoric creature
Key species: Mawsonia gigas

Pteranodon

Gliding through the air, this pterosaur kept a look out for fish or other small animals in the ocean below. Once food was in sight, Pteranodon swiftly swooped down, even diving underwater to catch its prey.

Three clawed fingers at the edge of each wing

Long crest on head

Its long, toothless jaws were similar to a pelican's beak.

Pteranodon's wings were large compared to the size of its body.

Weird but true!
The male Pteranodon had a long crest on its head. It was probably used to show off and attract females.

Super stats

Name: Pteranodon   **Pronunciation:** teh-RAN-oh-don
Name meaning: Toothless wing   **Period:** Cretaceous
Wingspan: 7 m (23 ft)   **Weight:** 40 kg (88 lb)
Diet: Carnivore   **Habitat:** Sky   **Location:** North America
Animal type: Prehistoric creature
Key species: Pteranodon longiceps

Protoceratops

Sheep-sized and tough, this little ceratopsian lived in the dry desert. Fossilized Protoceratops nests show that it may have cared for its young, and kept its eggs warm for 83 days or longer.

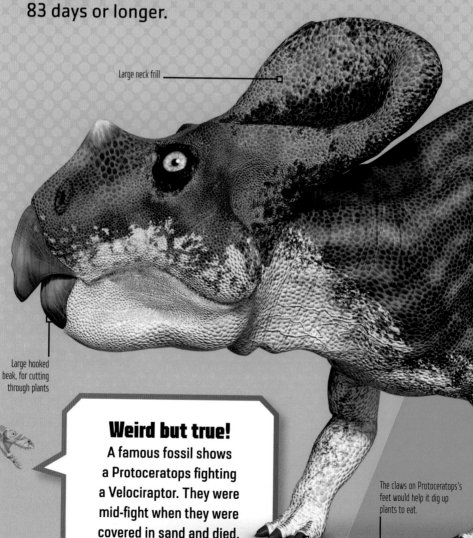

Large neck frill

Large hooked beak, for cutting through plants

The claws on Protoceratops's feet would help it dig up plants to eat.

Weird but true!
A famous fossil shows a Protoceratops fighting a Velociraptor. They were mid-fight when they were covered in sand and died.

Super stats

Name: Protoceratops
Pronunciation: PRO-toe-SERRA-tops
Name meaning: First-horned face   **Period:** Cretaceous
Length: 1.8 m (6 ft)   **Weight:** 180 kg (400 lb)
Diet: Herbivore   **Habitat:** Land
Location: Asia   **Animal type:** Dinosaur
Key species: Protoceratops andrewsi

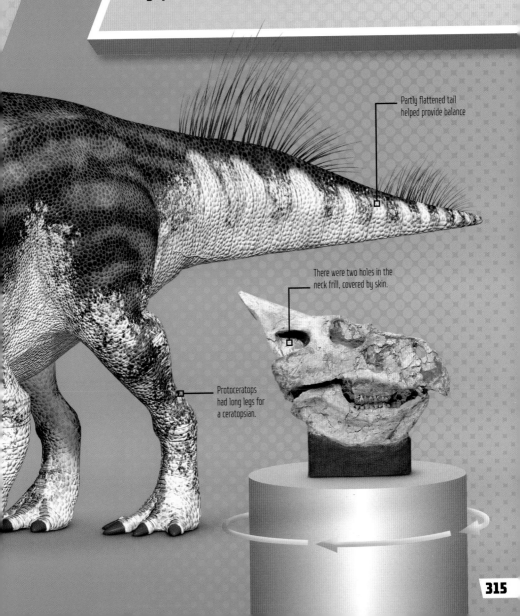

Partly flattened tail helped provide balance

There were two holes in the neck frill, covered by skin.

Protoceratops had long legs for a ceratopsian.

Under attack

This Tenontosaurus is in grave danger!
Its bird-like attacker, Deinonychus, was smaller
than Tenontosaurus, but was intelligent enough
to see the advantage of hunting in packs to take
down larger prey.

Dinosaur babies

Dinosaurs could differ in size, shape, speed, diet, and just about everything else! But they had one thing in common – as far as we know, they all laid hard–shelled eggs. The shape, size, and colour of dinosaur eggs varied greatly. The sauropod dinosaurs laid the biggest eggs that have been found so far. They were large, round, and bigger than a football.

Egg fossils

Scientists know surprisingly little about dinosaur babies, as fossilized eggs with baby dinosaurs inside are rare. Even if a fossilized egg is found, it is often hard to tell which dinosaur laid it.

Laying eggs

Eggs were produced by females. Most clutches (groups of eggs) were small, but some dinosaurs laid around 30 eggs at a time. One benefit of laying so many was that some might survive, because eggs and babies were often eaten by predators.

The smallest dinosaur egg found so far was only 3 cm (1.2 in) long. That's smaller than a golf ball. No one knows which dinosaur it came from.

Fossilized dinosaur nest

Hatching

Most dinosaurs did not sit on their eggs until they hatched. This is probably a good thing if the parents were heavy Argentinosauruses! It is likely that they built nests in safe places and perhaps used plants to keep the eggs warm.

Some dinosaurs, such as Citipati, sat on top of nests to keep their eggs warm, like birds, but this was not common.

Dinosaur parents

Most dinosaurs were not watchful parents. Many babies were able to stand up when they were born, so they did not need much looking after. They would have been in danger from predators, though.

Growing up

Baby dinosaurs grew quickly after hatching. Many hadrosaurs, such as Maiasaura, for example, would more than triple in size in their first year.

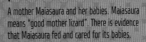

A mother Maiasaura and her babies. Maiasaura means "good mother lizard". There is evidence that Maiasaura fed and cared for its babies.

Aucasaurus

This theropod weighed about the same as a small car. Not much is known about how Aucasaurus behaved, but it is likely to have hunted other, smaller dinosaurs, possibly even other Aucasaurs!

Short, deep-snouted skull

Small ridges over the eyes

Very small arms

Outstretched, raised tail helped with balance when walking or running

Weird but true!
Aucasaurus is known from an almost-complete skeleton – only the end of the tail is missing.

Super stats

Name: Aucasaurus **Pronunciation:** AW-ka-SORE-us
Name meaning: Auca lizard **Period:** Cretaceous
Length: 6 m (20 ft) **Weight:** 1,000 kg (2,200 lb) **Diet:** Carnivore
Habitat: Land **Location:** South America **Animal type:** Dinosaur
Key species: Aucasaurus garridoi

Troodon

Bird-like and brainy (for a dinosaur), Troodon had binocular vision – its two eyes pointed forwards, like ours do, letting it see a single, 3D image. It was probably an opportunistic hunter, meaning it would eat whatever it could find.

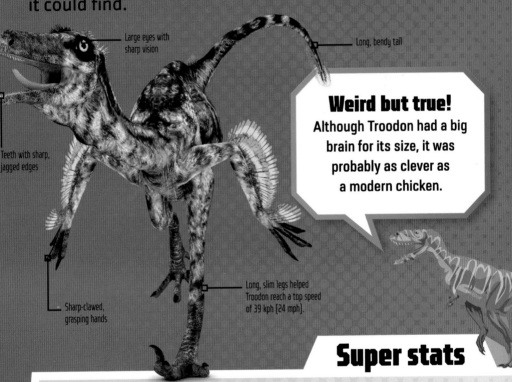

Large eyes with sharp vision

Long, bendy tail

Teeth with sharp, jagged edges

Sharp-clawed, grasping hands

Long, slim legs helped Troodon reach a top speed of 39 kph (24 mph).

Weird but true!
Although Troodon had a big brain for its size, it was probably as clever as a modern chicken.

Super stats

Name: Troodon   **Pronunciation:** TRUE-oh-don
Name meaning: Wounding tooth   **Period:** Cretaceous
Length: 1.8 m (6 ft)   **Weight:** 50 kg (110 lb)   **Diet:** Carnivore
Habitat: Land   **Location:** North America   **Animal type:** Dinosaur
Key species: Troodon formosus

Corythosaurus

To keep its big body working, this hadrosaur had to eat constantly. Corythosaurus used its hundreds of teeth to chomp away at plants. It is famous for the helmet–like crest on its head.

Weird but true!

Corythosaurus's head crest was filled with tubes, which may have let it blow its nose like a trumpet.

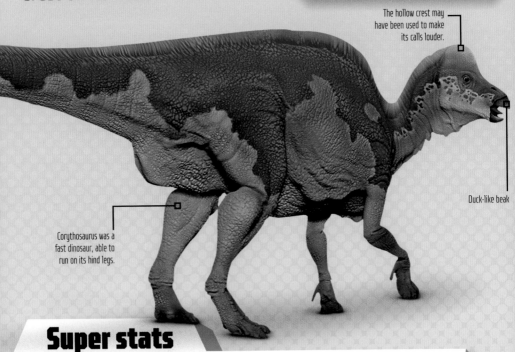

The hollow crest may have been used to make its calls louder.

Duck-like beak

Corythosaurus was a fast dinosaur, able to run on its hind legs.

Super stats

Name: Corythosaurus   **Pronunciation:** ko-RITH-oh-SORE-us
Name meaning: Helmet lizard   **Period:** Cretaceous
Length: 9 m (30 ft)   **Weight:** 3,500 kg (7,700 lb)
Diet: Herbivore   **Habitat:** Land
Location: North America   **Animal type:** Dinosaur
Key species: Corythosaurus casuarius

Pachyrhinosaurus

Instead of a horn, like other ceratopsians, Pachyrhinosaurus had a wide, flat bulge called a nasal boss. It may have used this lump as a weapon in head–butting fights over mates or territory.

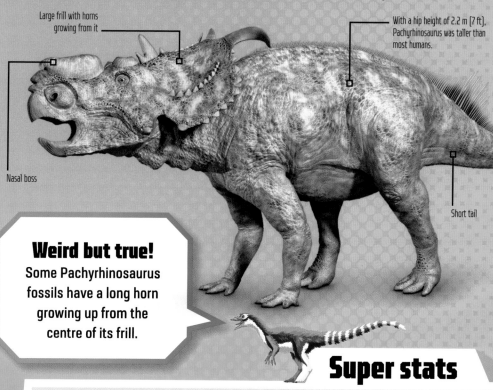

Large frill with horns growing from it

With a hip height of 2.2 m (7 ft), Pachyrhinosaurus was taller than most humans.

Nasal boss

Short tail

Weird but true!
Some Pachyrhinosaurus fossils have a long horn growing up from the centre of its frill.

Super stats

Name: Pachyrhinosaurus **Pronunciation:** pak-ee-ry-no-SAW-russ
Name meaning: Thick-nosed lizard **Period:** Cretaceous
Length: 7 m (23 ft) **Weight:** 3,200 kg (7,000 lb)
Diet: Herbivore **Habitat:** Land
Location: North America **Animal type:** Dinosaur
Key species: Pachyrhinosaurus canadensis

Skorpiovenator

This fearsome theropod did not have a very powerful bite. As well as clamping its jaws onto prey, it may have also used its head a bit like a club, forcefully smashing it into prey.

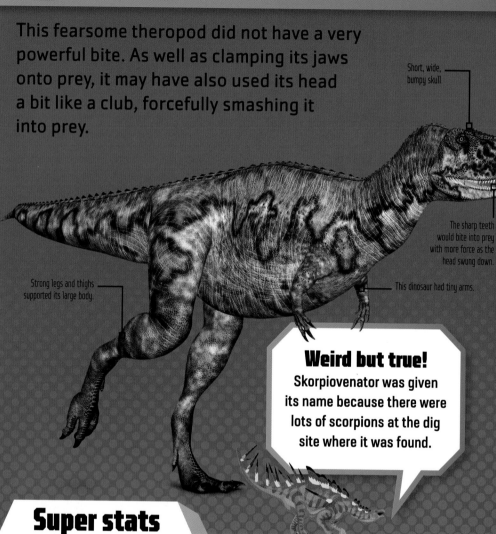

Short, wide, bumpy skull

The sharp teeth would bite into prey with more force as the head swung down.

Strong legs and thighs supported its large body.

This dinosaur had tiny arms.

Weird but true!
Skorpiovenator was given its name because there were lots of scorpions at the dig site where it was found.

Super stats

Name: Skorpiovenator **Pronunciation:** SKOR-PEE-oh-VEN-ah-tor
Name meaning: Scorpion hunter **Period:** Cretaceous
Length: 6.5 m (21 ft) **Weight:** 1,500 kg (3,300 lb)
Diet: Carnivore **Habitat:** Land
Location: South America **Animal type:** Dinosaur
Key species: Skorpiovenator bustingorryi

Tylosaurus

Fossils show that this gigantic, ocean–living reptile ate a huge range of different marine animals – including other mosasaurs! It had extra rows of teeth in the roof of its mouth, which may have helped direct food down its throat.

Super stats

Name: Tylosaurus
Pronunciation: tie-lo-SORE-us
Name meaning: Knob lizard
Period: Cretaceous
Length: 14 m (45 ft)
Weight: 9,000 kg (20,000 lb)
Diet: Carnivore   **Habitat:** Ocean
Location: North America
Animal type: Prehistoric creature
Key species: Tylosaurus proriger

Weird but true!

One fossil shows Tylosaurus had diamond-shaped scales, similar to those of modern snakes.

Inside Tylosaurus's long, skull were sharp, cone-shaped teeth. It may also have used its snout as a weapon.

Scaly skin

Its tail contained more than 80 vertebrae and was perfect for pushing Tylosaurus through the water.

Four paddle-shaped flippers were used for steering, rather than swimming.

Spinosaurus

Colossal, water-loving Spinosaurus was the largest carnivore ever to have walked the Earth. It lived next to rivers and lakes, and spent a large part of its day in the water, catching and eating fish.

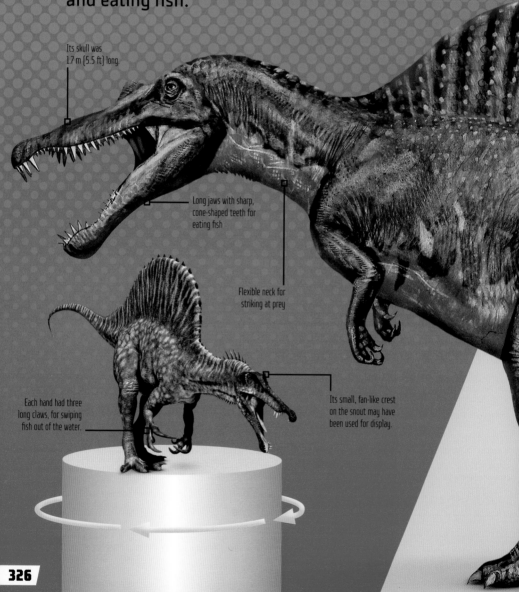

Its skull was 1.7 m (5.5 ft) long.

Long jaws with sharp, cone-shaped teeth for eating fish

Flexible neck for striking at prey

Each hand had three long claws, for swiping fish out of the water.

Its small, fan-like crest on the snout may have been used for display.

Super stats

Name: Spinosaurus
Pronunciation: SPY-noh-SORE-us
Name meaning: Spine lizard   **Period:** Cretaceous
Length: 15 m (49 ft)   **Weight:** 10,000 kg (22,000 lb)
Diet: Carnivore   **Habitat:** Land   **Location:** Africa
Animal type: Dinosaur   **Key species:** Spinosaurus aegyptiacus

Large sail on back

Long, flexible, paddle-like
tail for swimming

Weird but true!

Spinosaurus ate giant fish,
such as Mawsonia. A single
Mawsonia could be up to
6 m (20 ft) long – that's bigger
than the average car.

Archelon

This enormous turtle had a huge, leathery shell. The shell, along with Archelon's massive size, would have put off a lot of predators because plenty of other animals were easier to eat! Archelon's sharp beak was perfect for chopping up jellyfish into easy-to-swallow pieces, and it would have been able to give a painful bite if under attack.

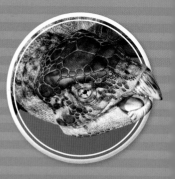

Tough, leathery shell to protect body from predator's teeth

Powerful flippers to push Archelon through the water

Archelon's closest living relative is the leatherback sea turtle.

The sharp beak could give a powerful bite.

Archelon: This mega turtle with a snapping beak will not give up without a fight!

Battle up!

The Cretaceous ocean was a dangerous place, full of huge, hungry predators hunting for their next meal. Archelon was a giant turtle, bigger than any alive today. Tylosaurus was a mosasaur – a predatory, water–living reptile.

Tylosaurus

Sharp teeth and a huge body made this colossal mosasaur the biggest and most dangerous marine predator of its day. It would have snapped up any large animals it could catch as it cruised the Cretaceous oceans. It might even have eaten dinosaurs that had ventured into the sea...

Tylosaurus probably surprised its prey by attacking suddenly, with a quick burst of speed.

Sharp, cone-shaped teeth for chomping on prey

Paddle-shaped flippers to help with steering

Tylosaurus: The terror of the deep closes in on its prey!

Who would win?

Tylosaurus would have been the clear winner in a fight with Archelon. The giant turtle had a shell, but it could not pull its head and legs inside to hide. It would have been nothing but a crunchy mouthful for one of the biggest mosasaurs in the Cretaceous ocean. Fossils show that Tylosaurus ate just about any animals that it could catch, including other ocean predators, such as plesiosaurs.

Winner!

Brontomerus

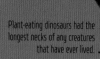

This super sauropod had one unusual feature – extremely large, powerful thigh muscles. These mega thighs supported Brontomerus's strong, long legs, and may have been useful for walking on rough ground.

Plant-eating dinosaurs had the longest necks of any creatures that have ever lived.

Hip bones were much larger than those of similar dinosaurs.

Weird but true!
Brontomerus's thigh muscles may have allowed it to kick predators that came too close.

Big, powerful thighs

Brontomerus was about the height of five 10-year-old children, stacked c top of each other.

Super stats

Name: Brontomerus   **Pronunciation:** bron-TOE-meh-rus
Name meaning: Thunder thighs   **Period:** Cretaceous
Length: 14 m (46 ft)   **Weight:** 6,100 kg (13,500 lb)
Diet: Herbivore   **Habitat:** Land
Location: North America   **Animal type:** Dinosaur
Key species: Brontomerus mcintoshi

Pelecanimimus

This dinosaur had rows of teeth inside its beak. The teeth were blade–like at the back of its beak and wider at the front. They probably helped this carnivore slice up food.

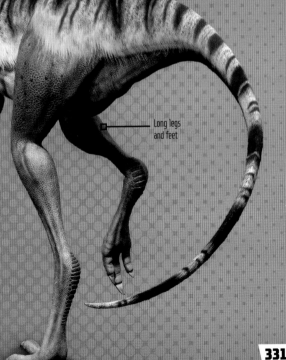

The fleshy crest on its head may have been used to attract mates.

Feathers all over body

Pelecanimimus had about 220 teeth in its beak.

Long legs and feet

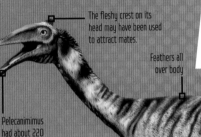

Weird but true!

Some scientists believe Pelecanimimus may have stored fish in its throat, much like a modern pelican.

Thalassodromeus

Large head crest

Long, sharp beak used to hunt fish, or animals on land

Toothless jaws

This crested pterosaur could fly, but it also crept along the ground or in shallow water looking for prey. When it spotted something tasty, it quickly stabbed it with its sharp beak.

Weird but true!
Thalassodromeus's head crest has been described as looking like a pharaoh's crown.

This pterosaur had a wingspan of 4.5 m (15 ft).

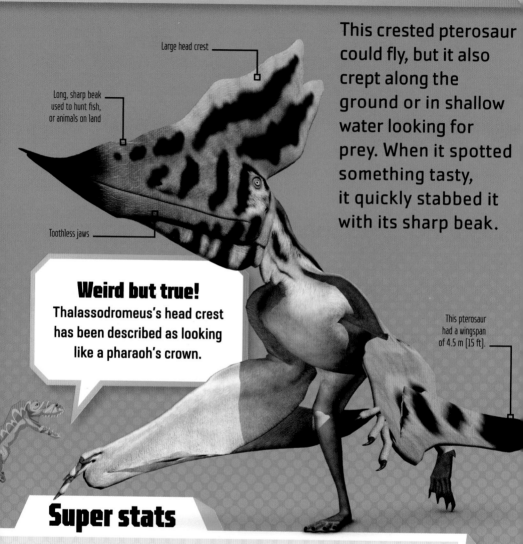

Super stats

Name: Thalassodromeus   **Pronunciation:** fah-LASS-oh-DRO-ME-us
Name meaning: Sea runner   **Period:** Cretaceous
Wingspan: 5 m (16.5 ft)   **Weight:** 18 kg (40 lb)
Diet: Carnivore   **Habitat:** Land / Sky
Location: South America   **Animal type:** Prehistoric creature
Key species: Thalassodromeus sethi

Dilong

A speedy, turkey-sized theropod, Dilong was one of the smallest known tyrannosaurs. Despite its size, it was a real threat to the smaller animals that lived alongside it in the forest. Dilong's body was covered in a layer of soft, warm feathers.

Sharp teeth

Skin covered in feathers

Short arms with three fingers were able to clutch food.

Short legs for a theropod dinosaur

Weird but true!
Dilong was one of the first dinosaurs discovered that showed clear evidence of feathers.

Super stats

Name: Dilong   **Pronunciation:** DYE-long
Name meaning: Emperor dragon   **Period:** Cretaceous
Length: 2 m (6.5 ft)   **Weight:** 25 kg (55 lb)
Diet: Carnivore   **Habitat:** Land
Location: Asia   **Animal type:** Dinosaur
Key species: Dilong paradoxus

Hungarosaurus

This heavily-armoured ankylosaur had strong bony plates called osteoderms covering its back and sides. It lived on floodplains with plenty of plants, and spent its days chomping on low-growing vegetation.

Defensive spikes

Hungarosaurus's short beak was ideal for munching plants.

Sauroposeidon

The neck of this sauropod was so long that it would have towered over most other dinosaurs – it was the same height as a seven-storey building. This incredible neck let it reach leaves that other herbivores could not.

Scaly skin

Weird but true!
For many years, the only known Sauroposeidon fossils were four huge neck vertebrae.

Bony plates covered its back and sides.

Weird but true!

Four Hungarosaurus fossils were found close together, so they may have lived in groups.

Super stats

Name: Hungarosaurus
Pronunciation: hun-GAR-o-SORE-us
Name meaning: Hungary lizard
Period: Cretaceous **Length:** 4.5 m (15 ft)
Weight: 650 kg (1,450 lb) **Diet:** Herbivore
Habitat: Land **Location:** Europe
Animal type: Dinosaur
Key species: Hungarosaurus tormai

A fully grown Sauroposeidon was probably safe from attack, as it was more than twice as long as the biggest predator.

Its extremely long neck was about a third longer than that of its relative Brachiosaurus.

Small head relative to its body size

Super stats

Name: Sauroposeidon
Pronunciation: SORE-oh-po-SY-den
Name meaning: Lizard god of earthquakes
Period: Cretaceous **Length:** 32 m (105 ft)
Weight: 60,000 kg (132,000 lb)
Diet: Herbivore **Habitat:** Land
Location: North America **Animal type:** Dinosaur
Key species: Sauroposeidon proteles

Wide, round feet

Sauroposeidon was an incredible 18 m (60 ft) tall. That's about the height of 13 10-year-old children stacked one on top of another.

Pachycephalosauru.

Bony-headed Pachycephalosaurus probably took part in head-to-head combat. It would have used its thick skull to smash into its opponents in fights over territory. Pachycephalosaurus fossils are rare, and no complete skeleton has ever been found.

The thick, bony, domed skull was made from a special type of bone that healed quickly.

Tough beak used for grabbing fruit, seeds, and plants

Super stats

Name: Pachycephalosaurus
Pronunciation: PACK-ee-SEF-ah-low-SORE-us
Name meaning: Thick-headed lizard   **Period:** Cretaceous
Length: 5 m (16.5 ft)   **Weight:** 500 kg (1,100 lb)
Diet: Omnivore   **Habitat:** Land
Location: North America   **Animal type:** Dinosaur
Key species: Pachycephalosaurus wyomingensis

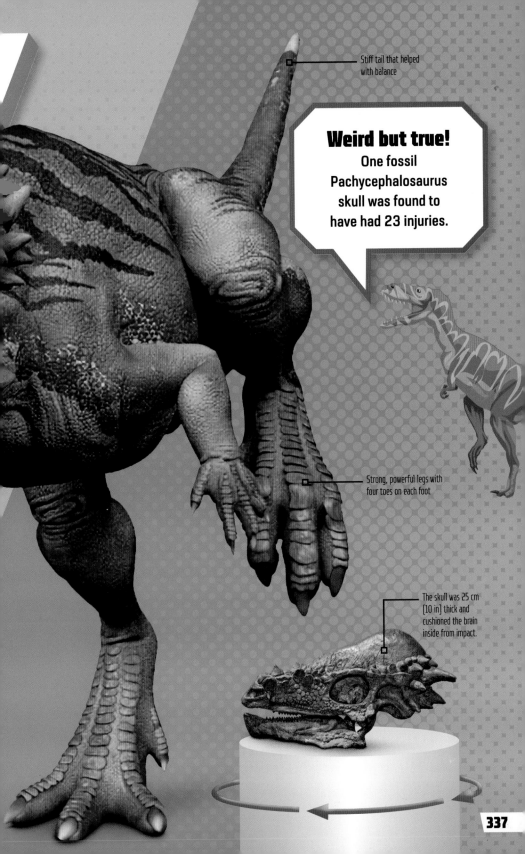

Stiff tail that helped with balance

Weird but true!
One fossil Pachycephalosaurus skull was found to have had 23 injuries.

Strong, powerful legs with four toes on each foot

The skull was 25 cm [10 in] thick and cushioned the brain inside from impact.

Territorial Troodon

Pairs of Troodon may have had to guard their territory – their patch of land and the prey that lived there – from other hungry Troodon. Many modern birds also have territory, and will fight to defend it.

Zuniceratops

Zuniceratops lived at least 25 million years before its famous ceratopsian relative, Triceratops. It was much smaller than later members of the ceratopsian dinosaur family, being about the same size as a cow.

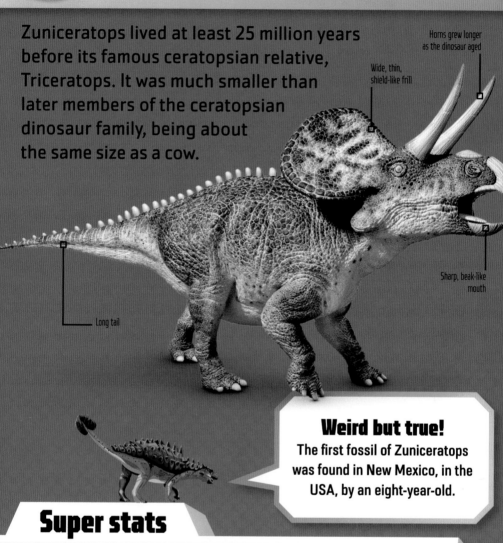

Horns grew longer as the dinosaur aged

Wide, thin, shield-like frill

Sharp, beak-like mouth

Long tail

Weird but true!
The first fossil of Zuniceratops was found in New Mexico, in the USA, by an eight-year-old.

Super stats

Name: Zuniceratops **Pronunciation:** ZOO-nee-SERRA-tops
Name meaning: Zuni-horned face **Period:** Cretaceous
Length: 3 m (10 ft) **Weight:** 200 kg (440 lb) **Diet:** Herbivore
Habitat: Land **Location:** North America **Animal type:** Dinosaur
Key species: Zuniceratops christopheri

Saltasaurus

Saltasaurus's partially armoured body was covered in thick bony plates that protected it from hungry carnivores. Even though it was already tall, it could reach even higher into trees by standing upright on its back legs.

Broad, spoon-shaped snout

Long, mobile neck with a small head

Bony oval plates on the body

Weird but true!
Saltasaurus had no toes on its front feet – those legs just ended in stumps.

Strong, pillar-like legs

Super stats

Name: Saltasaurus   **Pronunciation:** SALT-ah-SORE-us
Name meaning: Lizard from Salta   **Period:** Cretaceous
Length: 13 m (42.5 ft)   **Weight:** 6,700 kg (15,000 lb)
Diet: Herbivore   **Habitat:** Land
Location: South America   **Animal type:** Dinosaur
Key species: Saltasaurus loricatus

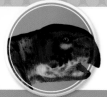

Psittacosaurus

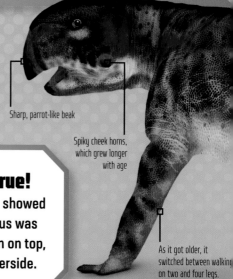

Psittacosaurus had a big brain and may have looked after its young. One fossil shows an adult with more than 20 babies. It ate plants, using its sharp beak to slice them up.

Sharp, parrot-like beak

Spiky cheek horns, which grew longer with age

As it got older, it switched between walking on two and four legs.

Weird but true!
One amazing fossil showed that Psittacosaurus was dark, reddish-brown on top, with a lighter underside.

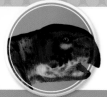

Therizinosaurus

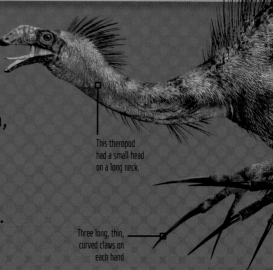

Standing on its back legs, this theropod could reach up into the trees. It used its enormous claws to hook branches down to its mouth, so it could eat the leaves. Its claws might also have been useful for swiping at predators that got too close.

This theropod had a small head on a long neck.

Three long, thin, curved claws on each hand

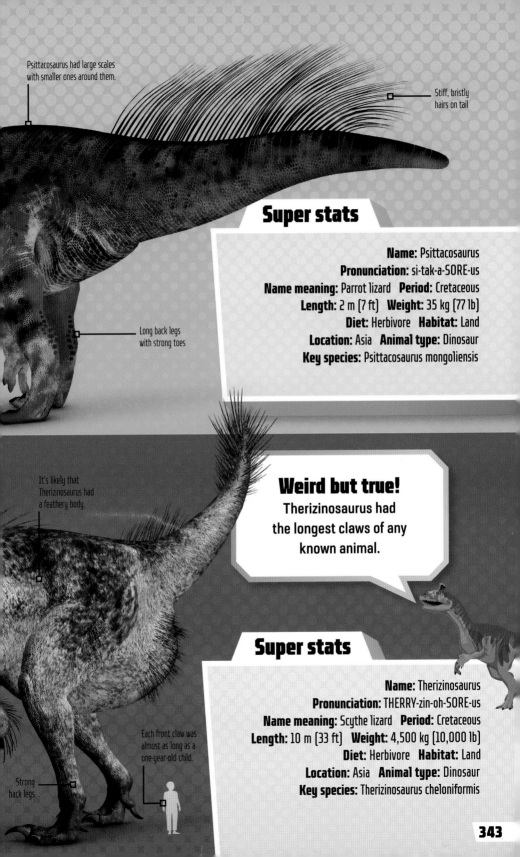

Psittacosaurus had large scales with smaller ones around them.

Stiff, bristly hairs on tail

Long back legs with strong toes

Super stats

Name: Psittacosaurus
Pronunciation: si-tak-a-SORE-us
Name meaning: Parrot lizard **Period:** Cretaceous
Length: 2 m (7 ft) **Weight:** 35 kg (77 lb)
Diet: Herbivore **Habitat:** Land
Location: Asia **Animal type:** Dinosaur
Key species: Psittacosaurus mongoliensis

It's likely that Therizinosaurus had a feathery body.

Weird but true!

Therizinosaurus had the longest claws of any known animal.

Each front claw was almost as long as a one-year-old child.

Strong back legs

Super stats

Name: Therizinosaurus
Pronunciation: THERRY-zin-oh-SORE-us
Name meaning: Scythe lizard **Period:** Cretaceous
Length: 10 m (33 ft) **Weight:** 4,500 kg (10,000 lb)
Diet: Herbivore **Habitat:** Land
Location: Asia **Animal type:** Dinosaur
Key species: Therizinosaurus cheloniformis

Zhejiangopterus

This flying fish eater was a pterosaur — not a dinosaur. Pterosaurs were one of the first vertebrates to take to the skies, long before birds. It lived in what is now China.

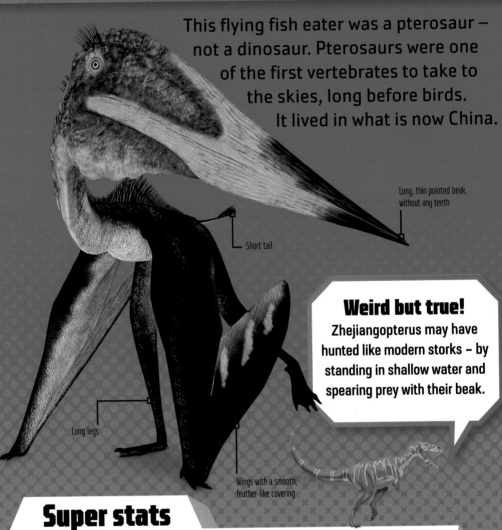

Long, thin pointed beak, without any teeth

Short tail

Weird but true!
Zhejiangopterus may have hunted like modern storks – by standing in shallow water and spearing prey with their beak.

Long legs

Wings with a smooth, feather-like covering

Super stats

Name: Zhejiangopterus
Pronunciation: ZEE-zhang-OP-teh-rus **Name meaning:** Wing of Zhejiang
Period: Cretaceous **Wingspan:** 3.5 m (11.5 ft) **Weight:** 8 kg (18 lb)
Diet: Carnivore **Habitat:** Land / Sky **Location:** Asia
Animal type: Prehistoric creature
Key species: Zhejiangopterus linhaiensis

Utahraptor

This giant, feathered dromaeosaur probably hunted in packs. A group of Utahraptors worked together to bring down large prey.

Weird but true!

Utahraptor had flexible toe joints, which let it lift the big claws on its back feet out of the way when it was running.

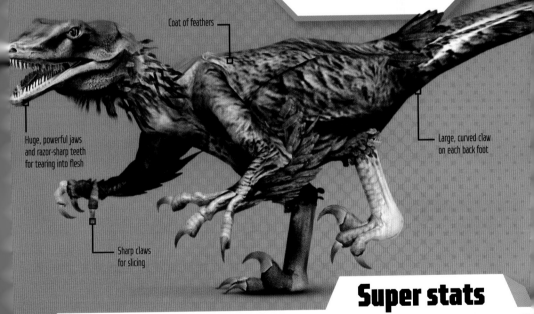

Coat of feathers

Huge, powerful jaws and razor-sharp teeth for tearing into flesh

Sharp claws for slicing

Large, curved claw on each back foot

Super stats

Name: Utahraptor **Pronunciation:** YOU-tah-RAP-tor
Name meaning: Utah's predator **Period:** Cretaceous
Length: 7 m (23 ft) **Weight:** 500 kg (1,100 lb)
Diet: Carnivore **Habitat:** Land **Location:** North America
Animal type: Dinosaur **Key species:** Utahraptor ostrommaysi

Velociraptor

Small, feathered, and fierce, this little carnivore may have hunted in packs. Velociraptors were fast predators with super-sharp killer claws on their hands and feet. They could not fly, but used their claws to pin animals down then tear them apart with their teeth.

Large eyes for spotting small prey

A super-sharp sense of smell helped hunt down prey.

Weird but true!
The long, curved claws on Velociraptor's back legs may have been used for slashing and fighting.

Big, grasping hands, with long claws

Super stats

Name: Velociraptor
Pronunciation: vel-OSS-ee-RAP-tor
Name meaning: Swift thief   **Period:** Cretaceous
Length: 2 m (6.5 ft)   **Weight:** 15 kg (33 lb)
Diet: Carnivore   **Habitat:** Land   **Location:** Asia
Animal type: Dinosaur   **Key species:** Velociraptor mongoliensis

Fine feathers all over body

Long, feathery tail used for balance while running

Velociraptor had about 15 razor-sharp teeth on each side of its jaw – perfect for slicing through meat.

Quetzalcoatlus

Not only was Quetzalcoatlus enormous and capable of fast flight, but it was also able to hunt on land. Toothless Quetzalcoatlus swallowed its prey whole, but that was not too difficult because its beak was as long as a ladder! Quetzalcoatlus could prey upon fairly large animals, perhaps including young Tyrannosaurus.

On land, Quetzalcoatlus walked on its arms and legs. It kept its large wings folded in at its sides.

This pterosaur's impressive neck was 3 m (10 ft) long.

Quetzalcoatlus could fly 10,000 km (6,000 miles) without stopping. This is further than flying from the USA to Africa!

Quetzalcoatlus: The giant of the skies is deadly on land!

Battle up!

Quetzalcoatlus soared in the skies above North America, searching for food. A young Torosaurus might have looked like tempting prey to the pterosaur, but the land-based dinosaur could fend off predators.

Torosaurus

Torosaurus was a large, armoured ceratopsian with an impressive neck frill and long horns. Its skull was the biggest of any known land animal. Torosaurus used its frill to show off to others of its kind, but the sharp, strong horns were used for battling against most predators.

Its huge skull was very strong and would be used against an opponent in a fight.

The frill was made from rather thin bone and not designed as a weapon.

Some experts think that Torosaurus was actually the adult version of Triceratops.

Torosaurus: This armoured beast had a head for defence!

Who would win?

Quetzalcoatlus would tower over Torosaurus. Its long beak meant it did not need to get too close. However, if hefty Torosaurus did land a blow to the pterosaur's soft body, it would cause serious injury. Despite Quetzalcoatlus's size, its lack of teeth was the problem here. Torosaurus's huge skull, with the added horns and frill, would not fit into Quetzalcoatlus's jaws, making it impossible for the winged wonder to succeed.

Winner!

The end of the dinosaurs

Around 66 million years ago, an asteroid about the size of Mount Everest struck Mexico. Its impact was so massive that it caused huge tidal waves, started wildfires around the world, and flung hot dirt and ash up into the Earth's atmosphere. The effects of this asteroid led to all non-flying dinosaurs, as well as many other species, dying out.

Climate change

The asteroid permanently changed Earth's climate. Dust and gases released by the impact blocked out the Sun, lowering the Earth's temperature. This meant that many plants and animals could not survive.

Weird but true!

A wide hole, called a crater, was left by the asteroid. It measured 160 km (100 miles) across and still lies beneath the Yucatán Peninsula in Mexico. It is known as the Chicxulub crater.

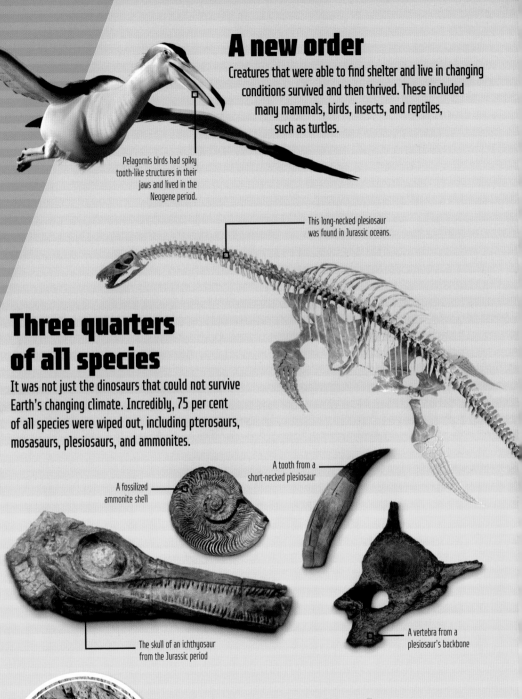

A new order

Creatures that were able to find shelter and live in changing conditions survived and then thrived. These included many mammals, birds, insects, and reptiles, such as turtles.

Pelagornis birds had spiky tooth-like structures in their jaws and lived in the Neogene period.

This long-necked plesiosaur was found in Jurassic oceans.

Three quarters of all species

It was not just the dinosaurs that could not survive Earth's changing climate. Incredibly, 75 per cent of all species were wiped out, including pterosaurs, mosasaurs, plesiosaurs, and ammonites.

A tooth from a short-necked plesiosaur

A fossilized ammonite shell

The skull of an ichthyosaur from the Jurassic period

A vertebra from a plesiosaur's backbone

Dinosaur extinction

Although many dinosaurs were killed by the asteroid, it was the effect on Earth's climate that led to their extinction. With fewer plants to eat, the large herbivores died off first. This left the carnivores with nothing to eat, so they died, too.

Cenozoic

Around 65 million years ago, an asteroid crashed into the Earth. It caused a dramatic change in the weather, wildfires, and a limited food supply. This brought an end to the Cretaceous period, and dinosaurs as we know them died out. As the new Cenozoic Era started, other creatures thrived, such as early mammals, insects, and reptiles. However, one group of dinosaurs also survived – birds.

Icaronycteris

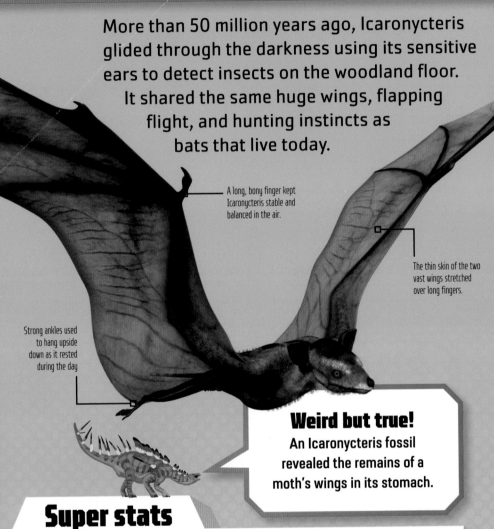

More than 50 million years ago, Icaronycteris glided through the darkness using its sensitive ears to detect insects on the woodland floor. It shared the same huge wings, flapping flight, and hunting instincts as bats that live today.

A long, bony finger kept Icaronycteris stable and balanced in the air.

The thin skin of the two vast wings stretched over long fingers.

Strong ankles used to hang upside down as it rested during the day

Weird but true!
An Icaronycteris fossil revealed the remains of a moth's wings in its stomach.

Super stats

Name: Icaronycteris **Pronunciation:** ICK-ah-roe-NICK-teh-riss
Name meaning: Icarus night flier **Period:** Paleogene
Wingspan: 37 cm (15 in) **Weight:** 20 g (0.7 oz) **Diet:** Carnivore
Habitat: Land / Sky **Location:** North America, Europe, and Asia
Animal type: Prehistoric creature
Key species: Icaronycteris index

Aenocyon dirus

Many Ice Age creatures lived in fear of this bloodthirsty, prehistoric predator. Bigger and heavier than modern wolves, Aenocyon dirus sniffed out prey and hunted in packs over long distances.

Gaping jaws with large teeth grabbed hold of prey

Stocky, powerful legs helped Aenocyon dirus to run at high speed.

Weird but true!
Aenocyon dirus fought with sabre-toothed cats in some of the deadliest clashes between early cats and dogs.

Super stats

Name: Aenocyon dirus **Pronunciation:** AY-no-SY-on DIE-russ
Name meaning: Terrible wolf **Period:** Neogene
Length: 1.8 m (6 ft) **Weight:** 75 kg (165 lb)
Diet: Carnivore **Habitat:** Land **Location:** North America
Animal type: Prehistoric creature **Key species:** Aenocyon dirus

Moeritherium

Looking like a strange cross between a hippopotamus and a pig, Moeritherium was at home in the waters of swamps and rivers. It had strong lips and long teeth, perfectly designed for feeding on marine plants.

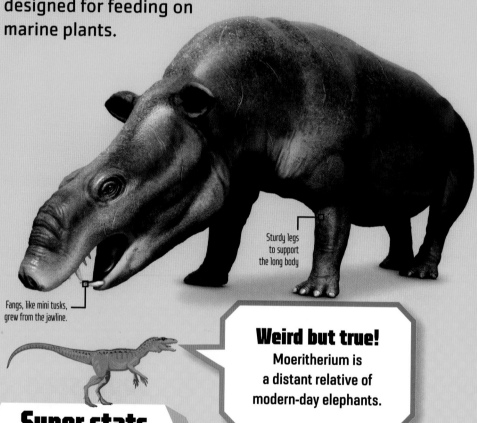

Sturdy legs to support the long body

Fangs, like mini tusks, grew from the jawline.

Weird but true!
Moeritherium is a distant relative of modern-day elephants.

Super stats

Name: Moeritherium **Pronunciation:** MEH-ree-THEER-ee-um
Name meaning: The beast from Lake Moeris **Period:** Paleogene
Length: 2.3 m [8 ft] **Weight:** 235 kg [520 lb]
Diet: Herbivore **Habitat:** Land / Water
Location: Africa **Animal type:** Prehistoric creature
Key species: Moeritherium lyonsi

Stegotetrabelodon

This ancient elephant was unique as it had four huge tusks. Stegotetrabelodon travelled around forests using its huge size and long trunk to reach the lushest leaves.

Super stats

Name: Stegotetrabelodon
Pronunciation: STEG-oh-TET-row-BELL-oh-don
Name meaning: Roofed four tusks
Period: Neogene   **Length:** 7 m (23 ft)
Weight: 10,000 kg (22,000 lb)
Diet: Herbivore   **Habitat:** Land
Location: Africa, Europe, and Asia
Animal type: Prehistoric creature
Key species: Stegotetrabelodon syrticus

Flexible trunk used to pick plants and drink water

Two pairs of tusks extended from the top and bottom of the jaws.

It had a shoulder height of 4 m (13 ft).

Weird but true!

Track marks possibly made by a herd of at least 14 Stegotetrabelodons have been found, dating back roughly 7 million years.

Paraceratherium

This prehistoric rhinoceros did not have a horn like modern rhinoceroses. Possibly the largest ever land mammal, Paraceratherium was taller than two men and weighed the same as five elephants.

Large, blunt teeth, suited to picking leaves off trees

Weird but true!

Paraceratherium was a great wanderer, travelling huge distances between forests to find the tastiest trees.

Its giraffe-like neck was much longer than that of a modern rhinoceros.

Paraceratherium's long legs were ideal for covering long distances.

Super stats

Name: Paraceratherium   **Pronunciation:** PARRA-serra-THEER-ee-um
Name meaning: Near the hornless beast   **Period:** Paleogene
Length: 8 m (26 ft)   **Weight:** 20,000 kg (44,100 lb)
Diet: Herbivore   **Habitat:** Land
Location: Asia   **Animal type:** Prehistoric creature
Key species: Paraceratherium bugtiense

Kyptoceras

Unique horns set this ancient antelope–like animal apart from other prehistoric plant eaters. Two bent horns curved over Kyptoceras's head, while two smaller horns stuck up from its nose.

Short, strong teeth tore off leaves to eat.

Weird but true!
Kyptoceras used its unusual horns to fight with rival males and scare away predators.

Long, slender legs could run at high speeds.

Super stats

Name: Kyptoceras   **Pronunciation:** KIP-toe-SER-as
Name meaning: Bent forward horns   **Period:** Neogene
Length: 1.6 m (5 ft)   **Weight:** 100 kg (220 lb)
Diet: Herbivore   **Habitat:** Land
Location: North America   **Animal type:** Prehistoric creature
Key species: Kyptoceras amatorum

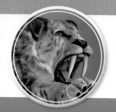

Smilodon

Smilodon struck fear into other prehistoric creatures. This sabre–toothed cat was instantly recognizable by its dagger–like canine teeth. A skilled predator, it hunted deer, tapir, and horses in grasslands and forests. It pounced from behind shrubs to deliver a deadly bite to the throat.

Two sharp canine teeth were Smilodon's ultimate weapons for stabbing and slicing prey.

Weird but true!

Smilodon could open its mouth nearly twice as wide as a modern tiger. This gave prey no chance to escape its gaping jaws.

Powerful paws pinned wriggling prey firmly to the ground

Super stats

Name: Smilodon

Pronunciation: SMILE-oh-don

Name meaning: Knife tooth

Period: Quaternary

Length: 2 m (6.5 ft)   **Weight:** 430 kg (950 lb)

Diet: Carnivore   **Habitat:** Land

Location: North America and South America

Animal type: Prehistoric creature

Key species: Smilodon populator

Strong neck muscles gave Smilodon control when attacking its prey.

Its coat is usually shown as being spotty, but Smilodon may have had plain or patterned fur.

Its long canine teeth were up to 20 cm (8 in) long.

Smilodon

Ferocious felines did not come much deadlier than this. This cat had a pair of enormous canine teeth, which it used to stab prey with devastating effect. Its muscular body, strong legs, powerful paws, and sharp claws also gave it a big advantage. This hungry predator prowled through forests tracking prey and attacking at high-speed.

Smilodon lived in forests and shrubland, so it probably had spots to help it hide among the trees and bushes.

The canine teeth were up to 28 cm (11 in) long.

Many Smilodon fossils show bone injuries from fatal fights with prey.

Fossil footprints likely belonging to Smilodon are bigger than a Bengal tiger's!

Smilodon: This sabre-toothed predator gives prey nothing to smile about!

Battle up!

Sabre–toothed Smilodon was speedy, super sneaky, and had terrifying teeth. Mighty Mammuthus had its size and powerful tusks for weapons. A bloody battle might result if the two creatures met.

Mammuthus

Beware the huge tusks of Mammuthus! These huge weapons did serious damage to predators, clattering into bodies and breaking bones. Mammuthus was a herbivore and did not hunt, but its huge size sent out a warning to predators.

Mammuthus relied on its massive size, colossal feet, shaggy fur, and frightening tusks to protect itself.

Scientists believe that its tusks may have been curved to push snow off the grass beneath it.

A record-breaking mammoth tusk measured more than 4 m (13 ft) long!

Mammuthus: The mammoth beast with tusks can make a point!

Who would win?

In a one-on-one fight, Mammuthus would easily force Smilodon away, using its strength and killer tusks. But, if Smilodon arrived with some of its friends and hunted in a pack, they would be too much for Mammuthus. With so many predators biting and tearing at its body, the herbivore would have had no chance. Smilodon would most likely win the fight, especially with a big dinner like Mammuthus at stake.

Winner!

Mammals

At the same time as dinosaurs roamed the Earth, tiny, rat-like mammals scurried around. Once the "terrible lizards" were extinct, it was the mammals' turn to shine. During the next 65 million years, with no ferocious dinosaurs or marine reptiles to stop them, mammals developed into bigger creatures. They became fearsome animals on land and in the sea.

Megazostrodon

One of the first mammals, mousy Megazostrodon burrowed underground during the Late Triassic and Early Jurassic periods, hoping to escape dinosaur predators.

Repenomamus

This badger-sized mammal did not always hide from the dinosaurs. One Repenomamus fossil had a baby Psittacosaurus in its stomach, showing that it ate small dinosaurs.

Mammuthus

Plant eater Mammuthus lived during the Ice Age. It is known as a woolly mammoth because of its long, shaggy fur.

Basilosaurus

Ocean-living Basilosaurus was an 18 m (59 ft) long whale, with sharp teeth and a crushing bite. It had a long, flexible body, but tiny back flippers.

Megatherium

As big as an elephant, this herbivore was known as the giant ground sloth. It used its tail as an extra leg, so it could stretch up to reach higher growing leaves.

Why did the mammals survive?

Almost all dinosaurs died after an asteroid hit the Earth and dust from the impact blocked out the Sun. Smaller creatures, such as burrowing mammals, would have been able to find food underground and were better equipped for survival.

Paraceratherium

Paraceratherium was the largest land mammal of all time. This herbivore could reach higher than a giraffe to feed on leaves from the treetops.

Smilodon

The largest sabre-toothed cat, Smilodon, terrorized other animals as early as 2.5 million years ago. Its enormous teeth grew as long as an adult human's hand.

Basilosaurus

Ancient giant whale Basilosaurus ruled the waves in prehistoric times. It used its eel-like body to move smoothly through the water on the hunt for fish, including sharks and marine mammals.

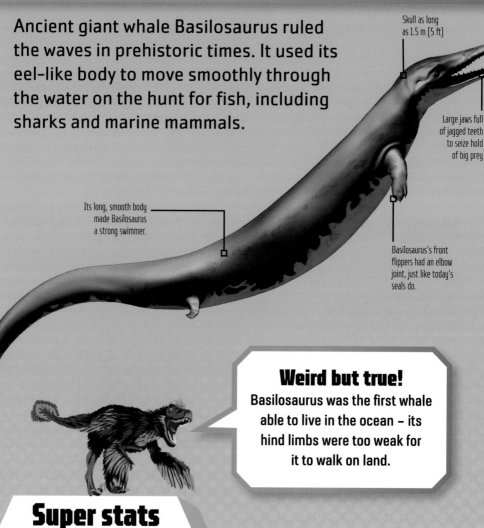

Skull as long as 1.5 m [5 ft]

Large jaws full of jagged teeth to seize hold of big prey

Its long, smooth body made Basilosaurus a strong swimmer.

Basilosaurus's front flippers had an elbow joint, just like today's seals do.

Weird but true!

Basilosaurus was the first whale able to live in the ocean – its hind limbs were too weak for it to walk on land.

Super stats

Name: Basilosaurus   **Pronunciation:** BASS-ill-oh-SORE-us
Name meaning: King lizard   **Period:** Paleogene
Length: 18 m [59 ft]   **Weight:** 18,000 kg [40,000 lb]
Diet: Carnivore   **Habitat:** Ocean
Location: Worldwide   **Animal type:** Prehistoric creature
Key species: Basilosaurus cetoides

Megalodon

The ultimate ocean hunter in prehistoric times was massive Megalodon. The largest and heaviest species of shark, it had super senses suited for hunting marine life in the deepest, darkest waters.

Weird but true!

Megalodon was three times the length of a great white shark.

Streamlined body shape powered the shark through water.

Hundreds of razor-sharp teeth were continually being worn down and replaced.

Super stats

Name: Megalodon **Pronunciation:** MEH-ga-lo-don
Name meaning: Big tooth **Period:** Neogene
Length: 18 m (59 ft) **Weight:** 50,000 kg (110,000 lb)
Diet: Carnivore **Habitat:** Ocean
Location: Worldwide **Animal type:** Prehistoric creature
Key species: Otodus megalodon

Darwinius

Darwinius swung through prehistoric forests in search of fruit and leaves to eat. This ancient primate looked a bit like modern lemurs, but amazingly, is a very distant relation of humans.

Thick fur provided a warm, protective covering.

Weird but true!
Darwinius was named to celebrate the 200th anniversary of naturalist Charles Darwin's birth.

A long tail helped Darwinius climb and balance in the trees.

Long fingers and toes gripped hold of branches tightly.

Super stats

Name: Darwinius   **Pronunciation:** dar-WIN-ee-us
Name meaning: After Charles Darwin   **Period:** Paleogene
Length: 58 cm (23 in)   **Weight:** 0.9 kg (2 lb)   **Diet:** Herbivore
Habitat: Land   **Location:** Europe   **Animal type:** Prehistoric creature
Key species: Darwinius masillae

Uintatherium

Mighty mammal Uintatherium grazed on grasslands and marshes. Although it had sharp canine teeth to fight with if attacked, its size scared away most predators.

Weird but true!
The six bony horns on Uintatherium skulls were probably used by males as weapons to fight rivals.

Only a male Uintatherium had three pairs of horns on top of its head.

Strong legs and clawed feet supported the massive body.

Huge canines stuck out from the mouth. Smaller teeth were used to chew leaves.

Super stats

Name: Uintatherium   **Pronunciation:** yoo-IN-tah-THEER-ee-um
Name meaning: Beast of the Uinta Mountains   **Period:** Paleogene
Length: 4 m (13 ft)   **Weight:** 2,000 kg (4,400 lb)
Diet: Herbivore   **Habitat:** Land
Location: North America and Asia   **Animal type:** Prehistoric creature
Key species: Uintatherium anceps

Entelodon

Entelodon was a scary sight on the prehistoric plains. This boar-like mammal munched on both plants and prey. Huge in size and fierce by nature, it was always up for a fight – and it usually won.

Huge head with raised bumps covering both of its cheeks

Its snout opened to reveal a dangerous mix of different teeth.

Weird but true!
Entelodon became known as the "pig from hell" because it was so aggressive.

Super stats

Name: Entelodon   **Pronunciation:** en-TEL-oh-don
Name meaning: Complete teeth   **Period:** Paleogene
Length: 2.3 m (7.5 ft)   **Weight:** 550 kg (1,200 lb)
Diet: Omnivore   **Habitat:** Land
Location: Europe and Asia   **Animal type:** Prehistoric creature
Key species: Entelodon magnus

Phorusrhacos

Prehistoric predator Phorusrhacos was a bird that could not fly. However, it could outrun almost any prey on the grasslands. Huge claws on its feet and a sharp beak were the perfect hunting tools to seize and swallow prey, such as small mammals.

Powerful beak with a hooked tip to grab hold of prey

Very long legs for chasing prey at high speed

Weird but true!
Phorusrhacos has been nicknamed "terror bird" because of its big beak, scary claws, and huge appetite.

Super stats

Name: Phorusrhacos **Pronunciation:** fo-russ-RA-koss
Name meaning: Wrinkle bearer **Period:** Neogene
Length: 2.5 m (8 ft) **Weight:** 130 kg (290 lb)
Diet: Carnivore **Habitat:** Land
Location: South America **Animal type:** Prehistoric creature
Key species: Phorusrhacos longissimus

Mammuthus

Mammuthus, or the woolly mammoth, stomped its way through the Ice Age, 400,000–4,000 years ago. With its colossal body, huge tusks, and powerful trunk, it looked a little like a modern Asian elephant – but this beast was even heavier and much hairier!

Shaggy fur coats kept mammoths cosy and warm on the freezing ice sheets where many lived.

Some hairs grew up to 1 m [3 ft] long.

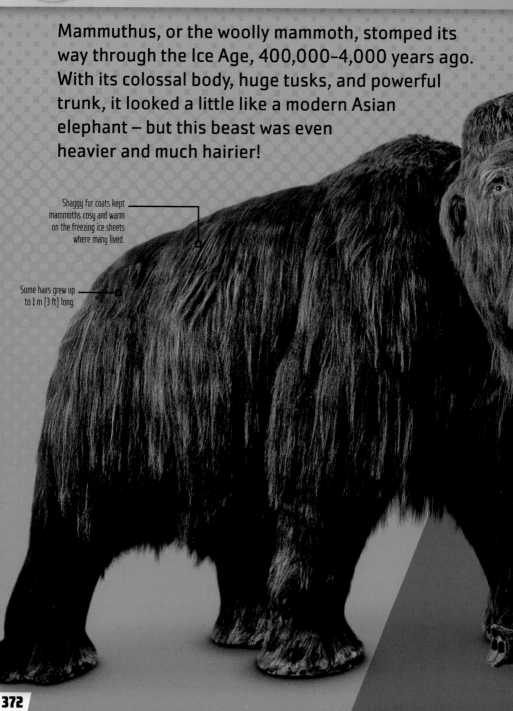

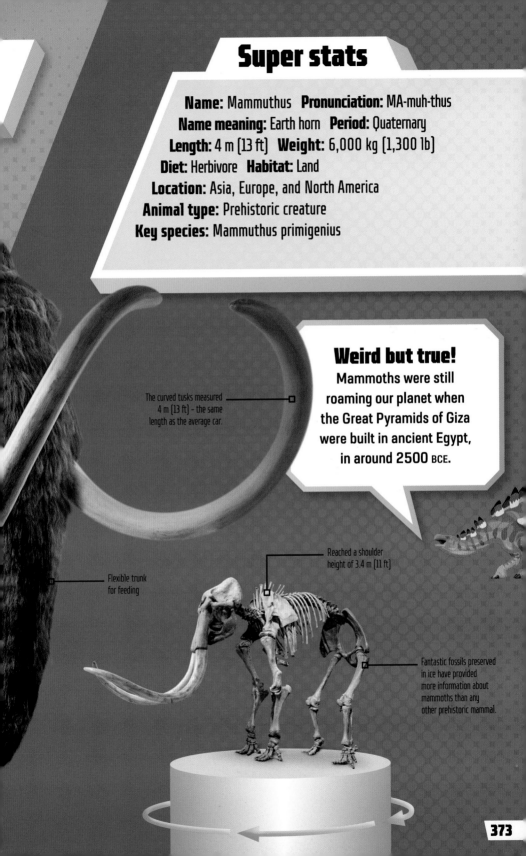

Super stats

Name: Mammuthus **Pronunciation:** MA-muh-thus
Name meaning: Earth horn **Period:** Quaternary
Length: 4 m (13 ft) **Weight:** 6,000 kg (1,300 lb)
Diet: Herbivore **Habitat:** Land
Location: Asia, Europe, and North America
Animal type: Prehistoric creature
Key species: Mammuthus primigenius

The curved tusks measured 4 m (13 ft) – the same length as the average car.

Weird but true!
Mammoths were still roaming our planet when the Great Pyramids of Giza were built in ancient Egypt, in around 2500 BCE.

Reached a shoulder height of 3.4 m (11 ft)

Flexible trunk for feeding

Fantastic fossils preserved in ice have provided more information about mammoths than any other prehistoric mammal.

Prowling predator

Aenocyon dirus was one of many predators in the Cenozoic Era. Stalking open plains for prey, this wolf-like creature also hunted in packs to take down the largest mammals, perhaps including young mammoths.

Megalodon

Megalodon was the largest shark of all time. It also had the strongest bite of any animal ever – about three times as powerful as Tyrannosaurus. It attacked its prey with its rows of razor-sharp teeth that were replaced before they could ever grow blunt. Like its modern-day relative, the great white shark, Megalodon could sense its prey and stalk it, even in darkness, with deadly accuracy.

Scientists have worked out that Megalodon grew up to 18 m (60 ft) in length.

Whale fossils have been found with bite marks from Megalodon's teeth.

There were up to 276 teeth in Megalodon's mouth at any one time, arranged in rows.

Its fins were probably as long as an adult human's body.

Megalodon: The mega shark that slams unsuspecting prey!

Battle up!

During a time known as the Miocene, the waters off the coast of Peru were ruled by two gigantic predators called Megalodon and Livyatan. It is certain that these two massive ocean killers would have come face-to-face.

Livyatan

Livyatan ruled the seas as a top predator, using its enormous teeth to kill large prey, including other whales. Scientists think it may have been able to hunt and track prey, possibly chasing a target to tire it out before going in for the kill - similar to how modern orcas hunt. However it hunted, Livyatan was a fearsome predator.

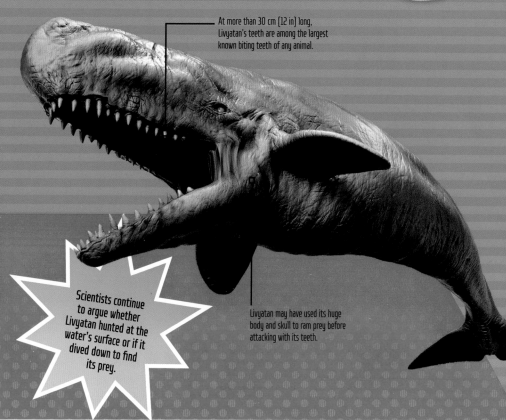

At more than 30 cm (12 in) long, Livyatan's teeth are among the largest known biting teeth of any animal.

Scientists continue to argue whether Livyatan hunted at the water's surface or if it dived down to find its prey.

Livyatan may have used its huge body and skull to ram prey before attacking with its teeth.

Livyatan: The monster whale with a huge body, huge teeth, and huge hunger!

Who would win?

Livyatan had bigger teeth and, as a mammal, a larger brain. Megalodon had a stronger bite, plus 420 million years of shark development to make it a successful ocean predator. If Megalodon launched a surprise attack, it could tear off one of Livyatan's fins to win the toothy fight.

Winner!

Titanoboa

This super-sized serpent was the largest, longest, and heaviest snake to ever live. Titanoboa was a distant relative of today's boa constrictors, but was three times as long and 20 times heavier.

Its flexible jaw and stretchy skin expanded to swallow large prey whole.

A forked tongue was used to detect fish and other reptiles living in tropical swamps.

Weird but true!
The first Titanoboa bones found were so big that scientists originally mistook them for crocodile bones.

Super stats

Name: Titanoboa   **Pronunciation:** ty-tan-oh-BO-ah
Name meaning: Giant boa   **Period:** Paleogene
Length: 14 m (46 ft)   **Weight:** 1,150 kg (2,500 lb)
Diet: Carnivore   **Habitat:** Land
Location: South America   **Animal type:** Prehistoric creature
Key species: Titanoboa cerrejonensis

Arctodus

During the Ice Age, Arctodus ranked among the biggest and strongest predators on land. This big bear hunted prey, or fed on the leftovers of other predators.

Weird but true!
We know Arctodus could run fast for short bursts, but palaeontologists are not sure what its top speed was.

Its short snout is why Arctodus is often known as the short-faced bear.

Longer and thinner limbs allowed Arctodus to move more freely than most bears.

Super stats

Name: Arctodus **Pronunciation:** ARK-toe-duss
Name meaning: Bear tooth **Period:** Quaternary
Length: 3.4 m (11 ft) **Weight:** 900 kg (2,000 lb)
Diet: Omnivore **Habitat:** Land
Location: North America **Animal type:** Prehistoric creature
Key species: Arctodus simus

Glyptodon

This ancient, armoured armadillo was the same size as a small car. Glyptodon's huge domed shell provided protection as it grazed on leafy plants in swamps and forests.

Weird but true!
Male Glyptodons fought one another for territory, using their bony tails as weapons.

Each shell had its own unique pattern of connected bony plates.

Spiky, armoured tail

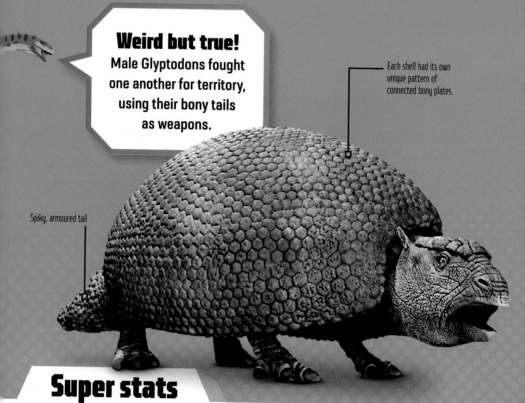

Super stats

Name: Glyptodon   **Pronunciation:** GLIP-toe-don
Name meaning: Carved tooth   **Period:** Quaternary
Length: 3.5 m (11.5 ft)   **Weight:** 2,000 kg (4,400 lb)
Diet: Herbivore   **Habitat:** Land
Location: North America and South America
Animal type: Prehistoric creature   **Key species:** Glyptodon clavipes

Mastodon

Majestic Mastodons stomped their way through the Ice Age searching for plants to munch. They were as big as modern elephants and are often confused with mammoths. But, Mastodons were smaller and had flatter heads.

Pair of long tusks

Its flappy ears were smaller than the ears of elephants today.

Legs like tree trunks to support the heavy body

Weird but true!
Like modern African elephants, male Mastodons had larger tusks than the females.

Super stats

Name: Mastodon **Pronunciation:** MASS-tuh-don
Name meaning: Nipple tooth **Period:** Neogene
Length: 4 m (13 ft) **Weight:** 8,000 kg (17,500 lb)
Diet: Herbivore **Habitat:** Land **Location:** Worldwide
Animal type: Prehistoric creature **Key species:** Mammut americanum

Megatherium

Mega by name and mega by nature, this giant sloth was the size of an elephant with an appetite to match. Although it was too heavy to climb trees, Megatherium could stretch up on two legs to reach the highest leaves in the prehistoric rainforests.

Its long claws ripped off leaves. Sharp teeth then sliced them up for swallowing.

Powerful tail supported Megatherium when standing on two legs

Weird but true!
In the 19th century, British naturalist Charles Darwin discovered fossilized giant sloths in South America.

Super stats

Name: Megatherium **Pronunciation:** MEG-ah-THEER-ee-um
Name meaning: Great beast **Period:** Neogene
Length: 6 m (20 ft) **Weight:** 6,000 kg (13,300 lb)
Diet: Herbivore **Habitat:** Land
Location: South America **Animal type:** Prehistoric creature
Key species: Megatherium americanum

Livyatan

Colossal killer Livyatan was an ancient sperm whale that ruled the prehistoric oceans. Its ferocious bite and terrifying teeth could kill any prey! It may even have lived alongside massive rival Megalodon.

Weird but true!
Livyatan melvillei was named after Herman Melville. He wrote a famous book called *Moby Dick* about a sperm whale.

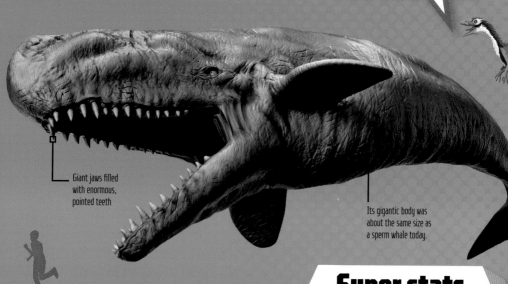

Giant jaws filled with enormous, pointed teeth

Its gigantic body was about the same size as a sperm whale today.

Super stats

Name: Livyatan **Pronunciation:** LIV-ya-TAN
Name meaning: Dire whale **Period:** Neogene
Length: 16 m (52 ft) **Weight:** 45,000 kg (100,000 lb)
Diet: Carnivore **Habitat:** Ocean **Location:** South America
Animal type: Prehistoric creature **Key species:** Livyatan melvillei

Purgatorius

The world's oldest primate was the prehistoric Purgatorius. This tiny creature was the size of a mouse. It spent most of its time scampering up and down prehistoric trees, looking for seeds, nuts, fruit, and insects to eat.

Its teeth were a similar shape to those of modern primates. This suggests that it ate lots of different things.

Purgatorius was lively and light on its feet.

Weird but true!
Fossils show Purgatorius might have been around when the asteroid struck the Earth 66 million years ago.

Super stats

Name: Purgatorius   **Pronunciation:** PER-gah-TORE-ee-us
Name meaning: After Purgatory Hill, in Montana, in the USA
Period: Possibly Cretaceous to Paleogene
Length: 15 cm (6 in)   **Weight:** 0.1 kg (0.2 lb)
Diet: Omnivore   **Habitat:** Land   **Location:** North America
Animal type: Prehistoric creature   **Key species:** Purgatorius unio

Elasmotherium

A single horn might have been the same height as an adult human.

Sometimes known as the "Siberian unicorn", Elasmotherium was a prehistoric rhinoceros. It was twice as heavy as a modern rhinoceros, and grazed in open grasslands.

Weird but true!

Elasmotherium fossils show that it lived as recently as 39,000 years ago, alongside humans.

A shaggy fur coat kept Elasmotherium warm during the Ice Age period.

Super stats

Name: Elasmotherium   **Pronunciation:** ell-AZZ-moe-THEER-ee-um
Name meaning: Thin plate beast   **Period:** Neogene
Length: 6 m (20 ft)   **Weight:** 4,500 kg (10,000 lb)
Diet: Herbivore   **Habitat:** Land   **Location:** Asia
Animal type: Prehistoric creature
Key species: Elasmotherium sibiricum

Coelodonta

One of the hairiest and scariest-looking prehistoric creatures during the Ice Age was the woolly rhinoceros, called Coelodonta. Although it was enormous and had two great horns, it was only interested in grazing on grass. Unlike modern rhinoceroses, this ancient animal was covered in a thick fur coat to stay warm in freezing temperatures.

Woolly fur covered
the entire body

Weird but true!

The ancient body of a young woolly rhinoceros was found in Siberia, in Russia. Its hair, hooves, horns, and organs were all preserved by the ice.

Heavyweight body was
similar to the bulky build of
rhinoceroses living today.

Name: Coelodonta
Pronunciation: SEE-low-DON-tah
Name meaning: Hollow tooth **Period:** Neogene
Length: 4 m (13 ft) **Weight:** 1,800 kg (4,000 lb)
Diet: Herbivore **Habitat:** Land **Location:** Europe and Asia
Animal type: Prehistoric creature
Key species: Coelodonta antiquitatis

It had horns for showing off and to defend against predators

Short, stocky legs to support its large body

Dinosaurs today

Although it is hard to believe, birds today are dinosaurs. Scientists now know that birds are living, breathing theropods. They have lots in common with dinosaurs that died out, but they are also different in some ways.

Early birds

In the Jurassic period, meat-munching, theropod dinosaurs walked upright on two legs. They had hollow bones and three toes. Some of them grew feathers and took flight. Most of these dinosaurs died out, but their features are similar to those of today's birds.

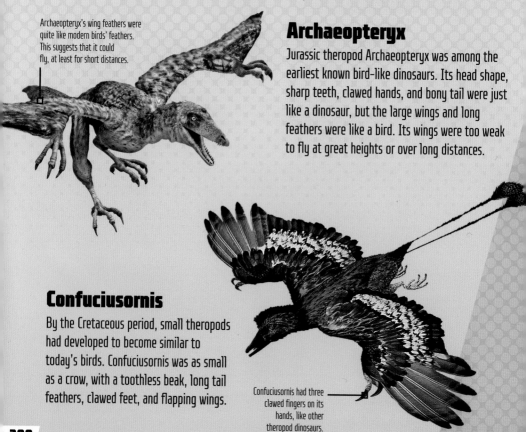

Archaeopteryx's wing feathers were quite like modern birds' feathers. This suggests that it could fly, at least for short distances.

Archaeopteryx

Jurassic theropod Archaeopteryx was among the earliest known bird-like dinosaurs. Its head shape, sharp teeth, clawed hands, and bony tail were just like a dinosaur, but the large wings and long feathers were like a bird. Its wings were too weak to fly at great heights or over long distances.

Confuciusornis

By the Cretaceous period, small theropods had developed to become similar to today's birds. Confuciusornis was as small as a crow, with a toothless beak, long tail feathers, clawed feet, and flapping wings.

Confuciusornis had three clawed fingers on its hands, like other theropod dinosaurs.

Some dinosaurs were the same size as a chicken, such as little Compsognathus.

Modern birds

The birds we see today and theropod dinosaurs are very alike. They share features, including beaks, lightweight bones, three toes, feathers, and wishbones. Over time, birds have developed many different wing and beak shapes to suit their diets and environments.

Chicken

At first glance, a chicken may not seem much like a dinosaur, but look more closely. Chickens have wings but rarely fly, just like the first birds. They have big head crests to attract mates, like some dinosaurs. They are covered in protective feathers, except for their clawed feet, just like some theropods. Chickens have even got toothless beaks, like Confuciusornis.

Just like a dinosaur

The biggest dinosaur today is the ostrich, while the smallest is the bee hummingbird. When it is a chick, the South American hoatzin bird has wing claws, just like some Cretaceous dinosaurs.

Bee hummingbird

Feathers help an ostrich to control its body temperature. Feathers may have helped some dinosaurs to do this, too.

Hoatzin

Glossary

amphibians
Cold-blooded vertebrates that have moist skin, lay their eggs in water, and can live in both water and on land. Examples include newts and frogs

ancestor
Relative from a long time ago

ankylosaur
Group of plant-eating dinosaurs that lived at the end of the Cretaceous period, about 68-66 million years ago. Their bodies were covered with bony plates to protect them

armadillo
Only living mammal to have bony plates covering its back, head, legs, and tail. Found in Central and South America and North America, armadillos feed on beetles, ants, and other insects

arthropod
Type of animal with no backbone, a hard skeleton on the outside of its body, and legs with joints. Examples include spiders, crabs, insects, and millipedes

bonebeds
Areas of rock and soil that also contain the fossilized remains of plants and animals, including bones and bone fragments

camouflage
How animals blend into their environment so that they cannot be seen

canine teeth
Four sharp, pointed teeth in the mouth. There are two on the top and two on the bottom of the mouth, which help to tear food

carnivores
Animals that eat the flesh of other animals to survive

ceratopsians
Mostly four-legged, plant-eating, and horned dinosaurs with bony frills and spikes on their heads

coprolite
Fossilized dinosaur poo

crustaceans
Type of arthropod that lives in water, such as crabs, lobsters, or crayfish. Arthropods have a hard outer skeleton and many legs with joints

denticles
Small bumps on a tooth that give it a sharp, cutting edge

dorsal fin
Fin found on the back of fish, whales, dolphins, and porpoises. It stops the animal from rolling over when swimming and helps it to make sudden turns